Green Filmmaking

Beyond the principles of reduce, reuse, recycle, this book looks at how every department on a production can minimize its environmental impact.

Is your filmmaking contributing to the environmental crisis, or is it part of the solution? How can film students make movies in a more ecologically friendly way so that our planet can continue to be inhabited by humans who watch their films? This book suggests step-by-step ways that each person and department on a film's production can make simple changes to reduce their project's environmental footprint, from including climate content to offering vegetarian craft service options.

It is an essential guide for film students, graduates, and professionals engaged in the practice of making movies.

Kent Hayward is a filmmaker, Associate Professor of Production at California State University Long Beach, and a cofounder and vice-Chair of the Green Film School Alliance, a consortium committed to integrating sustainable production practices into film school programs. Previously, Hayward worked in visual effects and editorial on films including *The Dark Knight*, *Inception*, and *Terminator 3: Rise of the Machines*, and on TV shows for NBC Universal, SyFy, and Lifetime. Hayward's films include *Lunar Estates*, *August*, *Sunset to Sunset*, and *Homestead Artifact*. He earned his BA at the University of Wisconsin-Madison and his MFA at the California Institute of the Arts. Currently, Hayward is working on an essay film on themes ranging from the environmental havoc that humankind has wreaked on the planet to the enduring mystery of Bigfoot.

Green Filmmaking
A Guide to Sustainable Movie Production

Kent Hayward

LONDON AND NEW YORK

Designed cover image: C.K. Wilde

First published 2025
by Routledge
4 Park Square, Milton Park, Abingdon, Oxon OX14 4RN

and by Routledge
605 Third Avenue, New York, NY 10158

Routledge is an imprint of the Taylor & Francis Group, an informa business

© 2025 Kent Hayward

The right of Kent Hayward to be identified as author of this work has been asserted in accordance with sections 77 and 78 of the Copyright, Designs and Patents Act 1988.

All rights reserved. No part of this book may be reprinted or reproduced or utilised in any form or by any electronic, mechanical, or other means, now known or hereafter invented, including photocopying and recording, or in any information storage or retrieval system, without permission in writing from the publishers.

Trademark notice: Product or corporate names may be trademarks or registered trademarks, and are used only for identification and explanation without intent to infringe.

British Library Cataloguing-in-Publication Data
A catalogue record for this book is available from the British Library

Library of Congress Cataloging-in-Publication Data
Names: Hayward, Kent, author.
Title: Green filmmaking : a guide to sustainable movie production / Kent Hayward.
Description: Abingdon, Oxon ; New York, NY : Routledge, 2025. | Includes bibliographical references and index.
Identifiers: LCCN 2024029206 (print) | LCCN 2024029207 (ebook) | ISBN 9781032545639 (hardback) | ISBN 9781032545622 (paperback) | ISBN 9781003425441 (ebook)
Subjects: LCSH: Motion pictures--Production and direction--Environmental aspects. | Motion picture industry--Environmental aspects.
Classification: LCC PN1995.9.P7 H44 2025 (print) | LCC PN1995.9.P7 (ebook) | DDC 791.4302/32--dc23/eng/20240627
LC record available at https://lccn.loc.gov/2024029206
LC ebook record available at https://lccn.loc.gov/2024029207

ISBN: 978-1-032-54563-9 (hbk)
ISBN: 978-1-032-54562-2 (pbk)
ISBN: 978-1-003-42544-1 (ebk)

DOI: 10.4324/9781003425441

Typeset in Sabon LT Pro
by KnowledgeWorks Global Ltd.

Access the Support Material: www.routledge.com/9781032545622

T&F is committed to sustainability across all aspects of the book production process, and this has been honoured in the production of *Green Filmmaking*. To find out more please see our website: https://taylorandfrancis.com/about/corporate-responsibility/sustainability/

To all my teachers who opened doors for me, especially Mr. Stamler (5th grade, Randall Elementary), Mrs. Meanwell (7th grade, Van Hise Middle), Mr. Keyes (12th grade, West High), and Mrs. Moen (12th grade, West High), who enlightened my young mind and encouraged a study of media and filmmaking in Madison, Wisconsin, in the 1980s; UW Madison College film professors David Bordwell and J.J. Murphy; and CalArts teachers James Benning, Berenice Reynaud, Jules Engel, and Thom Andersen. You inspired me and made a difference in my life. Thank you.

Contents

About the Cover and Illustrations — *ix*
Preface — *x*
Introduction — *xvi*
Acknowledgments — *xix*

1 An Introduction to the History and Context of Green Filmmaking — 1

2 Intersections and Production — 14

3 Why Be Green? — 19

4 How to Film Green – By Department — 26

5 Documentary — 39

6 Content, Development, and Climate Storytelling — 45

7 Preproduction: The Plan — 60

8 The Production Department — 73

9 Production Design, Art, Construction, Props, and Set Decoration — 84

10 Camera, Grip, and Electric — 92

11 Actors, Talent, and Casting — 105

12 Food: Catering and Craft Services — 110

13 Wardrobe, Hair, and Makeup	118
14 Transportation	125
15 Effects	131
16 Sustainable Sound Practices in Film Production	136
17 Editorial or Postproduction	142
18 Wrap	151
19 Green Filmmaking Case Studies and Jobs	156
20 Looking to the Future	168
Appendix A	*174*
Appendix B	*175*
Index	*177*

About the Cover and Illustrations

About the Cover

Currency collage artist Christopher Karl Wilde was born and raised in Madison, Wisconsin. In 1993, he founded Artichoke Yink Press, an imprint for artists' books that has published over 125 titles to date. In 1998, Wilde co-founded The Booklyn Artists Alliance, in Brooklyn, New York. He is represented by Rosamund Felsen Gallery in Los Angeles. C.K. Wilde's artwork can be found in over 70 collections worldwide, including at The Getty, The Metropolitan Museum of Art, and MOMA NYC and San Francisco. Find him at currencycollage.com.

About the Illustrations

Ramón Hone is a LEED Accredited Professional and a licensed architect in the United Kingdom and the United States. Free to draw on the walls of his London bedroom as a child, Hone developed a love of communicating ideas through illustration that flourished from a young age. He is committed to sustainable design practices and passionate about creating spaces that inspire and endure. Find him at www.3eggstudio.com

Preface

Extensive species extinctions. Widespread flooding. Severely compromised agriculture production. These are among the projected long-term effects of climate change.[1] Human activity is the dominant cause of greenhouse gasses[2] and climate warming,[3] and the biggest contributors are the energy, transportation, industry, agriculture, and construction sectors,[4] all of which the entertainment business depends upon to produce films and television.

For that reason, the entertainment industry has an obligation to significantly reduce its environmental impact. And since the business supports millions of jobs[5] held by millions of workers, their livelihood long-term depends on making the industry sustainable.

A 2022 Pew Research study found that 75% of people from the 19 countries surveyed felt that global climate change is a major threat to their country.[6] Another study in the United Kingdom found that 83% of respondents say that they are concerned about climate change.[7] Unfortunately, according to the 2023 WHO UN Climate Report "United in Science," the world is off track to meet our climate goals from the Paris Agreement, an international treaty signed in 2015 to combat climate change. In fact, at the halfway point to the 2030 target, only 15% of the sustainable development goals (SDGs) were on track.[8] As fossil fuel CO_2 emissions increase, we continue to experience the warmest years on record,[9] triggering widespread concern about the future of our planet. As the report warns, "urgent and ambitious mitigation and adaptation action is needed."[10]

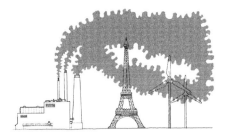

The Paris Climate Agreement was adopted by 196 parties at the UN Climate Change Conference (COP21) in Paris, France, on Dec 12, 2015. The world is not on track to meet the environmental targets set for 2030, according to experts.[11]

War and human conflict also contribute to the problem,[12] with the most vulnerable communities caught in the crossfire disproportionately affected. Urgent action is needed to stem the tide.[13]

We are all flawed, imperfect creatures. Unfortunately, we can't do the very best thing for everyone and everything 100% of the time. There is no magic bullet that will fix the planet, but making changes on an individual level adds up, and advocating for changes on a larger scale brings others along with us. We can change the world one step at a time.

And one step at a time in the film world can mean a lot. A 2019 report claims that an average day of filming a major movie release equates to more than one person's annual carbon footprint, and an average hour of filming equates to the carbon footprint of a round-trip flight between London and New York.[14] Fortunately, that production footprint is one thing that we can change.

Why I Wrote This

Writing a book, like making a movie, is difficult. So why do it? I teach film at California State University, Long Beach. I tell my students that you'd better believe in your movie because making anything is hard to do if you want to do it well. The project needs to be important for *you personally* in order to put all that effort and care into it. My personal connection to this project goes back to being a kid growing up in Wisconsin during the environmental movement of the 1970s, and what I carried from that time through my career in visual effects, editing, and teaching production.

The first Earth Day, conceived by Governor Gaylord Nelson of Wisconsin, was in 1970. It was a huge event. This was the same year that the United States created the Environmental Protection Agency and a milestone Clean Air Act under the Nixon administration. It was a monumental year that started an environmental decade of action – and the year I was born. Legislation in the 1970s was spurred by the social change and protests of the 1960s, which were inspired by the investigation of the pollution and pesticides of the 1950s, and the growth of the National Park system in the earlier half of the century. I remember the oil crisis in the 1970s, where my grandpa sat in long lines of cars to fill up the station wagon with gas and President Carter put solar panels on the White House. A public service announcement on television showed a Native American character with a tear running down his cheek as he looked at the polluted land around him. "People start pollution; people can stop it," the baritone narrator says. Other PSAs showed Woodsy the Owl combating litter, Smokey the Bear taking care of the forests, and a pollution-minded kid who spoke for me sitting on a swing to tell grown-ups to "give us kids our chance." All this in the glow of the moon missions and the iconic photo of our planet Earth, our "blue marble" rising from the edge of the lunar sphere.

There has been pushback on environmentalism since then. The Reagan administration removed the solar panels from the White House, climate science found its deniers, and the rainforests are still being cut down at an alarming rate. Nonetheless, there has been a tremendous reduction in pollution, toxic emissions, and littering, and a huge increase in the amount of alternative energy use since I was a kid. So many things are better. Still, it's complicated – more complicated and more interconnected than that baritone narrator could have imagined. So, when a student in my class recently said, "You boomers caused this climate change and you're leaving us to clean up your mess," I couldn't really disagree (even though the "baby boomers" were closer to my parents' generation, technically speaking). My generation could have done more. We still can. All of us can.

In my days working in visual effects and editorial, I was a small part of the machine making disaster movies about climate change and dystopian futures like *The Day After Tomorrow*, *The Core*, and *Terminator 3: Rise of the Machines*. Despite my love for some of the films and TV that I've worked on, I felt conflicted about the waste that they created and their reliance on dirty fuel and cheap labor. Not to mention the environmental footprint created by some of the other films and TV projects I worked on that were at times just ... well, kind of meaningless. Most of the really inane ones you've never even heard of because they went to the great rubbish pile of history. They're still there, too – their VHS cases and 35mm film reels left to decompose for another thousand years.[15]

The truth is that I love all kinds of movies, from the most esoteric experimental films to the saddest documentaries to the big, loud, popcorn franchise films. They form a collective mythology of our time and our culture. Our task as modern media makers is to create a new ideology for filmmaking and storytelling that incorporates sustainability.

I remember one big franchise film where the company I worked for had spent months making beautiful miniature sets, some full-sized fake caverns, and a restaurant set for the first unit to shoot on our stage. Film was shot, movie magic was made, and at the end of the shoot days, everything had to be wrapped and cleaned up ASAP so that production didn't have to pay for an additional day of stage rental, labor, etc. So, all the sets, flats, props, office furniture, supplies, signage, leftover food, packaging, and everything else had to be packed up, shipped, or thrown away. We piled the dumpsters sky-high with mixed-use waste. There just wasn't space to store most of it or time to go through it to recycle it or to find homes for things that could be reused. It felt so wasteful.

So, as I started teaching, I would set aside used items from my production jobs. Used diffusions, gels, props, worn-out gear, and leftover expendables headed for the trash would be saved for reuse by my students. As I told my classes about these shoots and the huge footprint of a few of the projects, some of my students and I became interested in the idea of conservation and sustainability in film production. In a later chapter, I will discuss some of the student projects that tried to introduce the use of sustainable practices on set. At the time I thought that we were one of only a very few filmmakers dipping our toes into green filmmaking, but I couldn't have been more wrong. There were many individuals in academia, scripted narrative production, documentary, broadcast production, media studies, and all through the global media landscape who were also working on sustainable solutions. I'll get into some of their work in upcoming chapters.

Before we jump in further, I want to acknowledge my own privilege at the start of this book. I am not a member of a significant minority or underrepresented group. If anything, I am a member of the most overrepresented, exploitative demographic on the planet. Statistically, as a white American male, I am a part of an imperialist patriarchy working in both the hegemonic Hollywood media machine *and* the Ivory Tower of academia. Ironically, however, even though the mainstream culture seems designed to support people just like me, the stories on television and in the movies don't always feel authentic to me, and the motives of the economic systems and sociopolitical machines that are reinforced by those stories often seem questionable.

It's time for some different new stories. We need new stories, ancient stories, diverse stories. Storytelling is a practice that has no boundaries, and cinematic storytelling should have no boundaries either. I work to overcome my biases as a storyteller and teacher and to use the privilege I was born with to effect change in my world with the tools I have been given.

Why You Should Read This Book

Maybe you're saying, "I already recycle, I never print scripts, I use efficient lights. I'm not the problem, it's the big corporate polluters and the giant media companies and other people who are the *real* problem." But as both individuals and members of larger groups, we are all the problem, and we can all make a real difference.

You should read this book because we each are part of a big company, university, generation, culture, or nation that has an ecological footprint. Holding other people accountable for pollution, waste, and misuse of resources is tremendously important. But we also need to acknowledge that we as individuals and members of various communities have the power to make change ourselves. The adage "think globally and act locally" couldn't be more fitting. Each of us can ask questions about the daily practices around us and be a part of the conversation. We can lessen our local footprint by 1%, 2%, 5%. When everyone does the same, it creates a sea change. A rising tide that lifts all boats. Or in this case, maybe not a rising tide, but a sea level that doesn't rise, thereby saving all the homes and habitats at sea level – a sea *not* changed, if you will.

You should read this because you want to help be a part of the sea not changing.

You should read this because you care about the people and creatures affected by climate change.

Why read this? Because you care. And because the practices suggested in the book will decrease the carbon footprint and environmental waste of your productions.

Why You Should Use This as a Textbook in Your Class

By now, we all know that sustainability and "being green" is important. If humans are going to meet the goals set at the Paris Agreement at *The 2015 UN Climate Change Conference* (COP21) in Paris, or any of the environmental goals that we've set since then, we're all going to need to pitch in. If your area of study is filmmaking, then that's one place that you can make a difference. This is the textbook to walk you through it.

Why use this book when there are so many free resources out there? Good question. There are some great free resources from Greenproductionguide.com, the Green Film School Alliance, Albert, and the Doc Society; we'll refer to them in later chapters, in fact. This book offers solutions, techniques, and resources, but there is no single authority on sustainability. We need to become our own authorities on our place in the world. Our job as ethical filmmakers is to look at all the resources and figure out how to apply them to our particular circumstances. This book will help you to navigate and understand the world of sustainability as applied to filmmaking, but more importantly how to *bring it into your practice* as a film student and future media maker, or into your pedagogy as a film teacher.

When I talk to my students about conservation, I see sincere interest and hear great ideas from them. My students get excited and even a little competitive about who can put together the most sustainable film production team.

This is not the definitive history of ecological sustainability in filmmaking. There are so many involved and so much happening. Just like the larger fields of sustainability and environmentalism, there are many leaders all over the world – some visible, some not.

There is no doubt that media content and production are incredibly influential drivers of our culture, our economies, and our global conversations. Film and art are like a frame that humans use to examine our world. When we look at a motion picture, we are looking at a reflection of ourselves – a powerful, intense, magnified reflection. When we make a motion picture, we have an incredible responsibility to use that power wisely. Teaching sustainability in student film production is a way to incorporate the best practices of production integrated with the science of sustainability and lessons in ethics.

The principal goal of the Green Film School Alliance and the Sustainable Entertainment Alliance is to "make *green production* just *production.*"[16] One of my goals as a film teacher is to impact the young filmmakers of tomorrow by bringing safe, thoughtful, and ethical "best practices" to their daily practices. As primatologist and conservationist Jane Goodall says, "You cannot get through a single day without having an impact on the world around you.

What you do makes a difference, and you have to decide what kind of difference you want to make."

So, do you want to work on film productions that make a difference for people and the environment?

What kind of difference do *you* want to make?

Notes

1. *What are the long-term effects of climate change? | U.S. Geological Survey.* https://www.usgs.gov/faqs/what-are-long-term-effects-climate-change
2. Unfccc.Int. *The Working Group Contribution to the Fifth Assessment Report of the Intergovernmental Panel on Climate Change (IPCC).* unfccc.int/topics/science/workstreams/cooperation-with-the-ipcc/the-fifth-assessment-report-of-the-ipcc. Accessed Jan. 3, 2024.
3. National Academy of Sciences. 2020. *Climate Change: Evidence and Causes: Update 2020.* The National Academies Press, p. 5. https://doi.org/10.17226/25733
4. *Annual EPA Report on Greenhouse Gas Emissions.* www.epa.gov/ghgemissions/sources-greenhouse-gas-emissions
5. Motion Picture Association, *Driving Economic Growth.* www.motionpictures.org/what-we-do/driving-economic-growth/
6. Pew Research Center. 2022, August. *Climate Change Remains Top Global Threat Across 19-Country Survey.*
7. BEIS Public Attitudes Tracker: Net Zero and Climate Change, Autumn 2022, UK. https://assets.publishing.service.gov.uk/government/uploads/system/uploads/attachment_data/file/1123571/BEIS_PAT_Autumn_2022_Net_Zero_and_Climate_Change.pdf
8. Fong, C. and Roy, D. 2023. *What are the UN Sustainable Development Goals? Council on Foreign Relations.* https://www.cfr.org/backgrounder/what-are-un-sustainable-development-goals
9. *NASA announces Summer 2023 hottest on record* (2023) *NASA.* https://www.nasa.gov/news-release/nasa-announces-summer-2023-hottest-on-record/
10. *WHO UN Climate Report.* https://library.wmo.int/idurl/4/68235
11. Unfcc.int. https://unfccc.int/process-and-meetings/the-paris-agreement
12. Rannard, G. (2022) *COP27: War causing huge release of Climate Warming Gas, claims Ukraine, BBC News.* https://www.bbc.com/news/science-environment-63625693.
13. A. L. Fanning and J. Hickel. 2023. Compensation for atmospheric appropriation. *Nature Sustainability*, Vol. 6, No. 9, pp. 1077–1086. https://doi.org/10.1038/s41893-023-01130-8
14. *A Screen New Deal a Route Map to Sustainable Film Production*, a Sustainability Report from a Collaboration between Albert, BFI, and Arup, 2019.
15. *Plastic planet: How tiny plastic particles are polluting our soil*, UNEP. https://www.unep.org/news-and-stories/story/plastic-planet-how-tiny-plastic-particles-are-polluting-our-soil
16. Green Film School Alliance. 2020. *Mission Statement.*

Introduction

Heidi Kindberg Goss, VP Sustainability, Warner Bros. Discovery (HBO/Max)

"Every piece of plastic ever made still exists."

Hearing that from Captain Charles Moore, a sailor and an oceanographer who discovered the great Pacific garbage patch, was my aha moment. It was then, at an Earth Day event at Sony nearly 15 years ago, when I knew that I wanted – no, needed – to somehow bring together my experience in production with my passion for sustainability.

Only sustainability wasn't even a common word yet, so what followed was a multidecade-long learning adventure defining, implementing, and sharing sustainable production practices with the unwavering goal of reducing the environmental impacts of physical production while increasing environmental awareness through content.

Although that quote about plastic changed my life, sustainable production is about much more. In the early days, when people first heard about sustainable production, they assumed we were only there to take away plastic water bottles and manage recycling on set. To be sure, we did, and still do, but that's just the surface. Both our work and this topic are much more complex, yet it is worth mentioning to recognize just how *symbolic* plastic water bottles are. They represent overconsumption, corporate responsibility – or the lack thereof – the health of our oceans, our personal health, and individual behaviors, not to mention the inappropriately placed responsibility on individuals when it comes to solutions. Further, bottom line, they're about fossil fuels, with a supply chain that is entirely petroleum-based. In other words, they are a direct connection to climate change and the epitome of a broken, unhealthy, and unsustainable system.

Inspired to action, I officially started this merged journey after film school and years of production experience (starting as a Production Assistant, then Production Office Coordinator, and finally producer, working on low-budget features, documentaries, sitcoms, and news programming), then a brief hiatus to be home with young kids, and finally a return to the industry with my first corporate job and going back to school to get a master's degree in urban sustainability. I think it's important to note that I started over as an assistant at this point in my career, for which I was grateful but also quite humbled. There is much to be said about work/life balance in this industry, which I try to bring up when talking with young people, and about the loss of career growth that mothers in particular face when they stay home – but that's all for another book. Even with these truths, this life path put me in the right place at the right time to pursue what has become, for me, a dream career, growing into Director of Sustainability at Sony Pictures and now VP of Sustainability for Warner Bros. Discovery's HBO and Max scripted productions.

I love the process of making content. After all these years, I'm still in awe of all the people and pieces that come together to make each day of shooting possible. Likewise, we all need to work together, no matter what our role, if we're going to succeed at this enormous task called "sustainability." This is nowhere else more evident than in the collaboration of the major studios and streamers.

While we were developing our sustainable production program in the early years at Sony, so were other studios; yet we were all working independently. In a short time, however, the six majors and the Producers Guild of America's Green Committee collaborated, forming what is now known as the Sustainable Entertainment Alliance (formerly the Sustainable Production Alliance, or SPA). Over a decade later, this group is composed of the biggest content makers in the world and still growing. The studios working together made sense because we're all constantly going to different places to shoot, but the same different places – so we shared information about resources near and far. We wanted to have a common language for our transient crews and a carbon calculator for like-measuring, allowing for industry-level insights and data aggregation. All of this and more, years of collaborative work, can be found on GreenProductionGuide.com. To this day, in this competitive Hollywood industry, we are still extremely collaborative in this space, speaking with a collective voice that can drive change more so than any one of the media goliaths could on their own. It's honestly something that I'm proud to have built and to be a part of – and it works.

In the beginning, we looked for the most impactful areas of film production and found that, in terms of biodiversity, it was the plywood used to build the set walls so this became a top priority to change. The industry-preferred ply, a tropical hardwood known as Lauan, was coming from Indonesia and Malaysia through a destructive supply chain. So, our first instinct was to stop using it and find a replacement. While we did end up discovering a good alternative, working with a non-profit, understanding the needs of construction crews through data collection and conversations, and identifying the mom-and-pop stores from which our shows buy, we also realized the better approach was to improve the system. Through collaborative work led by Sony Pictures when I was there, the major studios literally changed the supply chain throughout North America, bringing FSC-certified Lauan to local vendors supplying our industry.

As far as emissions are concerned, across scripted shows, the fuel used in vehicles and generators is together typically responsible for over half and often closer to 60% or even 70% of a production's emissions. Knowing this, our focus is heavily on clean energy solutions, specifically transitioning away from diesel fuel use. This must happen via behavior changes (downsizing generators, seeking grid power) and infrastructure improvements (transitioning to electric fleets) as well as innovative solutions (clean tech mobile power like battery, hydrogen, and sodium units), and fuels such as renewable diesel and green hydrogen. Suffice it to say that we're addressing the need to get off fossil fuels, and the SPA members' Energy and Climate Working Group is working toward just that.

While many other areas have an environmental impact, the final one I'll mention here is what's on screen – that is, modeling and messaging sustainable behaviors and the actual content itself. As studies have confirmed, individual behavior change can impact up to a quarter of emission reductions, and, as other research has shown, characters and stories are hugely influential. A quick internet search will prove this – try looking up *Cheers* and designated drivers or smoking on screen in general. Look no further than product placement to understand the financial value. Showing characters eating plant-based foods, installing solar panels, engaging in clean travel (e.g., public transport, electric vehicles, bicycling), composting, and yes, avoiding single-use plastics and recycling does matter. Again, together we're confronting this challenge.

The SPA and its many partners, including NGOs, governments, guilds and unions, private vendors, and of course, the Green Film School Alliance which boasts a similar mission: to bring sustainable production to students. This is perhaps the most important part of what we do – working intergenerationally to share knowledge, stay connected, and proliferate green practices so they become just the way it's done.

My continuing journey is to share, educate, and constantly learn as well as to bring sustainable solutions to crews, students, and viewers. We must alter how the dominant culture thinks about waste, convenience, responsibility, rights, and environmental issues. We need to challenge current realities and create new ones, portraying a future created by and for young people that implements solutions for the climate crisis. We must build a new normal, which includes conscious consumerism, ethical business practices, equitable living, and shared and protected resources.

This partnership includes you, the reader of this book. You will make decisions, whatever your role, as you create content, and those actions become our reality and will in turn create our new normal. Hopefully, you'll join as we will build a future where "sustainable production" is just "production."

Acknowledgments

I didn't come up with the content of this book. I drew from a community of film people who have been working passionately for years to make filmmaking more sustainable. Thanks to those folks for collectively beginning the work that we all continue.

Thank you to my family, who put up with all of this book-writing business: my incredible partner, wife, and first editor Elizabeth Hurchalla, and our amazing son, Dean. I am also grateful to my fellow Green Film School Alliance founders and executive committee members, Erica Elson and Harry Winer, and the GFSA membership, who encouraged me and contributed to the book, as well as to Sustainable Entertainment Alliance leaders Heidi Kindberg Goss, Jennifer Lynch, and Matt Halperin.

Thank you to my talented California State University Long Beach colleagues Seung-hoon Jeong, José Miguel Palacios, Helen Hood Scheer, Kevin O'Brien, Sharri Hefner, Susan Bloom, Ben Huff, David Waldman, Andrew Pearson, Nipper Knapp, and Adam Moore, who looked at chapter drafts and offered advice. Huge thanks go to the brilliant Larry Smith, who went above and beyond to give me his notes and insights on indigeneity and inclusion. CSULB staff members Riley Eggleston, Jose Sanchez, Sarah Len, and LaTanya Jones also deserve thanks for all the things they facilitated for this project too.

Professor and Associate Director of the Center for Environmental Filmmaking Larry Engel's advice and counsel was invaluable in the editing and review process, and Dr. Hunter Vaughan, author of *Hollywood's Dirtiest Secret: The Hidden Environmental Costs of the Movies*, gave me guidance as well.

I appreciate the helpful notes I got from student research assistants and Green Film School Alliance Student Ambassadors, including Soo Ahn, Habiba Hassaan, Riley Hodgson, and former student Claudia Villalta-Mejia.

Friends and industry insiders including Carol Stutz, Mark Weingartner, Matthew Gratzner, and Brian Rogers gave me suggestions and helped improve this book all around.

Kind contributors Lena Welch (Owner of Next Earth and consultant to numerous Netflix and HBO shows), Lydia Pilcher (Columbia University

School of the Arts & Climate School), Marieke Pielot (Das Gleiche in Gruen), Birgit Heidsiek (Green Film Shooting), Allison Begalman (Young Entertainment Activists, and the Hollywood Climate Summit), and Bibesh Roy (International Academy of Film and Media) not only answered my questions, they broadened the scope of the book to better address their specialties and areas of the world.

I thank Christopher Wilde for his amazing currency collage for the cover, and Ramón Hone for his incredible illustrations inside the book. Thanks also go to Routledge/Taylor & Francis team Claire Margerison, Rachel Feehan, Andrew Peart, Sarah Pickles, and Emma Morley for their patience and direction.

I owe a debt of gratitude to my family, Lori Hayward, Mark Hayward, Fred Hayward, and Linda Hunter for their unwavering support; and to Jean Hurchalla, who volunteered to proofread.

Thank you also to my students, who motivate me and keep me hopeful for the future.

I hope this book can inspire action and discussion, and that it is worthy of the excellent advice I got from all of these people.

1 An Introduction to the History and Context of Green Filmmaking

Movies make up an entertaining, spectacular mythology consisting of true crime stories, epic quests, impossible romances, superheroes, villains, sequels, remakes, quirky indies, deep fictional universes, and spicy reality stories. This mythology connects art, commerce, resources, and content. It's a mythology whose stories are sometimes treated like, and mined like, a commodity. Creators are constantly looking for new material, sometimes at the expense of the art of storytelling itself. It's as if somewhere around the introduction of the box office, things got mixed up and the story of the horse race got mistaken for the story of the horses. Putting the spotlight on profits took some of the magic out of the storytelling, leading some to bad business practices, poor safety regulations, unethical treatment of people and animals, pollution, and environmental waste – ecological degradation coming from the making of money and spectacle.

To complicate things, filmmakers and audiences both seem to enjoy the spectacle of our own destruction on screen. From the massive physical and metaphorical fires in the climactic burning of Atlanta in *Gone with the Wind* (1939), for which Selznick and collaborators torched much of the back lot of MGM, to the frequent digital VFX destruction of our major cities and landmarks like the Golden Gate Bridge, Big Ben, and the Hollywood sign. The Eiffel Tower, which is a UNESCO World Heritage Site, has been destroyed in at least a dozen movies, like *The Great Race* (1965), *War of the Worlds* (1953), Weird Al's *UHF* (1989), *Teenage Mutant Ninja Turtles* (1993), *Mars Attacks!* (1996), *Armageddon* (1998), *Team America: World Police* (2004), *GI Joe: Rise of Cobra* (2009), *Men in Black 4* (2019), and others. It doesn't help that we, as an audience, seem to want to see more and more waste, destruction, fire, apocalypse, and bigger, badder, more wasteful catastrophes. Some filmmakers even brag about how much inconvenience and mayhem they actually imposed on a location: the tires and gasoline burned for smoke effects in *Apocalypse Now* (1979), a ship dragged up and over a clear-cut rainforest mountain pass in *Fitzcarraldo* (1982). Is this self-destructive story getting old? Maybe we will never tire of watching Hollywood burn – or the rest of the world, for that matter.

DOI: 10.4324/9781003425441-1

2 An Introduction to Green Filmmaking

What's Old Is New Again

But maybe what we need, what we don't even know we're looking for, is a new mythology. One that's free from the burning, the strip mining, the money exchanging, and the excesses of the mythology we've settled for. Perhaps even a return to a very old mythology that reconnects us with the original magic of storytelling. A more inclusive storytelling that isn't about conquering nature or each other. Stories that show people as part of the natural world, not against it. Green film and green filmmaking offer a promise to inspire and rekindle some of that spark that storytellers and story lovers may not even know will make them whole again.

Mythologist and literature professor Joseph Campbell talks about the Native American reverence for nature and how Hollywood's dominant storytelling tradition has "lost our whole sense of accord with nature."[1] When you lose connection to the sacred in the natural world, he says, you miss the "matching of our own nature with this gorgeous nature of the land." He invokes Native American figure Black Elk's reminder that "anywhere is the center of the world."[2]

Look at the enduring Seventh Generation Principle, from the nearly 1,000-year-old Great Law of the Iroquois, which says "in every deliberation, we must consider the impact on the seventh generation."[3] It's true in environmental stewardship and sustainability, but it applies more broadly too. It applies to deliberations about natural resources, deliberations regarding cultural relationships, the implications of the hero's journey, and other things too. It's a valuable outlook, even though it's sometimes over-quoted to sell dish detergent, paper towels ... or books like this one.

The idea of green film production is more than just recycling drink containers and donating leftover food from set. An important part of green filmmaking is re-popularizing a mythology that connects us to the sacred in the natural world.

Sustainability and Ecomedia

In order to get a handle on what green filmmaking is and what it can be, it helps to define a couple of related terms. Sustainability can mean several different things. One simple definition is "meeting the needs of the present without compromising the ability of future generations to meet their own needs."[4] Another definition, "the ability to be maintained at a certain rate or level, as in, the sustainability of economic growth." Or finally, the "avoidance of the depletion of natural resources in order to maintain an ecological balance" – for example, "the pursuit of global environmental sustainability."[5] Sustainability is often broken into three intertwined categories: *social sustainability*, *economic sustainability*, and *environmental sustainability*. Together, these three forms of sustainability are known as the three pillars of sustainable development.

Ecomedia is the study of film and media and its relationship to the natural environment. It examines representations of the environment in media and the environmental impact of the media itself. For example, ecomedia looks at how the TV and movie biz crashed into the natural environment in a mostly unsustainable way during the Anthropocene (the period since the Industrial Revolution when human activity started significantly impacting our planet). There are many related areas of study, like environmental communication, environmental media studies, ecocriticism, and ecomaterialism. Scholar Pat Brereton suggests that the mass media is especially persuasive in speaking of injustices, like those generated by climate change.[6]

There is a tangled chain of sprocketed frames that links the film industry, the way that nature is depicted on screen, the climate crisis, and the potential that film has to inspire change. This chapter discusses cinematic representations of nature, introduces some connections between sustainability and film, and offers a look at ecomedia studies for production students. Some scholars propose that incorporating sustainability in media demands a new three-pronged strategy including content, production, and policy.[7] This book focuses on the first two because it is written from the perspective of the media makers.

A Glimpse into Film History

Filmmakers need to understand more than lenses and blocking; they need to also study film history (what other filmmakers have done) and media studies (the way that films and society affect each other). Knowing about the context of the films of the past will inform your projects and make them much richer.

Humans have unquestionably transformed the natural world. From logging to transportation to large-scale agriculture, the imprint of industry and progress has consumed the resources of our earth and resulted in pollution and global warming. In many ways, the history of cinema parallels the history of human industry and presents a photographic record of our interaction with the natural world.

The way that films show nature and our place within it has gone from a naive adventure in its early days to a more complex conflict-based mentality in mid-century cinema to a more nuanced relationship with nature that demands a certain amount of eco-literacy on the part of the viewer today.

Early Days of Film – A Simplistic View of Nature

Since its inception, cinema (meaning film, all flavors of analog and digital video, and all the other motion picture technologies) has made images that showcase our interaction with the natural world. Some of the greatest metaphors for humans versus nature can be seen in the first movies ever made. *Rough Sea at Dover* (1895) is a one-shot film from the UK by Birt Acres featuring substantial waves crashing into a breakwater. Waves hit bricks, pounding the stone and concrete in a time-tested exercise in futility. Erosion, entropy, and time will eventually win, and as sea levels rise, the shores and cliffs of Dover will get smaller. But that's a more contemporary reading of a film that was created more as a spectacle, or a novelty. The force of those crashing waves captured on celluloid and projected for an audience was remarkable for spectators of the day. One photography publication wrote of these moving pictures: "We all know how beautiful ordinary, instantaneous effects of breaking waves appear on the screen, but when the actual movement of nature is reproduced in addition, the result is little short of marvelous."[8] Enthusiastic rapt viewers tried to "avoid the spray of the sea foam" in early screenings.

On the other hand, the Edison Company's *Electrocuting an Elephant* (1903) and the Pathé Frères film *The Polar Bear Hunt in the Arctic Seas* (1910) both witness a human clash with wild animals that ends in the death of the noble creatures.[9] There were also the famous early films of Teddy Roosevelt on safari in Africa depicting man versus wild. Roosevelt had a great love and respect for nature but also a strong desire to shoot at it.

Nanook of the North (1922) is Robert Flaherty's famous/infamous ethnography of an Inuit clan and a great example of this naive, adventurous view of Mother Nature. The first few shots of the film that situate us afloat in the Arctic Ocean are majestic and beautiful, clearly positioning the human subjects as small creatures in the grandeur of a vast, natural world.

Flaherty's ground-breaking documentary is also an important touchstone for the discussion of ethics in filmmaking and showcases the entanglement of all the intersecting issues that society and filmmakers are still trying to sort out 100+ years later (see Chapter 2: "Intersections and Production"). Can an outsider (especially one from a colonizer group) make a film about another person's culture? How exploitative of the environment (and the Inuit) was Flaherty? How does that sit with the fact that he originally did survey work for mining concerns? These are some of the contradictions that brought about the Flaherty Seminars on ethics in film. Author Nadia Bozak makes some interesting analysis of *Nanook* in her book *The Cinematic Footprint: Lights, Camera, Natural Resources*, looking at the hunted seal as an extracted resource for the hunter, and the hunt and the life of the Inuit family as the extracted resource for Flaherty.[10] *Nanook* is a romanticized man versus nature story with a Western point of view. Flaherty's storytelling is a blending of fact and fiction – the adventures are staged, the women who travel with Nanook are not actually his wives … even his name is invented.

Taking a step back, the very act of placing anything inside the rectangle of the film frame means that the filmmaker is making choices about meaning – what to include, exclude, highlight, exploit, or downplay. With the use of the camera, films literally and figuratively frame the natural world in relation to human technology. The tension between nature and human culture is a collision – there is an effect, a wake, an aftershock. The aftershock becomes particularly apparent in mid-century films.

Mid-Century Monsters

One of the (literally) biggest figures representing humanity's recklessness and nature's revenge is *Godzilla* (1954). As the song by Blue Oyster Cult says: "History shows again and again, how nature points out the folly of men. Go, go, Godzilla!" Spawned in the atomic era from A-bomb testing at the Bikini Atoll (and within the historical context of the US bombing of Hiroshima and Nagasaki), Godzilla is a Force of Nature. Like his kaiju brethren Mothra and Rodan, who were awakened by mining, Godzilla doesn't care much for human irritants, on whom he is frequently stomping, and blitzing their cities. Godzilla's destructive powers grow with radiation, in contrast to its negative effects on humans.

Ecohorror is a genre of films representing fears related to the natural world. The creature movies of the 1950s showed us the consequences for messing with nature in schlock movie classics like *Them!* (1954) featuring giant ants mutated from atomic bomb tests rampaging over civilization. Other movie monsters like Hedorah, AKA *The Smog Monster* (1971), are literally spawned from pollution. Similar themes can be seen in *The Creature from the Black Lagoon* (1954), *It Came from Beneath the Sea* (1955), *Tarantula* (1955), *Attack of the Crab Monsters* (1957), and later films that would follow in their footsteps like *Night of the Lepus* (1972), *C.H.U.D.* (1984), *Alligator* (1980), and *The Host* (2007).

In the introduction to *Science Fiction Film and Television*, Bridgette Barclay and Christy Tidwell argue that "creature features provide a space for considering environmental issues. Through fun and fear, they often lead viewers to identify or empathize with the creatures and against the humans making bad decisions, and such responses make creature features especially fruitful texts for environmental messages and analyses."[11]

Sustainability in Film and the Green Monster

An interview with Brian Rogers, Producer on *Godzilla* (2014), *Godzilla: King of the Monsters* (2019), *Godzilla vs. Kong* (2021), and *Godzilla x Kong: The New Empire* (2024)

Around 2003, there was a Godzilla 3D IMAX treatment going around (*Godzilla 3D to the Max*) featuring the smog monster Hedora, a character named Deathla, the Iguazú Falls, and the Great Pacific Garbage Patch in the Sargasso Sea. There is a whole history in Godzilla films about humans harming nature, and nature getting its revenge…

Yes. In the Legendary Pictures films about Godzilla, we really tried to keep the original spirit of Godzilla – because he was created by atomic energy that was misused. So Godzilla – is he a good guy or a bad guy? He straddles the world in between the two – especially in *King of the Monsters*, which has some heavy ecological subtext – man destroying the world and monsters solve it/fix it.

In terms of sustainability, in the movies, there is a tremendous amount of waste. In *Godzilla 3*, we had to make a huge skull out of foam and then had to throw it away. This skull was so big that we needed a cherry picker just to get to the top of it to sculpt it. I asked, "What are you going to do with the skull? Can you give me one of the teeth?" There was no good answer for what to do with the waste. Styrofoam is used all the time, but it's a problem because there's no way to get rid of it. Papier mache won't work – there's just nothing else that does the same job. So, we gotta use what works.

It would be great to see more of a green infrastructure – a place where other productions, especially low-budget ones, could advertise to reuse or repurpose leftover materials. Obviously, you can't reuse a copyrighted set – craftspeople have put all their creativity into it and it would be weird to see it in some awful cheap film, but there must be other ways to reuse the materials.

Luckily, some projects now have sustainability coordinators trying to find homes for cleared items after wrap, but storage is a real challenge.

Yes. Space is sometimes a more valuable commodity to film schools and studios than being able to reuse existing materials. I've seen some recycling initiatives on sets, but on most shoots, you do end up with all this crap at the end that you need to get rid of. I don't know how they put it out there to get it to people. You should get some students to create a company with a clearinghouse for film materials. I bet there are some really clever entrepreneurs coming out of school now who could take that on. Good luck to you and all the young filmmakers out there!

Sea-level rise, superstorms, tsunamis, and even monsters are part of the cinematic revenge of Mother Earth in some disaster movies.

Sustainability and the Films of Today: "It's Complicated"

One way to show the aftershock of the intersection of humans and nature is through the visual spectacle of the climate disaster movie. *The Day After Tomorrow* (2004), based on the book *The Coming Global Superstorm* by two of my favorite scholars of mystery, myth, and conspiracy, Art Bell and Whitley Strieber, is perhaps the most often cited example. In *Avatar* (2009), it's space-faring human miners who threaten the ecosystem of the moon Pandora on behalf of a greedy corporation. Likewise, the series *The Last of Us* (2023) shows a dystopian world ruined by the consequences of climate change.

Ironically, many of these films produce huge carbon footprints. Roland Emmerich's *The Day After Tomorrow* (2004) is reportedly the first Hollywood studio film to address the greenhouse gases of its own production.[12] The 10,000 tons of carbon emissions were offset with a $200,000 donation by Emmerich for planting trees.[13]

However, RARE Conservation, an environmental organization, reports that audiences interested in climate don't always want to see disasters and dystopia; in fact, according to one study, seven out of ten audience members prefer to see more climate-friendly actions on screen.[14] Indeed, in this era of accelerating climate change, humans are catching up to the effects of a simplistic, colonialist, anthropocentric attitude toward nature. Many recent films include a more nuanced acknowledgment that humans have negatively affected the environment and that the answers aren't as easy as they seemed in earlier movies.

Indeed, directors including Terrence Malick, Hayao Miyazaki, and Chloé Zhao highlight positive, lovely representations of nature. In one interview, *Nomadland* (2020) director Zhao said "you have to humble yourself to the weather, to the land, to the animals…. I think I'm attracted to telling stories that are somehow related to nature because it's a reflection of humanity."[15]

Notably, some Terrence Malick films even have interstitial nature shots woven into the narrative. In *The Thin Red Line* (1998), *Days of Heaven* (1978), and *Tree of Life* (2011), we see these "pillow shots" showing nature in concert with humans, or more accurately, nature moving along despite humans and human chaos.

In *Sasquatch Sunset* (2024), the family of Sasquatch is a part of the beautiful forest in which they live – a forest threatened by human campers, loggers, and encroaching development. Yet the film lovingly shows the beauty of the creatures' natural environment.

The same can be said for Ghibli studios films like *My Neighbor Totoro* (1988), *Ponyo* (2008), *The Secret World of Arrietty* (2010), and *Princess Mononoke* (1997), which all feature nature as a lovely character in the story. The natural world and magical spirit world are linked through tree spirits and blowing winds, and creatures. Very often an establishing shot or interstitial shot will linger on a landscape, or winds blowing through trees or grass.

The texture of nature is rich and magical in Ghibli animations, and there is a feeling of hope and an ultimate righteousness of nature and its plight.

"You mustn't give up! We'll find a way! The Forest Spirit is with us. Go on planting the trees, and someday, we will beat them!" says San in *Princess Mononoke*.

In Akira Kurosawa's *Dreams* (1990), the old man in the Village of the Watermills lays it down pretty well for us:

> People today have forgotten they're really just a part of nature. Yet, they destroy the nature on which our lives depend. They always think they can make something better. Especially scientists. They may be smart, but most don't understand the heart of nature. They only invent things that, in the end, make people unhappy. Yet they're so proud of their inventions. What's worse, most people are, too. They view them as if they were miracles. They worship them. They don't know it, but they're losing nature. They don't see that they're going to perish. The most important things for human beings are clean air and clean water.

It is the more nuanced, complex, and "deepening relationship between our environment, culture, and media"[16] that Environmental Media Studies and similar disciplines look to examine.

Nature Documentaries

Unlike their narrative Hollywood cousins, documentaries tend to explore a more contemplative approach to nature. Perhaps it's the smaller crew size that lends itself to a different perspective on the natural world – and often a more mindful, modest ecological footprint as well. Consider IMAX documentaries like *Pandas* (2018) or *Jane Goodall's Reasons for Hope* (2023). Immersive naturescapes, virtual 360 nature meditations, and nature travel films like *Ecosphere* (2020) or *Kingdom of Plants* (2022) call back to the earliest travel films of the 1890s in which a faraway waterfall or a view from the front of a train passing through the forest were brought to an audience of eager novelty seekers in special film parlors.

From early TV series like *The Undersea World of Jacques Cousteau* (which initially ran from 1968 to 1976) and *Mutual of Omaha's Wild Kingdom* (which initially ran from 1963 to 1988), documentaries have also long inspired viewers to pay attention to the planet and its inhabitants. David Attenborough began his more than 80-year career as a nature writer and presenter on the British documentary series *Zoo Quest* (1954–1963), which followed London Zoo staff members to a faraway location to capture an animal for their collection, standard practice at the time. The series, which gave audiences a rare look at animals in their native habitats, made Attenborough famous – and made fans care about animals they'd never seen or likely even heard of.

Today, documentaries have moved beyond simply shooting species in the wild (albeit with a camera rather than a gun) to portraying the interconnectedness of humanity and the rest of the natural world. Some, like *Racing Extinction* (2015), stress the importance of biodiversity. Others take a more intimate approach; for example, in *My Octopus Teacher* (2020), a cephalopod who lives in the waters off diver and filmmaker Craig Foster's beach home teaches Foster (and the rest of us) an important lesson – to "feel that you are a part of this place, and not a visitor. And that's a huge difference." Likewise, nonnarrative documentaries like *Koyaanisqatsi* (1982) and *Samsara* (2011), which take the viewer on a meditative visual journey across the planet without narration or dialogue, emphasize humanity's place within the larger web of life.

Other documentaries highlight the beauty of nature – and its fragility. David Attenborough's *Our Planet* (2019–2023) and *Planet Earth* (2006), as well as the much-loved *March of the Penguins* (2005) and *Chasing Coral* (2017), for example, bring the awesome spectacle of the natural world to an appreciative audience who couldn't otherwise see these wonders – while also pointing out that climate change has put the delicate balance of life in peril.

Independent and Experimental Approaches

Joris Ivens' observational art film *Rain* (1929) shows the simple natural beauty of rain falling in Amsterdam. In this lyrical film poem, we are witness to a meditative view of raindrops falling, puddles forming, and light reflecting off water. It's a lovely visual collage typical of the experimental landscapes and independent films of the avant-garde.

In *The Garden in the Machine: A Field Guide to Independent Films about Place*, Scott MacDonald looks at landscape, place, and history of landscape in art, painting, dioramas, and the Lumiere-like films of the American Avant-Garde. He credits experimental filmmakers such as J. J. Murphy, Kenneth Anger, Marie Menken, Carolee Schneemann, Stan Brakhage, James Benning, and George Kuchar with creating their own artful landscapes that offer an alternative point of view of the natural world. The filmmakers "provide cinematic vistas that allow viewers to sample, if only for a long moment, something in that meditative sense of landscape that invigorates the painting of a previous century. Each filmmaker creates a 'Garden' within the machine of Cinema and of contemporary society."[17] They also exhibit an economy of production that lends itself to a low-impact, small footprint.

The same can be said of many other experimental art films. For example, Peter Hutton's landscapes and Bill Viola's images of water and mirages examine nature and time while experimenting with photography – and all with a small carbon footprint.

Remember the floating discarded plastic bag in *American Beauty* (1999)? That beautiful and disturbing metaphor for waste in modern society is even more profound in indie filmmaker Jem Cohen's *Lost Book*

Found (1996), which was likely where the metaphor originated. *Lost Book Found* is a look at the city of New York, the bustling city's castoff relics, the discovery of a lost book of lists and numbers, and that floating, swirling plastic bag showing how trash too is subject to the natural eddies of the wind.

Stan Brakhage's *Mothlight* is not a film about climate change or the effects of humans on the insect world. Instead, it's a piece of art using physical aspects of nature, including moth wings and leaves, taped onto a human technology – film. It forces the viewer to consider the relationship between humans and the natural world in a new way – in an integrated way instead of an oppositional way.

A Further Study of Sustainability in Film

The focus of this book is sustainability in the writing, creation, and production of films and screen content. There are many other related areas of study that we can also include in the larger category of sustainability in film. I mention a few in this section for those who want to explore further but recognize that each is much more nuanced than I can address here.

Green Screen: Environmentalism and Hollywood Cinema, by David Ingram, looks at film studies and environmental history and politics as a way to discuss cultural criticism informed by "green" thought. Ingram argues that Hollywood cinema has perpetuated romantic ideas about nature and participated in "greenwashing."[18] The book also examines the rise of environmental concerns in the movies, and the approach to wilderness, wild animals, and land use in films.

The book *Environmental Management of the Media: Policy, Industry, Practice*, by Pietari Kääpä, looks at the history of ecomedia and related fields, including the work of David Ingram, Lisa Parks, Nadia Bozak, and many other scholars looking at media's footprint and brainprint. *The Environmental Management of the Media* is a study of the ecological content of media and the management of media organizations and their production strategies. The publication from the *FilmForum 2022 XXIX Udine International Film and Media Studies Conference* in Udine, Italy, includes extensive essays for those seeking further study.[19]

We might also look at films, television shows, and games in relation to degrowth, environmental justice, our desire for spectacle, and the environmental footprint of our productions, as well as the footprint of their distribution and consumption.[20] The loss of biodiversity[21] as a result of unsustainable and irresponsible film production practices is also related. Performing a complete study of sustainability in film means taking a holistic approach. As Naomi Klein says in her book *This Changes Everything*, "That means laying out a vision of the world ... that resonates with the majority of people on the planet, because it is true: That we are not apart from nature, but of it."[22]

Cleaning Up in Film Production

Capitalism and the Industrial Revolution have been tough on the environment, so it's no surprise that filmmaking has taken its own ecological toll. However, the damage has been farther reaching than you might think.

For example, *Mad Max: Fury Road* (2015) reportedly "left tire tracks on an untouched, fragile landscape in Namibia ... and *Pirates of the Caribbean: Dead Men Tell No Tales* (2017) was accused of spilling chemical waste into a creek in Australia."[23]

Danny Boyle's film *The Beach* (2000) bulldozed a beach in Ko Phi Phi Le, Thailand, removing native bushes that prevented erosion and planting coconut palms to fit the filmmakers' preferred aesthetic, sacrificing the area's natural defenses against monsoons and ending in a lawsuit against Fox studios.[24]

The gigantic replica of the *Titanic* for the 1997 movie of the same name in Rosarito, Mexico, took over a shoreline, generating waste and messing with the sea urchin and other creature populations. The result was reportedly permanent damage to the ecosystem.[25]

In *Hollywood's Dirtiest Secret – The Hidden Environmental Cost of the Movies*, author Hunter Vaughn asks, "Would you accept the extinction of a species of fish in exchange for your favorite movie? How about a species of rabbit? How many trees would you cut down in order to have *Transformers: Dark of the Moon* (2011)? Does that change if the question is about *Singin' in the Rain* (1952) or *Moonlight* (2016)?"[26] How many old growth Redwoods would you trade for a classic film like *Casablanca* (1942)? How many elephants would you give up? Or people?

The British Academy of Film and Television Arts (BAFTA) project called "albert" (with a lower-case "A") reports that "the average television programme produces tens of tonnes of carbon dioxide, a feature film is in the thousands. This is a public relations and moral conundrum that the industry must address and one that we have precious few years in which to do so."[27]

According to albert's *Screen New Deal* (2020), "for a typical tentpole production, resource consumption data analysis shows that its:

- total energy consumption could power Times Square for 5 days
- total fuel consumption could fill an average car tank 11,478 times
- total waste generation equates to the weight of 313.5 blue whales
- total plastic bottle usage equates to yearly average use of 168 people"

That said, the fledgling efforts of the entertainment industry to mitigate waste and control its footprint are commendable. albert, EcoProd, the Sustainable Entertainment Alliance (formerly the Sustainable Production Alliance or SPA), Reel Green, and other industry initiatives have made some important, impressive progress. The task ahead is to continue the work, improve upon it, and transfer successful practices to other production groups, other countries, and other scales of filming.

However, there are challenges. There is no other production group that has the resources, workflow, access, or financial backing that Hollywood does. Does Hollywood's data and workflow even translate to the rest of the world? The larger problem is arguably with capitalism, corporate profit-making, old-world colonialist roots, and human greed. But as Desmond Tutu once said, "there is only one way to eat an elephant: a bite at a time."

In a way, the success of eco-filmmaking changemakers is in spite of outside pressures. Surely we can transfer and translate some of these practices to other kinds of filmmakers too. And surely the solutions coming from all the people and places in the world with often unheard voices can be applied to the Hollywood model and beyond. It's time to hear from everyone.

The cli-fi (Climate Fiction) novel *The Ministry for the Future* by Kim Stanley Robinson supposes a not-too-distant future where climate change is over the tipping point and radical action is needed to change human industry and the atmosphere to stop global warming. One character in the novel suggests that humanity needs a "new religion" with new values and new goals that are not based in capital gain, and extractive practices.

Similarly, environmental scientist Brian Ashenfelter, a teacher at the American Musical and Dramatic Academy (AMDA), writes in his sustainability class materials *How We Got to Now* that humans need a new philosophy – one dedicated not to material success, but that integrates the successes of the natural world and human achievement as a part of the same system – the same team. One of the missions of this book is to consider what that new mythology might be like. It may not be new at all. It may be a re-examination of an overlooked or maligned mythology. It may be a Campbell-style "monomyth" that we see through a new, more sustainable lens.

The project of this book is to assist in the transition to more sustainable screen storytelling. Most of the chapters include specific sustainable production practices for your future projects and some robust checklists and other tools to help you make them happen. But before we get to the specific practices, let's look at another lens through which we can measure the effects of our sustainability efforts: the lens of intersectionality.

Exercises/Homework

1. What does sustainability mean for you?
2. What are your personal sustainability goals? What about goals for your community?
3. Write an analysis of three films, one from before 1950, one from 1950 to 2000, and one from 2002 to present, discussing how they portray environmental issues and how effective they are at promoting eco-friendly behavior.

Notes

1. Joseph Campbell, Phil Cousineau, and Stuart L. Brown. 2003. *The Hero's Journey Joseph Campell on His Life and Work*. Novato, CA: New World Library.
2. Ibid.
3. Often attributed to The Great Peacemaker, and The Great Law, or constitution of the Iriquois Confederacy (c. 1190).

4 The 1987 United Nations Brundtland Commission.
5 Oxford Languages Dictionary.
6 Pat Brereton. 2022. Cinema, ecology, and environment. *The Routledge Handbook of Environment and Communication* (Ch. 22). Milton Park, UK: Routledge.
7 Pietari Kääpä, and Hunter Vaughan. February 2022. A companion to motion pictures and public value. In *From Content to Context (and Back Again): New Industrial Strategies for Environmental Sustainability in the Media*, edited by Mette Hjort and Ted Nannicelli (Ch. 14). https://doi.org/10.1002/9781119677154.ch14
8 *Amateur Photographer*, January 24, 1896. https://www.youtube.com/watch?v=L7HJAohiuuo
9 "Nature Films." n.d. Film Reference. http://www.filmreference.com/encyclopedia/Independent-Film-Road-Movies/ Nature-Films-EARLY-HISTORY.html
10 *The Cinematic Footprint: Lights, Camera, Natural Resources – Bozak.*
11 Bridgitte Barclay, and Christy Tidwell. Autumn 2021. Introduction: Mutant bears, defrosted parasites and cellphone swarms: Creature features and the environment. *Science Fiction Film and Television*, Vol. 14, No. 3, pp. 269–277.
12 "The Emmerich Effect." 2019. Green Film Shooting. October 3, 2019. https://greenfilmshooting.net/blog/en/2019/10/03/the-emmerich-effect/.
13 "Sustainability in the Motion Picture Industry" November, 2006. UCLA, California Integrated Waste Management Board, Publication # 440-06-017. http://personal.anderson.ucla.edu/charles.corbett/papers/mpis_report.pdf
14 Rare. 2024. "7 In 10 Americans Want Climate-Friendly Behaviors in Film and TV – Rare." June 20, 2024. https://rare.org/research-reports/audiences-are-demanding-climate-friendly-behaviors-on-screen.
15 A Spirituality That Comes out of Nature | Chloé Zhao | Studio 9 | TIFF 2017.
16 Meryl Shriver-Rice, and Hunter Vaughan. Jan 2020. What is environmental media studies? *Journal of Environmental Media*, Vol. 1, No. 1, pp. 3–13 (English). https://doi.org/10.1386/jem_00001_2
17 Scott MacDonald. December 2001. *The Garden in the Machine: A Field Guide to Independent Films about Place.* Berkeley, CA: University of California Press.
18 David Ingram. 2004, January 1. *Green Screen: Environmentalism and Hollywood Cinema.* Exeter: University of Exeter Press.
19 Published collection of essays from *FilmForum 2022 XXIX Udine International Film and Media Studies Conference – (Un)bearable Lightness of Media* (cfp 2022). Udine: Critical Approaches to Sustainability in Film and Audiovisual Production, Mimesis Circulation and Preservation. 2024.
20 Green(ing) Media (Studies). December 13, 2021. *in Autumn 2021_#Futures*. https://necsus-ejms.org/greening-media-studies/
21 "Biodiversity – Albert." 2024. Albert. July 29, 2024. https://wearealbert.org/biodiversity/.
22 Naomi Klein. 2015. *This Changes Everything: Capitalism vs. the Climate.* New York, NY: Simon & Schuster.
23 "Lights, Camera…Action for Nature?" n.d. Convention on Biological Diversity. https://www.cbd.int/article/film-industry-and-sustainability.
24 Something like: "The Beach Film Location" n.d., Vice, https://www.vice.com/en/article/7k8wpb/the-beach-film-location-thailand
25 Columbia University Press Blog. 2023. "5 Classic Films That Charmed the Industry and Devastated the Environment – Columbia University Press Blog." *Columbia University Press Blog – Publishing a Universe of Knowledge for Readers Worldwide* (blog). April 4, 2023. https://cupblog.org/2019/04/19/5-classic-films-that-charmed-the-industry-and-devastated-the-environment/.
26 Hunter Vaughn. *Hollywood's Dirtiest Secret – The Hidden Environmental Cost of the Movies.* New York, NY: Columbia University Press, p. 7.
27 "Why – Albert." 2021. Albert. September 22, 2021. https://wearealbert.org/why/.

2 Intersections and Production

When we pan that bright, hot 2000W mighty mole onto the business of film and media production and its connection to sustainability, a host of intersecting issues are illuminated. How does filmmaking go through the crossroads of race, gender, class, and nature? How are crew, cast, and content affected by diversity and inclusion? Looking at filmmaking through a sustainable, intersectional lens means examining the ways that representation and social justice show up in our storytelling.

Everything, Everywhere, All at Once, Connected

Everything is connected. This chapter has to do with the interaction between film production, climate change, and social justice – noting with special emphasis the way that underrepresented populations are disproportionately affected. The UN Sustainable Development Goals and associated research outline the ways that the common good is affected by a whole bunch of other issues, including the economy, fossil fuel use, hunger, and gender equality. We can help address these issues in our filmmaking.

Intersectionality is a complex business all the way around. In media studies, its roots are connected to lots of other areas of philosophy and cultural studies,[1,2] but this chapter's focus will be limited to intersectional issues as they relate to green film production.

The term **intersectionality** comes from "Demarginalizing the Intersection of Race and Sex,"[3] a 1989 paper by Professor Kimberlé Crenshaw that describes how race, gender, class, and other characteristics "intersect" with one another. In recent years, the term has been connected to brand-new areas like environmentalism and even film production.

In her book, *The Intersectional Environmentalist: How to Dismantle Systems of Oppression to Protect People + Planet*, climate activist Leah Thomas defines the term **intersectional environmentalism** as "an inclusive form of environmentalism that advocates for the protection of all people and the planet." As Thomas puts it, "We can't save the planet without uplifting the voices of its people, especially those most often unheard. As a society, we often forget that humans are a part of our global ecosystem

DOI: 10.4324/9781003425441-2

and that we don't exist separately from nature; we coexist with it each and every day."[4]

Good Energy, a screenwriters' **climate storytelling** resource group, looks at intersectional environmentalism in film this way: "The climate crisis isn't an issue—it contains all issues. When we write climate stories, it's important to recognize how this emergency intersects with our other identities and harms everyone differently."[5] The Good Energy Playbook has a section that speaks to the different ways that climate justice intersects with human vulnerabilities in areas of race, gender, sexuality, class, disability, and others. Does the film and television industry have a role to play in the ways that the environment connects with these issues? As a major cultural industry and economic driver, can the entertainment business support sustainable development to make improvements in some of these areas?

The development of a culture of sustainability in film is what we're talking about, and it's not a fringe or radical idea. Like other industries, the film business needs to become sustainable. It's that simple.

If we are trying to develop a culture of sustainability in film (or anywhere else), the UN sustainable development goals are a good place to start (Figure 2.1).

Some of the goals, such as "Responsible Production and Consumption," "Climate Action," and "Decent Work and Economic Growth," have concrete target areas like landfill waste, water use, and pollution. These are not easy, one-shot fixes, but they are quantifiable objectives for the entertainment industry. After all, we can measure things like water use, aluminum recycling, or particulates in the atmosphere and make changes within the systems that we are measuring. It gets more complex when we start to think about goals like gender equality, poverty, sustainable communities, and reducing inequality. But tackling intersectional goals like these is just as important.

How Filmmaking Physically Impacts Marginalized Communities

For starters, the lithium we use in our camera batteries, EVs, and computers is mined in Argentina, Bolivia, Zimbabwe, and many other countries in the developing world. This mining involves separating the lithium from iron ore using sulfuric acid, which is toxic, but many of the miners are from these countries' Indigenous populations and are so poor that they have little choice but to participate, creating an intersection of filmmaking, environmentalism, and social justice.

In some respects, the filmmaking business is like the oil drilling business. Movies are an extractive industry. Productions come in, they extract, leave, and usually don't follow up with the community. That's not a sustainable way to work. "The bottom line is that production is inherently not sustainable. You are building stuff that is going to be moved, shot, disassembled, and quickly discarded. And that's just the construction department, but it's the same for food, props, and everything else," says Lena Welch, owner of Next Earth and consultant to numerous Netflix and HBO shows. Filmmakers

16 *Intersections and Production*

Figure 2.1 The UN Sustainable Development Goals.

Intersections and Production

should consider that these practices particularly impact those who live in the community where a film is shot, even if the harm is accidental.

In 2023, the co-directors of *Everything Everywhere All at Once*, Daniel Kwan and Daniel Scheinert (The Daniels), were interviewed by Emellie O'Brien (CEO of Earth Angel) in a talk at the Academy of Motion Picture Arts and Sciences about "accelerating climate innovation and justice work in Hollywood."[6,7] In the words of Daniel Kwan, "There is no cavalry coming to save us, we are the cavalry." He continued, "We are not here to make what I call fast entertainment – think fast fashion, fast food. How much stuff can we pump out? How much attention can we suck and extract from our audiences?" Instead of producing fast entertainment, he called for "sneaking in the vegetables" and working around limitations in sustainable productions.

Daniel Scheinert suggested "cutting costs, not labor," – that is, linking with the labor movement, partnering with diverse groups of people, and "collaborating with the universe."

How Climate Justice Is Depicted in Movies

Intersectionality also shows up in the content, casting, and crews of films like *Parasite* (2019), *Nomadland* (2020), and *Black Panther: Wakanda Forever* (2022) (see also Chapter 6: Content, Development, and Climate Storytelling).

As Young Entertainment Activists (YEA!) CEO Allison Begalman put it in an interview with Walking Softer, a conservation nonprofit, "Climate is one of

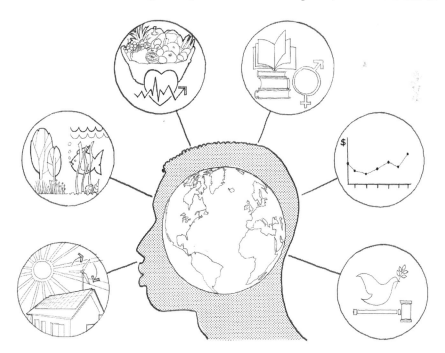

Figure 2.2 Climate, labor, justice, energy use, and life in the seas all intersect.

the most pressing and intersectional issues of our time, yet it has barely been mentioned in television and film."[8] In a panel for the 2023 Hollywood Climate Summit, *Abbott Elementary*'s creator and star Quinta Brunson agreed, adding, "I feel like no one is focusing on the climate crisis in conjunction with race."[9]

"Holding the villains accountable, and speaking truth to power is what it's about," according to environmental journalist Emily Atkin in the same talk. "The villains in these climate stories have convinced themselves that what they are doing is right." She continued, "Listen to the frontline communities and environmental groups who are trying to be heard. Look harder for climate stories. The major polluters are the villains. Tell stories about them."

Killers of the Flower Moon (2023) explores how members of the Osage tribe, who had been resettled onto Oklahoma land rich with oil, were exploited and ultimately murdered under mysterious circumstances in the 1920s. According to Angela Lawson, a member of the Northern Arapaho Nation of Wyoming and assistant professor of cinema studies and ethnic studies at the University of Colorado Boulder, director Martin Scorcese consulted with 200 community and tribal leaders and hired some Osage tribe members as crew.[10] That said, Lawson also voiced broader concerns about there not being more contemporary films about Native Americans and more Native American directors telling authentic Native American stories.

So what can we do? "We can be activated, tell climate stories, plan for seven generations. Make change where we are," climate activists Nalleli Cobo and YoNasDa Lonewolf implore at the HCS. "Show up. No apathy."

Notes

1. For more information on the wider topic, see other cited texts in these footnotes and the bibliography.
2. Michael Mikulewicz, Martina Angela Caretta, Farhana Sultana, and Neil J. W. Crawford. 2023. Intersectionality & climate justice: A call for synergy in climate change scholarship. *Environmental Politics*, Vol. 32, No. 7, pp. 1275–1286. https://doi.org/10.1080/09644016.2023.2172869
3. Kimberlé Crenshaw. 1989. *Demarginalizing the Intersection of Race and Sex: A Black Feminist Critique of Antidiscrimination Doctrine, Feminist Theory and Antiracist Politics*. University of Chicago Legal Forum, Vol. 1989, No. 1, Article 8. Available at: http://chicagounbound.uchicago.edu/uclf/vol1989/iss1/8
4. Leah Thomas. 2022. *The Intersectional Environmentalist: How to Dismantle Systems of Oppression to Protect People + Planet*. Hachette Book Group.
5. Sheehan, Ryan. n.d. "Climate Justice and Intersectionality." Good Energy. http://www.goodenergystories.com/playbook/climate-justice-and-intersectionality.
6. Weinstein, Allison Begalman Heather Fipps, and Ali. 2023. "Recalibrating the Culture of the Climate Crisis—How Stories Shape Our Future | Opinion." *Newsweek*, July 11, 2023. https://www.newsweek.com/recalibrating-culture-climate-crisishow-storiesshape-%20our-future-opinion-1811676.
7. HCS website. https://www.hollywoodclimatesummit.com/
8. Walking Softer. *Young Leaders Award*. https://www.walkingsofter.org/changemakers/checking-in-with-allison-begalman
9. Hollywood Climate Summit 2023. https://www.hollywoodclimatesummit.com/
10. "'Killers of the Flower Moon' and Indigenous representation in film." n.d. CU Boulder Today. https://www.colorado.edu/today/2023/11/22/killers-flower-moon-and-indigenous-representation-film.

3   Why Be Green?

"It's not easy being green," says *Sesame Street*'s Kermit the Frog. But being green isn't as difficult as some humans would have you believe.

Sure, sometimes the last thing that you want is another set of regulations and protocols to follow. Take the COVID-19 pandemic. To keep people safe, we had to devise and follow new testing protocols, observe distancing and masking, use the zone system on set, employ remote technologies, generate all kinds of paperwork, and appoint whole new teams on the crew to manage all of it. It was a big pain. But we were happy to be back to work on set after isolating in lockdown. Good filmmakers would do whatever they had to do to keep their team members safe and healthy.

Sustainable production practices are not the same as preventative practices for a global pandemic but think of the planet as one of your crew members. You wouldn't deny safety equipment or a 12-hour turn-around between workdays for your crew, would you? We need to keep the Earth safe and healthy too. As one of my students put it, "We want there to be a planet for us to keep making movies on in the future." A little extra care now will mean the world later.

Why Be Green?

Given the state of the world and some of the statistics we've outlined, it seems like a better question would be why *not* be green? It makes sense for filmmaking and for every other industry too. Humans will be better off, other creatures will benefit, and everyone's happy, right? Seems pretty obvious, but some people still need convincing. Here are some persuasive arguments to try on your colleagues, producers, teachers, clients, or bosses who are reluctant to "start a whole new thing."

The Economic Argument

Appeal to their bottom line. Ultimately, being sustainable is all about the conservation of resources. Using resources sparingly and wisely saves money. If we can save the cost of filling up the gas tank on our production vehicle one time, or pay out for fewer miles on the PA's car that she uses for production

DOI: 10.4324/9781003425441-3

runs, that saves money. Turning off generators, lights, and equipment that isn't in use is an obvious fix – having someone whose job is to help the whole team remember to do things like that (like a sustainability coordinator) is a win-win. Why is production paying for the kilowatt hours to charge everyone's phones and devices? Set up a solar panel charging station – that's free electricity. If we reuse set pieces or get them from a secondhand store instead of fabricating them, we save money and we're practicing "reduce, reuse, recycle." You're probably already being frugal with your budget, so adding some sustainable practices is just helping you do something that you're already doing. The greener you get, the more money you'll save.

Many filmmakers think that going green costs production time and money. To be sure, there are labor costs and expenses related to sustainable production that should be acknowledged. For example, adding a sustainability person who gets a paycheck and wants to buy more expensive materials, food, and utensils may take more money upfront. In the long run, however, savings in other areas often more than make up for any additional costs, and there is much more than what appears in our budget that is saved too. We don't budget to cover the hidden ecological costs from a production, but we know that they exist – for example, long-term harm to our environment, medical costs due to pollution, further endangering at-risk species, etc. In the thick of a production, know that conserving resources and being efficient is easier on the planet – *and* the budget. "I tested this in my $75,000 documentary *Potato Heads: Keeper of the Crops*," says filmmaker Larry Engel. "I saved about $5,000, mainly in printing and travel costs, which I then put toward better film finishing and sound mixing."

A 2014 New York study of productions using sustainable practices entitled *Going Green and Saving Green*[1] shows that sustainable practices can yield run-of-show cost savings as high as 51% on water, 40% on waste, and 58% on disposable batteries.

Bottom line: Being green saves money.

The Ethical Argument

It's the right thing to do. Appeal to your producer's sense of morality. If the filmmakers care about things like safe working conditions, equal opportunity, gender equity, and paying to license artists' original music, then they care about being ethical. Ethics extends to things like reusing rather than buying new, and not dumping trash or unused paint at your filming location. Showing that the production is being green shows everyone who comes in contact with the project that you are responsible, good people. There's just nothing wrong about doing the right thing.

The Audience Likes It

The viewers will feel good when they see a "certified green" seal in your credits or the marketing materials for your film. They will have a positive association with the film when they see on-screen characters using reusable water bottles or a recycling bin. Imagine learning that the film you just watched prevented 200 plastic water bottles from going into the waste bin or that the crew reduced its carbon emissions by 50% while making the project. You'd feel pretty good about that. As a consumer, buying a bag of coffee or sugar that is labeled "free trade," "organic," "cruelty-free," or "sustainably farmed" makes you feel good. Maybe one day we'll want to start labeling our movies like we label our food products. Imagine choosing between two great-looking comedies on a Saturday night with your friends, with one film labeled "certified carbon neutral" or "cruelty-free." That would help you to decide which movie to spend your money on, right? The audience likes to feel virtuous.

It's Inspiring

Eco-positive films inspire us. Think about how many people were fired up by Al Gore's climate change documentary *An Inconvenient Truth* (2006), a film that spurred conversation, affected policy, and encouraged environmental action for years after its release. Other groundbreaking movies, including *Erin Brockovich* (2000), *Wall-E* (2008), *Okja* (2017), and *My Octopus Teacher* (2020), also inspired audiences and changed outlooks. Even a 30-second commercial can make a big impact. Take, for example, environmental organization WildAid's ads featuring NBA star Yao Ming and heartbreaking footage of a shark that couldn't swim because its fins had been cut off. These ads, which began airing around the 2008 Beijing Olympics, explained that 70 million sharks were killed each year for shark-fin soup.[2] Seeing is believing: By 2016, China's CITES (Convention on International Trade in Endangered Species of Wild Fauna and Flora) Management Authority reported an 80% decline in Chinese shark fin soup consumption.[3]

It's the Future

More and more, studio television shows, feature films, documentaries, shorts, and all kinds of projects are starting to incorporate sustainability into their content and production. In its 2021 report, British Academy Film and Television Art (BAFTA) albert calculated an increase of 146% in completed carbon action plans. The report highlights that trainings on sustainability in production are up and it looks as though they will continue to increase in the future. Projects that are not considering sustainability are stuck in the old paradigm. Be future-thinking, be proactive, be smart: be green.

Job Training

There are jobs out there now for Sustainability Coordinators, Eco-PAs, and other positions that need workers who are knowledgeable about sustainability. Learning about green production is just good job training. Learning how to coil cables, set a c-stand, read a budget, or do coverage on a script is a normal part of getting ready for working in production; those skills make you more employable. Your sustainability IQ makes you more employable too. If you know how to save 20% on fuel costs in your budget, or keep batteries recharged longer with solar, or run the PEACH or albert tools, then you have a skill set that makes you attractive to prospective employers.

It Makes You Look Smart

Managing your resources well is the hallmark of being a good producer. Making a little look like a lot is just being clever, whether we're talking about money, set design, extras, lighting, or whatever. Conserving money and materials means that you can have more resources for when you really need it. Saving the day with those leftover resources or funds makes you look like a production genius. Everyone wants to work with a smart team.

Greenwashing – Watch Out

This book comes from a perspective of optimism, but the reality is that some studios will want to "be green" solely for the optics. Caring for the environment is good for their image, but their commitment is only skin deep. Throwing a little bit of money at something relatively ineffective to make a company look good is called **greenwashing** (see also Chapter 4). For example, a coal mining company might create an advertisement that shows lush green forests that the company is "giving back to" by spending research money on biodiversity in the rainforest. The footage may all be from a stock library, and the research may not even benefit a real environmental cause. This kind of hypocritical behavior is more about marketing than contributing to the cause of conservation or environmentalism. Filmmakers and film producers need to be aware of easy fixes like purchasing carbon offsets, which may represent more a surface change than a substantive one.

Figure 3.1 Corporations, businesses, and production companies engage in greenwashing when they say that they are being environmentally sustainable and make a minimal, visible contribution but fail to make substantive changes.

It is very important that as we begin a sustainability program in preproduction, we carefully consider our own effectiveness. We do not want to inadvertently engage in greenwashing. The plan that we set up needs to be impactful and real, not just wishful thinking and pretty pictures. The best way to measure the effectiveness of your green plan is to gather data. Using checklists and tools like the ones outlined in the next chapters will keep you honest and give you metrics by which to make meaningful comparisons.

Other Filmmakers Are Doing It

One of the biggest roadblocks that we face is one that we create in our own minds. The questions that we ask ourselves can discourage action. Can the individual really do anything that will matter? Isn't it the government, the corporations, and society that need to change?

Katie Patrick has a podcast and book called *How to Save the World* that looks into the psychology of being green. In one episode of the podcast, she refers to the research of Thijs Bouman, assistant professor in the Environmental Psychology Group at the University of Groningen in the Netherlands, regarding the relationship between group and individual environmental values. The research suggests that humans are highly influenced by the groups we interact with and that we tend to underestimate the pro-environmental values of others. Individuals tend to be discouraged from participating in pro-environmental practices that they believe in if they see that their community doesn't seem to care about those practices. When we start to see that the group *does* care as much or more than we as individuals do, it reinforces our own green values. In other words, check your assumptions and realize that other people *do* care about this stuff, which will motivate you in turn.

There are filmmakers out there already employing green practices. As we just learned, individuals are more likely to engage in environmental practices if they see that their community cares about those practices. So, tell your people that lots of other people are interested in being sustainable. You're reading a whole book about it. The Green Film School Alliance, for example, is a group of schools and student filmmakers who are getting into the practice. Groups like The Sustainable Entertainment Alliance, albert, EMA, docsociety, the IDA, and the *Journal of Environmental Media* are deep into it. Other people – good people – are doing it too.

The Science

According to statistics from the UN Report *Provisional State of the Climate 2022*,[4] "increasing levels of greenhouse gases in the atmosphere due to human activities are a major driver of climate change."

Greenhouse gases, which trap heat in the air, have been increasing since the Industrial Revolution in the 18th century, when our machines, powered by fossil fuels, began to emit pollution on a large scale. Since then, CO_2

emissions are up 149%, and methane is up 262%. Nitrous oxide and fluorinated gasses from agriculture and industry also contribute to the greenhouse effect, which traps heat in Earth's atmosphere, raising temperatures. As a result, the ocean's temperature is also rising, leading to coral bleaching, the loss of marine habitats, sea level rise, and a negative impact on many species.

Our planet is currently 1.2°C warmer than pre-industrial temperatures. The Paris Accord at the 2015 United Nations Climate Change Conference agreed to a 1.5°C limit on temperature rise by 2030. It's "Code Red for humanity,"[5] declared the *2021 UN International Panel on Climate Change* report.[6] If we continue like this, millions could be exposed to heat waves, sea level rise, and extreme weather and become climate refugees. Furthermore, air pollution has become the biggest environmental risk for early death, killing more people than war, terrorism, malaria, and drugs, according to a *Lancet* report on planetary health.[7] And the damage is disproportionately affecting economically disadvantaged and historically marginalized communities – which is the very definition of *environmental racism*.[8]

The BAFTA project albert claims that green filmmaking is "simply about building an industry that works more efficiently, creatively, and collaboratively. We believe our future industry will exclusively contain individuals and organizations who realize this, the others falling away with the passing of time."

In his book, *Unstoppable*, author and TV Science Guy Bill Nye says it's like living in a house that's on fire. "You can run all the cost-benefit calculations that you like, but when you see those flames, the decision is made: you have to act. You can't afford not to. When it comes to safeguarding our planetary home, it's the same deal. We have no option but to act. Fortunately, there is still just enough time."

It is time for us to act to save our home using the tools we have as filmmakers.

Exercises/Homework

1 Imagine that you have to convince your supervisor at work to "go green" on your next task. Write a letter or email to your employer about practices like composting, purchasing recycled materials, and reducing, reusing, and recycling. What would you say to convince them that they should engage in these practices? After you've written it, send the letter or email. See what they say.
2 Pick a practice at your school or institution that could be improved. Maybe there is too much packaging used for something. Maybe something could be purchased locally instead of shipping it from long distances. Research the proper office, job title, and gatekeeper to approach about it. Request a meeting and visit their office in person to talk.

Notes

1 Emellie O'Brien. 2014, April. *Going Green & Saving Green: A Cost-Benefit Analysis of Sustainable Filmmaking.* https://greenproductionguide.com
2 WildAid. 2009. "WildAid PSA - Yao Ming: Shark Fin Soup." https://www.youtube.com/watch?v=mJG7RaLX-DM.
3 "Sharks - WildAid." 2019. WildAid. May 23, 2019. https://wildaid.org/programs/sharks/.
4 UN Report. 2022. *Provisional State of the Climate 2022.* https://storymaps.arcgis.com/stories/5417cd9148c248c0985a5b6d028b0277
5 UN Press Release. 2021, 9 August. *Secretary-General Calls Latest IPCC Climate Report "Code Red for Humanity," Stressing "Irrefutable" Evidence of Human Influence.* https://press.un.org/en/2021/sgsm20847.doc.htm
6 Intergovernmental Panel on Climate Change (IPCC). 2021. State of Global Climate 2021. *Intergovernmental Panel on Climate Change (IPCC) Report.* https://www.un.org/en/climatechange/reports
7 *Lancet Review*, Vol. 6, Issue 6, E535-E547, June 2022.
Landrigan Fuller and Bathan Balakrishnan. 2022, May 17. *Pollution and Health: A Progress Update.* https://doi.org/10.1016/S2542-5196(22)00090-0
8 Ibid.

4 How to Film Green – By Department

How can you make a sustainable movie? What is the secret of filming green?

> NARRATOR
>
> ```
> What is the secret of Soylent Green? It's the year
> 2022.... People are still the same. They'll do any-
> thing to get what they need. And they need Soylent
> Green.
> ```
>
> SOL
>
> ```
> You know, when I was a kid, food was food. Before
> our scientific magicians poisoned the water, polluted
> the soil. Decimated plant and animal life. Why, in
> my day you could buy meat anywhere. Eggs, they had.
> Real butter. Fresh lettuce in the....
> ```
>
> DETECTIVE THORN
>
> ```
> I know, Sol. You told me before. A heat wave all
> year long. A greenhouse effect. Everything burning
> up.
> ```
> —Soylent Green (1973) promotional trailer

It's no secret that there's a climate emergency and humans are a big part of that problem. We've also established that we *filmmakers* can be part of the solution.

What do we do now? And how do we do it?

Do we gather everyone up and make *Soylent Green*? Do we release a virus to depopulate our ravaged planet like in *The Maze Runner* (2014)? Do we bio-engineer a race of tasty super-pigs to feed the hungry like in *Okja* (2017)? Do we release particles into the atmosphere to reverse global warming like *Snowpiercer* (2013)?

No. No, we don't. We do what we always do when we go into production:

(Cue mobilization montage)

DOI: 10.4324/9781003425441-4

We take out our Sharpies and our checklists (or our stylus and tablet), we break down the tasks into manageable parts, we delegate jobs, we collect the best data that we possibly can, and we roll camera on the best content. We make the plan in preproduction, attack it department by department in production, and then we shape it, hone it, and sometimes fix it in post.

So, let's break it down by departments. Whether your team is just four people or one hundred and four, the opportunities are there to make a difference in writing, production design, photography, editing, and every other part of the process. It's up to you to decide how deep you want to go and how much you can do.

Checklists

Checklists are scientifically proven to be effective tools for managing people, resources, time, and tasks. Atul Gawande, author of *The Checklist Manifesto*, reminds us that our modern lives are very complicated, and a simple, effective checklist can help keep us on track. Gawande makes the argument that we can better navigate our complex tasks by using simple, effective checklists made by experts in their respective fields.

There are many examples of effective daily checklists in a variety of fields: a preflight checklist for a passenger airliner, a checklist for a complex medical procedure or surgery, NASA "go/no-go" prelaunch checklists, a checklist of building materials for constructing a commercial apartment building. As Gawande puts it, "good checklists … are precise. They are efficient, to the point, and easy to use even in the most difficult situations."[1]

Many film schools use a "greenlight checklist" to help their students navigate the complex process of production and preproduction paperwork, permits, risk assessment, insurance, and safety checks. The camera team might have a checklist for examining locations or a camera assistant's checklist for packing the gear.[2] Having a checklist makes it all work.

Figure 4.1 Checklists work – for rocket launches, for surgery, and for sustainability in your production.

Research backs up this claim. Studies by the National Institute of Health (NIH) and the science journal *Nature* were written up in a publication on transparency and the use of checklists.[3] The studies show how appropriate checks can ensure accuracy in medical procedures, scientific research, peer review, and other areas.[4,5]

The act of breaking down a complex task into organized, compartmentalized sections allows us to take it on in smaller bits. For a sustainable film project, breaking down the work by department makes it manageable. For their part, writers can include a scene about the toxic effects of pollution or write a joke about a compost bin, gaffers can use biodiesel in the generators or try a rechargeable power unit, and makeup artists can look for organic cosmetics or biodegradable applicators. There are tasks to be done in each area, and a checklist helps us to delegate and keep track of them. This is the simple idea behind a sustainability checklist for student filmmakers like the PEACHy tool.

Production Environmental Action Checklist for Young Filmmakers (PEACHy)

A good checklist is made by multiple specialists in the field who each have input in the process based on their specific experience so all partners are empowered in the process being tracked. Around 2011, film industry workers and environmental experts from the Sustainable Entertainment Alliance (SEA) and PGA Green (a committee of the Producers Guild of America) created the Production Environmental Action Checklist (PEACH). In 2021, the newly formed Green Film School Alliance (GFSA) adapted the PEACH tool for student use as PEACHy, the Production and Environmental Action Checklist for young filmmakers. Film professionals and film educators Erica Elson (American Film Institute) and I (California State University, Long Beach), with the guidance of Heidi Kindberg (SPA), made the changes. PEACHy is intended for all college-level and graduate-school productions, large and small. It can also be used by high schools with a film program. Although PEACHy was primarily designed for scripted narrative fiction production, it can easily be adapted to documentary or other forms of media production.

The PEACHy is a comprehensive checklist tool for student film productions that walks each department through actions that they could take to lessen the environmental footprint of their production. Students run through the checklist during preproduction and again after wrap (probably during postproduction). It's good to have a designated sustainability person (a Sustainability Coordinator, Sustainability PA, Eco-Rep, Producer, or PA) to handle the checklist and follow through on items that need further attention. Each green action earns points for the production. The higher the score earned, the greener the production's footprint. There is even a pie chart that changes as you enter data – it sort of gamifies the experience. It's fun for student filmmakers taking a production course to compete to see who can earn the most points on their checklist.

There are fields on the form for all the production details (title, director, etc.), student and faculty representatives, and even a place to put your school's logo.

How to Film Green 29

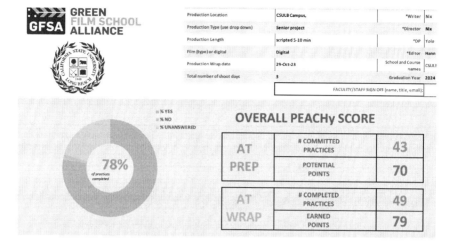

Figure 4.2a Your PEACHy score is calculated out of 100.

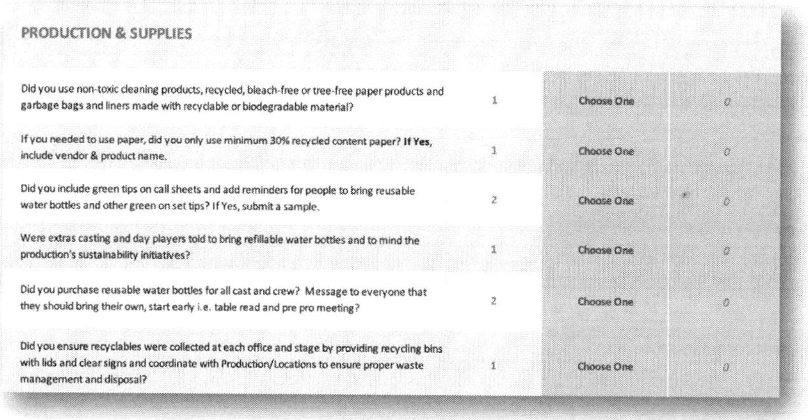

Figure 4.2b PEACHy asks productions to consider implementing specific green practices.

The tool divides the work into departments so that tasks can be delegated and given specific attention. PEACHy is comprehensive enough to list practices that may or may not be possible for the size and scope of your project, but not so many practices that it's as complex as industry versions (for example, PEACH+ or albert's carbon action plan).

30 How to Film Green

CAMERA, GRIP & ELECTRIC		At prep		At wrap	
Answered by (Name/Title): Anna Nguyen / Sustainability Coordinator					
Did you shoot digitally instead of on film?	2	YES	2	YES	2
Was at least 50% of your lighting package energy efficient set lighting such as LEDs? If Yes, confirm who provided the percentage.	3	Choose One	0	YES	3
Did you save the lights by dimming down in between takes and shut off when not in use? When prelight is complete, power down.	1	YES	1	YES	1
Did you reuse and donate expendables?	1	NO	0	YES	1
On location, did you utilize house power or tie into the grid instead of using generators (where you typically would)? If Yes, provide examples.	3	YES	3	YES	3
Did you avoid using generators completely, or if not, use diesel-fuel alternatives such as renewable diesel, electric generators or battery packs? If Yes, include vendor name.	4	Choose One	0	YES	4
Total	14		6		14
Insert Additional Comments, Notes, or Suggestions in this section					
We also tried using re-usable t-marks (metal ones, and bean-bag markers) instead of single use-tape marks. This turned out to be good on the locations floors too. DATA: saved about 3 rolls of paper tape.					

Figure 4.3 An example of the camera, grip, and electric section of the PEACHy checklist. Students select *yes/no* for each item at prep and at wrap. *Yes* selections earn points that are tallied up at the end of each section.

Going through the whole checklist the first time allows the Sustainability Coordinator the opportunity to check in early with each department and bring them into the conversation. Crew and department heads are more effective and involved if they are offered buy-in, and they will have more focused ideas for being green in their area. Crews of five and crews of 55 alike will have suggestions to contribute to the common cause if they are asked early. This also improves the effectiveness of your production's sustainability goal.

By clicking *yes* in the "at prep" or "at wrap" column, a point value is added for each line to the project's total score. If a project earns, for example, 30 points or more, the school might give a prize and/or green badge to the film. If a project scores 50 or more, it becomes eligible for the Environmental Media Association (EMA)[6] Green Seal for Students. The PEACHy form serves as the primary part of the EMA application.

The "Notes" section allows students to add data like the number of single-use plastics they avoided by refilling water bottles, or their ratio of landfill trash to recycling to compost collected. The more information collected, the better. Having data allows filmmakers to show how well they did, and also allows for comparison studies with other films and schools. The GFSA keeps a file of the checklists and data for use in future studies. Maybe there is an aspiring scholar reading this right now who is looking for a dataset like this to analyze for an academic paper. (Reach out and contact the GFSA – why *not* you?)

PEACHy isn't the only student film sustainability checklist, and it's far from the first. In fact, film schools including AFI, the American University, CSULB, NYU, UCLA, and USC all did some research into sustainable filmmaking and in some cases experimented with their own versions of a simple student checklist before PEACHy was created; a UCLA report even refers to research and work in sustainability in the entertainment business going back as far as 1991.[7] However, PEACHy is the most comprehensive for student projects so far – and if everyone uses the same checklist and collects similar data, then it becomes easier to compare and track the effectiveness of our collective efforts. Furthermore, for the graduating student, the PEACHy has the advantage of being very similar to the PEACH industry checklist and therefore serves as training for work in the field. In other words, knowing how to use this tool makes you more employable.

In the near future, we as an industry will need to start to use more robust tools like PEACH+, PEAR, PLUMB, and the carbon calculator tools provided by albert, EcoProd, Reel Green, and others. Solid numbers and hard data will give us a concrete way to measure progress and track across schools.

The Green Film School Alliance (GFSA) – Cofounder Erica Elson

The Green Film School Alliance was created in 2020, on Zoom, during the height of the global pandemic. Beginning with several of the top film schools in North America, the Green Film School Alliance quickly expanded and now includes more than 30 member schools and programs on four continents, all dedicated to the practice of sustainability in film and media production. The group aims to create a future where sustainable production is synonymous with production by integrating environmentally responsible practices into film school curricula globally.

In the United States, there have been two primary schools of thought in terms of how to reduce the effects of climate change. One focuses on the individual who embraces a sustainable life – recycling, composting, taking the train, not eating meat, not flying, going to protests, encouraging others to do the same – the hope being that if enough people change their behavior, large industries (beef, energy, transportation, etc.) will be forced to change how they operate. The other school of thought is that governments and top 10 corporations must change because they have such a massive impact that individual actions don't matter much in the grand scheme of things.

There is a third option, however, which I hope the GFSA will help to spread awareness about. This philosophy is that any individual, at any level in their workplace, can come together with other like-minded individuals to revolutionize the industry they work in. Just as a single person who works for a large corporation can implement a new strategy or create a new product if they can execute it without it causing a financial burden, the same is true of adopting sustainable practices. With the support of organizations like SPA and GFSA, an individual can create a small team (or alliance) that could change the entire way their field does something – and set an example for others, just as the streaming platforms recently jumped on the sustainability train because the studios were doing it for years.

The Green Film School Alliance offers teaching tools to help educators incorporate environmental sustainability into their filmmaking courses. The GFSA also supports sustainably-minded students through their Student Ambassador program, which helps students from all around the world meet and brainstorm ideas, resources, and solutions for their green production challenges. Representatives hail from places including, Vancouver, Iceland, Bangladesh, South Africa, Oregon, New York, Louisiana, and California. Each region faces its own unique challenges, both in terms of climate change and production resources, and the GFSA aims to provide tools that can serve all areas of the world. The PEACHy is one of many tools offered to member schools and collaborators in sustainability on the GFSA website. Sustainability courses, panels, and competitions are also offered, all free of charge.

When I worked at AFI, my supervisor and I worked together to create a plan to implement sustainable production by 2019. I gathered a group of passionate students to suggest ideas and provide feedback, and we started with basic action items like eliminating single-use plastics on set and working with greener caterers. We then presented a plan to senior leadership explaining why they should support the "AFI Green Initiative" – and they couldn't say no. Whether it was because they cared about the environment, wanted to support a mission the students wanted to pursue, or just thought it was a good look for the organization, department heads slowly started to adopt their practices. We made it easy for them to implement greener solutions, such as using Scriptation instead of printing scripts, or investing more in LED lighting so the students could use battery-powered generators. Backed by the school, students felt empowered to set new standards on their set and encourage outside collaborators to do the same.

Two years later, I met Heidi Kindberg at the SEA, and she introduced me to Kent Hayward. Together, we helped start and publicly launch the Green Film School Alliance and created and implemented the PEACHy. That year, I saw 10 of AFI's graduate thesis films receive the new Environmental Media Association's Student Green Seal. One of them was the Student Academy Awards' bronze medal winner, the first-ever student production to use the PEACHy. One year later, the number of films earning the Student Green Seal had doubled. Positive change requires time, but not as much time as you might think, especially if you have the right people to push the boulder up the hill. In our case, that group was the SEA and the many educators who were ready to heed the call to implement sustainable practices. I believe that every industry has a group like this, and the ecologically minded folks just need to find each other.

Part of the difficulty in fighting climate change is that it often feels hopeless. There is often a feeling that a single corporation could ruin all the actions that millions of people are taking to do their part every day. And, there is often a serious lack of infrastructure and resources for these practices to make real change possible. However, through the GFSA, we have realized not only what an impact we can make in the film industry but also beyond. Someone in marketing could adapt the PEACHy to their work and use it on all their photo shoots, commercials, and branding projects. Every college campus in the United States could create their own school-wide checklists based on the PEACHy and adapt similar practices in several departments. And perhaps most importantly, we can train students in every country to adopt sustainable actions off *and* on-screen so that in the future, creating media does not have as negative of an impact, and positive behaviors are modeled on screens for individuals in all parts of the world to see.

Other Green Film Checklists

Encouragingly, there are a number of other amazing tools and checklists in use today from many places around the world:

- **PEACH** (Production Environmental Action CHecklist; greenproductionguide.com) is a checklist of best practices in the film industry created by the SEA.
- **PEACH+** (greenproductionguide.com), also from the SEA, is a longer and more comprehensive sustainability tool.
- **PLUM** (Production Lumber Materials; greenproductionguide.com) is a tool for tracking plywood, lumber, and building materials like Luan, a rainforest wood commonly used for building sets.
- **PEAR** (Production Environmental Accounting Report; greenproductionguide.com) is a carbon footprint calculator for tracking energy use, fuel, and emissions.
- **albert** (wearealbert.org), based in the UK, offers a robust and comprehensive process for greening your film and calculating its carbon footprint. There are also many resources and studies available on their site. One helpful section called In Your Role even breaks down what you can do by job (sound, PD, post, etc.)
- **Principles and Practices Checklist** (cmsimpact.org/resource/code-best-practices-sustainable-filmmaking) from the American University's *Code of Best Practices for Sustainable Filmmaking* was introduced in 2009 by filmmaker and professor Larry Engel and Producer Andrew Buchanan.

- **Docsociety's Green Doc Protocol** (docsociety.org/greendocprotocol) specifically addresses the needs of documentary filmmakers.
- **The Clean Energy Toolkit** (creativebc.com/reel-green/toolkits) from Reel Green in British Columbia, Canada, offers training, resources, checklists, certification, and media assets for the promotion and use of green practices in production.
- **EcoProd** (ecoprod.com) in France has some excellent practical worksheets, checklists, and guides on green film practices in the office and on set (e.g., downloadable guide for the AD, for make-up, for post workflow). Their carbon calculator is called Carbon'Clap.
- **Go-Green Checklist** (wrapbook.com/resources/go-green-checklist), from production payroll platform Wrapbook, offers some simple green tips to get you started on your sustainability in film journey.
- **"ABCs of Sustainability" poster** (greenfilmshooting.net) is available for download from Green Film Shooting, based in Germany, along with resources and best practices.
- **Directors Guild of America (DGA) Sustainability Pro Tips** (dga.org/The-Guild/Sustainable-Future-Pro-Tips) list and tools for directors of different stripes, ADs, UPMs, locations, and more.

Green Film Shooting, Green Screen Ontario, EcoProd, and other organizations also offer data, strategic plans, studies, reports, and other resources on the green film movement. In general, the European and Canadian film groups have a huge head start over US counterparts regarding green practices, with government mandates and funding or incentives for green productions.

The European Film Commission Network has a list of green film initiatives in Europe on their site, eufcn.com/green-filming, and the Green Production Guide website, greenproductionguide.com, has an excellent list of international green film groups and resources from Italy, the United Arab Emirates, South Africa, Sweden, Estonia, Australia, and everywhere in between.

Beware the Greenwashing Trap

The term greenwashing derives from the term whitewashing, meaning to simply paint over a problem with cheap white paint. Whitewashing makes a surface look better, but it doesn't fix the problem. Likewise, greenwashing makes a person or company's practices look environmentally friendly on the surface level without making real, impactful changes.

Greenwashing can be malevolent and purposeful, or like unconscious bias, it can be unintentional or accidental.[8] Companies like Chevron, British Petroleum, Dupont, and Amazon have been publicly accused of purposeful greenwashing in the recent past as an attempt to erase or counter any negative environmental impact they are responsible for.

Does it happen in filmmaking? Yes. The public at large is generally in favor of "being green." Telling consumers that a production employed sustainable practices, or better yet, "harnessed cutting-edge eco-technologies" makes that production look ethical and forward-thinking. Humans want to feel like they are on the right side of progress; no one wants to be the bad guy on a TV show. But we are complicated characters, and sometimes we don't even know that we are making a mess just by participating in a consumer-driven culture – and that includes the films we make.

In an article about Hollywood greenwashing entitled "Vegan food, recycled tuxedos – and billions of tonnes of CO_2: can Hollywood ever go green?"[9] the *Guardian* points out the mixed messaging (or downright hypocrisy) of wealthy stakeholders touting vegan catering yet contributing to the estimated 15 million tons of CO_2 emissions that the industry reportedly produces each year. Even Roland Emmerich's environmentally themed film *The Day After Tomorrow* (2004) produced 10,000 tons of carbon (although the production reportedly contributed $200,000 to environmental groups to offset their footprint).[10] By any measure, Disney, Universal, Sony, and all the majors still contribute large amounts of CO_2 from film production despite positive environmental messaging, recycling, and electric vehicle promotion.

Hunter Vaughn's book *Hollywood's Dirtiest Secret* lays out a litany of egregious examples of waste, pollution, and environmental degradation at the hands of the film business and their related greenwashing marketing companies. Classic films like *Singing in the Rain* (1952) wasted an unconscionable amount of water for that rain, the fires set for scenes in *Gone with the Wind* (1939) were massive polluters, and some of the beautiful painted deserts of Antonioni's *Zabriskie Point* (1970) and other films were ironically painted with toxic pigments.

It's easy to find examples of bad actors and hypocrisy in Hollywood and other major production cities. The greenwashing in the entertainment industry is as bad as it is in any big business. It's an easy target in a global marketplace of easy targets. But the silver lining is that there are people in the business, including celebrities, executives, and above-the-line and below-the-line workers, who really do care and are earnestly striving for a greener future. Recent studies have indicated that film productions are slowly making improvements on becoming more efficient, less wasteful, and using more renewable energy[11] – although more data is needed.[12] Big players, independents, experimental artists, academics, sports broadcasters, and every other kind of media maker have the ability to make a change in the way we make our projects. That's where people like you come in. Commit to doing more. Use the checklists and the toolkits that are out there. Make green practices a standard part of all filmmaking. As the Onceler says in *The Lorax*, "Unless someone like you cares a whole awful lot, nothing is going to get better. It's not."

Collect Data and Find Experts

If you are reading this, you have noble intentions and are looking for sustainable solutions. So, how do you ensure that you are making meaningful change and not just doing lip service? Collect data. As creatives, we filmmakers don't always think about the numbers and the measures, but that's the only way that we can make real comparisons to see what's working. Checklist tools, like PEACHy, PLUM, and albert's carbon calculator, are your guide to gathering meaningful data.

There are a growing number of experts in the industry collecting data now too. And in fact, there is a need for more experts. As interest in green production grows, so too does the job market grow for those who have training in green filmmaking. Industry consultancies like Earth Angel, Green Spark Group, Green Eyes, The Same in Green, and many others have certified, trained experts with excellent ideas for making productions in an ecologically sustainable manner.

Teaching Sustainable Film Production at NYU

Harry Winer

Associate Arts Professor
Director of Sustainability
Kanbar Institute of Film and Television
NYU Tisch School of the Arts

One of my goals in teaching sustainable practices for film production is to bring awareness that sustainable film production is not just about bringing reusable water bottles to the set or using public transportation instead of individual cars, etc. It is about reconceiving how we interact with the world around us.

I share the story provided by the cellular biologist Siddhartha Mukharjee in his book *Song of the Cell* – how we begin as a singular cell that divides and divides again until there are millions of cells each evolving with separate functions, some becoming hair, eyes, skin, limbs, blood, a beating heart and a brain that can think, feel, create. It is a miracle of life. A miracle that could only occur in a healthy ecosystem that enables these cells to thrive. We are as dependent on this healthy ecosystem for us to create whatever we envision as the ecosystem is dependent on us to help preserve its health.

My goal is to bring to my students' awareness and understanding of our interdependence on all living beings. If I harm one precious life, it has an impact on my own. Then, as we go forward to tell the stories we tell through the film, medium we can better understand why sustainable practices are as integral to the process as where to place the camera. Without us understanding our responsibility to maintain a healthy environment, our own health and that of our potential audience is at risk, and it undercuts our ability to summon the fortitude and presence of mind needed to conceive of and produce the stories we wish to tell.

To get this message out, I have found engaging dedicated students as collaborators is the most effective means of raising students' awareness about sustainable production practices. These student "ambassadors" help disseminate the information and tools covered in this book that we have developed. The students know best how to use social media and speak, or the language that might best resonate with their peers. They also are on the front lines of production and can identify the needs of those producing student films. Meeting with student representatives on a regular basis keeps me abreast of sustainability our progress in the department and it keeps me informed about issues that need to be addressed to make green sustainable production as easy as possible for our students.

I have also found it is essential to get buy-in from the rest of the faculty. They will be the ones in their individual production classes to remind and encourage and remind students to use the PEACHy checklist and/or other relevant tools and integrate sustainable practices in their productions. The goal is for an Eco-Rep or Sustainability Steward to become as much a part of a production team as a DP or Production Designer so that sustainable practices become an integral step in the process of bringing our visions to life, in student films and beyond.

Exercises/Homework

1 Take a look at one of the checklists or toolkits mentioned in this chapter. Which listed practices seem the most effective to you? Which items do not apply to your kind of filmmaking? How are the practices listed paid for? What kind of data can you collect for future review with this checklist?
2 A campaign from Greenpeace prompts: "Every day, Americans are bombarded with advertising about environmentally friendly goods and services. But how many really are green, and how many are just pretending?" Find an advertisement that engages in greenwashing and do a breakdown of the rhetorical strategy that it uses, and the images employed to deliver its message. What are some ways that we can identify greenwashing? How can we address it as informed citizens?

Notes

1. Gawande, Atul. *The Checklist Manifesto*. Profile Books, 2011.
2. Jack Anderson. 2012. *Shooting Movies without Shooting Yourself in the Foot: Becoming a Cinematographer*. Routledge.
3. National Academies Press. 2020, March 24. *A Workshop and Study of Checklists: "Enhancing Scientific Reproducibility in Biomedical Research through Transparent Reporting."* National Academies Press. https://www.ncbi.nlm.nih.gov/books/NBK556610/
4. B. D. Winters, A. P. Gurses, H. Lehmann, J. B. Sexton, C. J. Rampersad, and P. J. Pronovost. 2009. Clinical review: checklists – Translating evidence into practice. *Critical Care*, Vol. 13, No. 6, p. 210. https://doi.org/10.1186/cc7792. Epub 2009 Dec 31. PMID: 20064195; PMCID: PMC2811937.
5. Rebecca K. Frels, Bipin Sharma, Anthony J. Onwuegbuzie, Nancy L. Leech, and Marcella D. Stark. 2011. The use of a checklist and qualitative notebooks for an interactive process of teaching and learning qualitative research. *Journal of Effective Teaching*, Vol. 11, No. 1, pp. 62–79.
6. The nonprofit organization, The Environmental Media Association (EMA), has been working in environmentalism and production for over 30 years. They describe themselves as "a diverse subsection of entertainment industry influencers, entrepreneurs in business, and green icons dedicated to the mission of promoting environmental progress" through "celebrity role-modeling, campaign work, social media messaging, year-round programs … to help our planet."
7. UCLA. 2006, November. *Sustainability in the Motion Picture Industry*. UCLA.
8. Forrester. 2022. "You're Probably Greenwashing, but You Don't Know It." *Forbes*, April 25, 2022. https://www.forbes.com/sites/forrester/2022/04/22/youre-probably-greenwashing-but-you-dont-know-it/.
9. Hoad, Phil. 2021. "Vegan Food, Recycled Tuxedos – and Billions of Tonnes of CO2: Can Hollywood Ever Go Green?" *The Guardian*, August 25, 2021. https://www.theguardian.com/film/2020/jan/09/vegan-food-recycled-tuxedos-and-billions-of-tonnes-of-co2-can-hollywood-ever-go-green.
10. Ibid.
11. BAFTA albert Annual Review, 2022.
12. I. E. Sørensen and C. Noonan. 2022. Production, policy and power: The screen industry's response to the environmental crisis. *Media, Culture & Society*, Vol. 44, No. 1, pp. 172–184. https://doi.org/10.1177/01634437211065697

5 Documentary

Any production, even one about climate change, leaves a substantial carbon footprint. As Louie Psihoyos laments in his documentary *Racing Extinction* (2015), "the worst thing you can do to the environment is to make a film about it. We did a carbon assessment of the first two years of production [for *Racing Extinction*] and I was horrified at how much energy it takes to do what I do."

Documentary's smaller crews, more limited use of generators, minimal or no construction, and less artificial lighting tend to result in lower environmental impact than that of narrative films. Nonetheless, documentary or otherwise, filmmaking creates significant emissions.

That said, there are areas for improvement and opportunities for green innovation, including in the areas of content, gear, and production practices. For example, working with local partners and "fixers" will make your production more efficient and attuned to the community you're filming in. Being conscious of local culture, environment, and worldview helps to keep your production authentic, supportive, and collaborative (rather than extractive, like an oil well), which is essentially the definition of "decolonizing" documentary filmmaking, a practice that producers like those in the Center for Environmental Filmmaking encourage.[1]

The importance of ethics in documentary filmmaking is hardly a new topic. Documentary filmmakers have long struggled with the question of what is truth ... and whose truth is it? To a filmmaker concerned with ethical storytelling, it's not much of a leap to think about green filmmaking as a practice within that goal. Environmentally responsible filmmaking is a part of ethical filmmaking.

Sustainability in the Content

The most direct way to incorporate conservation into documentary filmmaking is to make a film that addresses a specific sustainability issue. A film like *Chasing Ice* (2012), which looks at the melting of glaciers; *A Life on Our Planet* (2020), David Attenborough's look back at a world changed over the course of his lifetime; or *Seaspiracy* (2021), which deals with the

DOI: 10.4324/9781003425441-5

impact of the fishing industry on the environment, are just three examples. Jacques Cousteau's *The Silent World* (1956), Jane Goodall's *Reasons for Hope* (2023), and so many others represent direct calls to care for our fragile planet and its ecosystems.

That said, you don't have to make a film about the environment to make a film with a green message. Consider the 17 UN Sustainable Development Goals (SDGs) (see Chapter 2 and/or globalgoals.org), intended to be the "blueprint to achieve a better and more sustainable future for all." Goals include not just climate action but also quality education, the eradication of poverty, gender equality, and clean water. Let's say your project is about an amazing math teacher at an underfunded school. SDG #4 is Quality Education, the foundation of many other SDGs. "When people have access to quality education they can break from the cycle of poverty. Education helps to reduce inequalities, reach gender equality, and empowers people everywhere to live more healthy and sustainable lives."[2] That insight might lead you to look at other SDGs like pollution in the area, the availability of nutritious, organic foods, or other salient areas of exploration for your film. If there isn't an obvious way to make the connection, don't force it. A heavy-handed mention can feel forced, preachy, or like greenwashing.

How can you make a difference? Studies show that audiences who watch documentaries on social and climate justice are energized and eager to follow up with action.[3] Films have the power to move hearts and minds more than perhaps any other medium. Speak truth to power.

Visual Content

Chapter 10 on the Camera Department and Chapter 6 about Content both look into the idea of incorporating the natural world into your frame and your edit. If some of what we are doing as green filmmakers is redefining our relationship to the environment and challenging the human versus nature mythology, then we should consider putting more nature in our movies. Establishing shots can include plants and trees, solar panels, or a wind turbine in the background instead of framing them out. See chapter 9 on Production Design for thoughts about set dressing for expert interviews. Documentary filmmakers can also add shots of nature or footage of green-positive images.

The Gear

The crew on a documentary, more than on any other type of film, has the potential to be fully circular in its electricity use – that is, the team can be self-sufficient, even finding its own power sources. While very few cameras are still powered by hand cranking (with a few rare holdouts like some vintage Bolex 16mm film cameras), there are many other sustainable ways to generate power to charge batteries, including solar panels, small wind turbines, and even hand-crank generators. In this era of new technologies, an ideal, lightweight green documentary kit to take to remote places where electricity is scarce might include:

- Camera with 4 batteries and 2 chargers, and field bag/run bag
- Audio recorder with lavs, mixer, directional mic, and boom kit
- Rechargeable AA and 9V batteries for audio gear, plus chargers
- Lightweight carbon-fiber tripod
- LED lights with soft light attachments
- Lightweight light stands
- 5-in-1 collapsible reflectors
- Rechargeable battery pack (aka power bank) for lights, laptops, phones, etc.
- 20-to-50-Watt solar panels
- Hand-crank generator or dynamo (for emergencies)
- Battery pack with solar panels and wind turbine

There are other items that you might want to take, but these are a few ideas to get you started on your own research. Some of the power banks and solar panels can be purchased in camping supply stores like Atwool's or REI or in hardware stores like Home Depot, Lowe's, or ACE. Maybe you can put together an ideal list for your city or region.

Finally, keep in mind that your gear must be portable and lightweight. Lighter gear is easier for you to carry, of course, but it also uses less fuel to transport (via car, plane, train, etc.). More difficult to assess and compare are the environmental practices of your equipment manufacturers, vendors, and rental houses. A research project or survey as a class assignment or guided paper topic about effective green practices of film equipment vendors could be very revealing and helpful to others in the field.

Sustainable Production Practices

Many of the practices in this book lean toward scripted narrative projects because that is the largest sector of production, but that doesn't mean that the practices can't be adapted to documentaries, multi-cam studio shows, and even experimental projects. The practices in the Pre-Production, Production Department, Food, Camera, Sound, and Transportation chapters, like reducing fuel use, recycling, and reusing materials, are all critical for sustainable production, regardless of discipline. Checklists like PEACHy or the albert toolkit are easily translated to documentaries. But there are best practices and checklists made strictly for docs too.

One of the first green checklists out there was the Center for Media and Social Impact's *Code for Best Practices in Sustainable Filmmaking*, which was introduced in 2009.[4] Documentary filmmaker and American University Professor Larry Engel, one of the architects of the Code, described it as "the first clear, comprehensive guide in sustainability supported by scientific review and specifically designed to account for the challenges filmmakers face on a daily basis."[5] While not exclusively for documentaries, the Code was praised by the International Documentary Association (IDA).

Since then, the UK's Doc Society has come out with a checklist designed just for documentary films. As *The Green Documentary Protocol* puts it, "switching your production methods doesn't have to be challenging, and as a documentary community we all need to work together, spreading a message that it is possible to sustainably produce documentaries and encouraging others to do the same!"[6] They also suggest that you share your green filmmaking stories on social media using the hashtag #DocsGoGreen.

Here's a brief overview of practices that documentary (and other) filmmakers can use to shrink their film's carbon footprint:

- **Hire local fixers and crew**: Instead of flying someone in to be a production assistant, save the cost of the flight and the emissions by hiring a local expert to take care of the logistics instead. Many productions already make a habit of hiring local "fixers" because they know the territory and can save you time and money. Hiring local also increases the likelihood that your production will work with and support the community where you're filming rather than taking advantage of it, even if inadvertently. Hiring local crew can help in that direction too.
- **Reduce air travel**: According to the 2021 Sustainable Entertainment Alliance report "Close-Up: Carbon Emissions of Film and Television Production,"[7] unscripted productions show the largest percentage of their carbon footprint as air travel emissions. The 2021 BAFTA albert annual report draws similar conclusions.[8] To lessen that impact, use rail or bus instead of air travel for domestic transportation and/or choose hybrids or electric vehicles.
- **Switch to sustainable energy sources**: Contact your power company to see if you can sign up to use majority sustainable power or take part in a green energy initiative.
- **Limit cloud-based data storage and transfers**: These processes use more energy than you might think. The DocSociety's Green Documentary Protocol cites one forecast predicting that "by 2025 cloud storage will be responsible for a fifth of the world's CO_2 emissions. Think before you upload or send those files via the internet."[9-11] (See also Chapter 17.)
- **Reuse and recycle**: They may seem obvious, but there are many more areas to implement these ideas than you might imagine, including recycling e-waste, using rechargeable batteries, reusing sets and other aspects of production design, and recycling food packaging.
- **Switch to meatless meals**: One of the lesser practiced, higher impact techniques for reducing your footprint is going meatless.[12] Trying it for even just one day of your shoot decreases your film's environmental consequences.
- **Reduce the use of air conditioning**: Instead, open windows and/or use fans in pre-production and post-production office spaces.

- **Rely on house power**: Plug your gear into the wall whenever possible instead of using batteries. When you do use batteries, use rechargeable ones.
- **Clean up**: Just as you learned in elementary school, clean up after yourself. Your documentary crew should not act like a mining company or clearcutting forester, extracting your content and leaving. Make sure you leave your location the way you found it – or cleaner. This is an important practice, especially for expedition work, or work in fragile ecosystems. Of course, trash and food waste should be minimized and managed, but so should invisible pollution like carbon dioxide or microplastics. Even actual footprints can be damaging to certain places and creatures. Respect the environment and the culture of the places that you visit as a documentarian.

If this is the only chapter of this book you've read so far because you are strictly a documentary person, you might be surprised to see how much crossover there is with other kinds of production. Take a look at the chapters on Pre-Production, the Production Department, Food, Camera, Sound, and Transportation. There are so many practices that overlap with the creative nonfiction world.

Doing Your Part and Making Your Own Way

Ocean explorer and environmentalist Jacques Yves Cousteau once said that

> Water and air, the two essential fluids on which all life depends, have become global garbage cans.

The Great Pacific garbage patch is a testament to that. But he also said that

> "the future is in the hands of those who explore … and from all the beauty they discover while crossing perpetually receding frontiers, they develop for nature and for humankind an infinite love." It's that infinite love that documentaries can help cultivate.

To quote another environmentalist, Jane Goodall said, "There is still so much in the world worth fighting for. So much that is beautiful, so many wonderful people working to reverse the harm, to help alleviate the suffering. And so many young people dedicated to making this a better world. All conspiring to inspire us and to give us hope that it is not too late to turn things around, if we all do our part."

Finding a way to do your part can be tough in an industry that tends to favor exploitative, wasteful practices, especially if you are an outsider in some way. Making your own way is hard. "If you're doing something outside of dominant culture, there's not an easy place for you," according to Ava DuVernay, director of documentaries including *13th* (2016) and *Origin* (2024) "I'm not going to continue knocking on that old door that doesn't open for me. I'm going to create my own door and walk through that."[13]

Speak your truth, do your part, and make your own door. Your efforts make a difference.

Exercises/Homework

1 Make a one-page treatment for a documentary on an environmental issue. How would you approach it? Who would you partner with?
2 Do a behind-the-scenes doc on green filmmaking, exploring the sustainability data from your last film project or someone else's upcoming film. Use the PEACHy or Doc Society checklist as part of your documentation.
3 Research some of the popular manufacturers of camera or lighting equipment. Do some have greener practices than others? Make a report and share it with a filmmaking group or environmental organization.

Notes

1 "The Center for Environmental Filmmaking." 2001. American University. October 19, 2001. https://www.american.edu/soc/environmental-film/.
2 "Education - United Nations Sustainable Development." United Nations Sustainable Development. October 19, 2023. https://www.un.org/sustainabledevelopment/education/.
3 CSMI and Kaniphnath Malhari Kudale. 2023. Screening social justice: Brave new films and documentary activism. *Social Identities*. https://doi.org/10.1080/13504630.2023.2249421
4 "Code of Best Practices for Sustainable Filmmaking - Center for Media and Social Impact." 2017. Center for Media and Social Impact. February 8, 2017. https://cmsimpact.org/resource/code-best-practices-sustainable-filmmaking.; "PEACHy Checklist Redesigned." n.d. Google Docs. https://bit.ly/FMAGFSA.
5 "New Code Released to Help Filmmakers Go Green." 2009. International Documentary Association. February 4, 2009. https://www.documentary.org/blog/new-code-released-help-filmmakers-go-green.
6 "Doc Society." n.d. Doc Society. https://docsociety.org/greendocprotocol/.
7 Sustainable Entertainment Alliance. 2021, March. *Close-Up: Carbon Emissions of Film and Television Production*.
8 Albert. 2021. Creating a sustainable future. *Annual Review*. https://wearealbert.org/category/annual-review/
9 DocSociety Green Protocol. https://docsociety.org/greendocprotocol/; Justin Adamson. 2017, May 15. Carbon and the Cloud: Hard facts about data storage. *Stanford Magazine*; Nicola Jones. 2018, 12 September. How to stop data centers from gobbling up the world's electricity: The energy-efficiency drive at the information factories that serve us Facebook, Google and Bitcoin. *Nature*.
10 *Climate Change News*. 2017. "Tsunami of data" could consume one fifth of global electricity by 2025. *Climate Change News*. https://www.theguardian.com/environment/2017/dec/11/tsunami-of-data-could-consume-fifth-global-electricity-by-2025
11 Anders Andrae. 2017. Total Consumer Power Consumption Forecast. By Dr. Anders S.G. Andrae (Huawei) at the Nordic Digital Business Summit, Helsinki, Finland, 2017, October 5.
12 J. Poore and T. Nemecek. 2018, May 31. Reducing food's environmental impacts through producers and consumers. *Science*, pp. 987–992. https://doi.org/10.1126/science.aaq0216 (6392)
13 Reporter, Guardian Staff. 2017. "'Think About the Bigger Picture': Life Lessons From Meryl Streep and Other Successful Women." *The Guardian*, December 1, 2017. https://www.theguardian.com/lifeandstyle/2017/jan/21/think-bigger-picture-life-lessons-meryl-streep-successful-women.

6 Content, Development, and Climate Storytelling

It used to be that all stories were about the natural world. Geologically speaking, it was only yesterday when all of our campfire stories and cave wall paintings were about animals, migration, and the seasons. At some point, humans decided that we were no longer a part of the natural world, and our stories – our collective mythology – began to reflect that idea. Of course, it's not true. Humanity is still intrinsically connected to the natural world; we've just sort of forgotten to talk about it.

One of the most powerful ways to effect change in film is to incorporate sustainability and green practices *into the content itself*. Whether the project is a documentary, live multi-camera broadcast production, scripted narrative, or even experimental film, the subject matter can raise important questions about our relationship to the environment. In other words, as filmmakers, we have an opportunity to go green in what we say and how we say it.

A Call to Action

The National Resources Defense Council (NRDC) is a US-based environmental advocacy group that began in 1970 with a focus on litigating polluters; its first milestone success was the Clean Water Act of 1972. Since then, the group has expanded its work to include actions to protect forests, campaigns to reduce climate emissions, and support of artistic events inspiring and promoting environmental action. The NRDC's "Rewrite the Future" campaign points to the power that movies and TV shows have to call attention to environmental issues. Their materials explain that over the years,

> the entertainment community has focused its creative power on other social problems – the Vietnam War, racism, women in the workplace, the AIDS epidemic, marriage equality – and helped bring about cultural transformations. But Hollywood hasn't told many stories about climate change.... [What the world needs is a] new climate narrative. A narrative that will help us face reality ... and inspire us to action. We need Hollywood to help us rewrite the future.[1]

This chapter covers some ways to do just that.

DOI: 10.4324/9781003425441-6

Climate Change Screenwriting 101

Rewrite the Future – The NRDC offers lessons on sustainability in storytelling through presentations, workshops, panels, in-person and streaming events, and event sponsorship. Workshops and talks from past events at Sundance, and other panel talks are available on their site as well as a tip sheet for sustainability ideas, and a writing fellowship in collaboration with the Black List, the Redford Center, and the CAA Foundation. (https://www.nrdc.org/RewriteTheFuture)

UK-based sustainability in production super-group Albert (aka We Are Albert) has a resource for writing environmentally focused content called "**Telling Climate Stories**: A practical pocket guide for including sustainability in any genre." The pocket guide and related full report discuss not only the impact of screen stories and the behavior changes that they can inspire, but also offer practical tips on writing eco-content. "Make climate action normal," for example, might include a character in your script simply turning off some lights, or walking instead of driving. Seeing environmentally responsible behavior modeled on television makes for effective persuasion. The guide also suggests that content stay positive (as opposed to the tired gloom and doom routine), show as well as tell, collaborate in an inclusive way, and show how actions are a part of the bigger picture. The complete guide and larger study can be downloaded from wearealbert.org.

Good Energy, a "nonprofit story consultancy for the age of climate change" provides a guide by writers and for writers called "The Playbook for Screenwriting in the Age of Climate Change."[2] The playbook talks about seeing things through a "climate lens" and gives examples from existing TV shows and films like *Succession* (2018–2023) and *Beasts of the Southern Wild* (2012). The playbook makes a distinction between climate placement (where climate-friendly behaviors are shown or included in the production design), climate mentions (where a character mentions climate in passing), climate world (where climate drives a meaningful event in the story), and climate characters (where characters and plot are primarily driven by climate change). The guide also includes case studies of many modern examples in TV and Film, and even self-care for writing about climate. In addition, they also provide workshops and consulting for writers' rooms, schools, and companies.

According to a Good Energy/USC study of over 37,000 scripted TV episodes and films during 2016–2020, only .6% used the term "climate change," and only 2.8% of all scripts included any climate-related terms like "global warming" or "solar panels."[3]

The **Good Energy Playbook** debunks some myths about eco-writing too – that climate is too big, too depressing, or too controversial to take on. If climate is indeed part of our daily lives, then we are already taking it on. We're already talking about it, and dealing with it, so writing about it in our scripts shouldn't be a big leap. Tell those stories.

Content, Development, and Climate Storytelling 47

Figure 6.1 Writing sustainability-related content into your film can be as simple as showing a behavior like drinking from a refillable coffee cup or driving an alternative fuel vehicle.

We don't want to make propaganda. Messages that are preachy or condescending don't work. Your movie doesn't even have to be a movie about climate change. Just writing in something related to sustainability whether it's something from your own experience or something that you've read about in the news, is helpful and appropriate. It's writing what you know. Did you wonder which bin your paper plate should go in today? That's a human moment to write about. Is someone in the parking lot having trouble with the electric car charging station? That's an authentic bit of scene description for your screenplay. Flooding in your town, nearby wildfires, water use, pollution – all of these are real things that we talk about every day … but not too often in the movies. Maybe we should.

As screenwriting guru Robert McKee says, "Storytelling is the most powerful way to put ideas into the world." The cinematic arts are particularly effective at delivering stories. Since they are visual, dramatic, and time-based (like our lives), they have a unique ability to enter our consciousness. Filmmaker and Oceanic Preservation Society cofounder Louie Psihoyos echoes that idea in *Racing Extinction* (2015). "The power of an image is transformative," he observes. "I think it's in our DNA to take care of future generations. And if you can find that way in, you can reach people really quickly and change them."

It's not all about scripted narratives either. A documentary about carbon emissions and an experimental film about moths and lightbulbs can stimulate our imaginations about life, death, and the natural world. And whether the film is Stan Brakhage's *Mothlight* (1963), or Roland Emeric's *The Day After Tomorrow* (2004), the subject is environmental. The viewer is ultimately asked to consider the relationship between nature and human culture.

"Until the lions have their own historians, the history of the hunt will always glorify the hunter." – Nigerian proverb. So, who are we in the story: the hunter, the lion, the storyteller, the earth, or someone else maybe?

Environmental Films

The most direct way to talk about conservation is to make a film that directly addresses environmental issues. A conservation documentary-like *Seaspiracy* (2021) that deals with factual evidence about the impact of the fishing industry on the environment is a good example. David Attenborough's *A Life on Our Planet* (2020) is another documentary commenting on the state of our natural world using footage from the field and facts. How many young naturalists have been inspired by environment-focused films like *Chasing Ice* (2012), *The Undersea World of Jacques Cousteau* (1968), or Jané Goodall's movies featuring chimpanzees? Your documentary might be the next *Who Killed the Electric Car?* (2006), *The Cove* (2009), *Before the Flood* (2016), or *Polar Bear* (2022).[4]

Fictional narratives like *Princess Mononoke* (1997), *Snowpiercer* (2013), and *Don't Look Up* (2021) also tackle the issues of climate change and environmental crisis. The subjects of these films are their environmental message.

As actor Laura Dern put it, "It's really exciting when storytelling can resonate with the greatest issue of our time. There can be no greater focus than saving our home."[5]

If you want to use your voice to tell sustainability-driven stories, film is the perfect medium. There is no shortage of environmental subject matter to use as the A story, the B story, or even a side gag. The story material is there, why not use it?

Write in Environmental Moments

Talking about the environment in a relevant, positive way doesn't have to be exclusive to stories that are climate-driven – we can incorporate environmental moments into any film. For example, the character in your movie who makes a basket in the trash bin does it with an aluminum can in the recycling bin instead. There are a million ways to include the environment in the writing of jokes, actions, settings, and even scene descriptions ... and so many ways that screenwriters can help to save the planet according to the article "How Screenwriters are Ruining the Planet."[6]

In school and making their first films, students of screenwriting begin to learn the power of their words. "INT – SUPERMARKET – DUSK. It's raining." Mood, place, time, and weather are all conveyed in that description. Those five words affect our production design, schedule, and budget. Changing "Market" to "Space Shuttle" would change our budget dramatically, obviously. But what if we change "raining" to "cloudy"? Suddenly we don't need to use special effects anymore. That could affect our water use too. Even something as simple as changing "INT" to "EXT" can totally change our ecological footprint. Does it have to be an interior? If we can shoot at an outdoor farmers' market, or in front of the outdoor produce display of a grocery store, then we've just eliminated our need to bring in most of our lighting. Zero lighting may not be a possibility for the cinematographer's or director's vision every time – but if it is possible sometimes, then why not? You can do so much with bounce light and negative fill. Even changing "dusk" to "day" might work. Fewer lights can save you money on equipment rental too. Using daylight instead of artificial light saves money, electricity, and time. (See Chapter 10.)

We can do more with this simple scene description too. If we are in a grocery store, or a farmers' market, we have lots of opportunities to normalize sustainable behaviors in production design. We can put subtle signs in the produce aisle, like "local," "sustainably raised," "organic," etc.

Writing Paperless

For the actual typing part, paperless software solutions like Final Draft, Celtx, Fade In, and StudioBinder are a few of the popular writing tools out there with great formatting tools and the ability to easily export to a PDF, making paperless distribution simple.

Your writing, development, and preproduction people will likely be working with a fully digital workflow, including digital writing and digital preproduction tools. There are some great annotation tools out there like Scriptation that allow you to mark up your drafts, schedules, and other "paperwork" digitally. And if you have a tablet or touchscreen device, you can scribble notes and diagrams, sign digitally, and do real script breakdowns on it too.

Being all digital and avoiding paper doesn't mean that you don't have a footprint though. It's just a different footprint. (See the upcoming chapters 8 and 17 on digital technology and e-waste in the Production Department and Post-Production Departments.)

> **Incorporating Climate Justice into Storytelling**
>
> At the 2023 Hollywood Climate Summit, a panel called "Decolonizing Climate Storytelling: From Hip-Hip 50 to Land Back" highlighted important issues surrounding climate justice and changing the dominant mythology that is frequently reinforced in storytelling. Here, we share some excerpts from that discussion.

Faviana Rodriguez, President, the Center for Cultural Power and Interdisciplinary Artists

I come from a community that has been plagued by pollution and environmental racism since I was born. White communities were protected, while my community ingested toxic diesel fumes that cut my lifespan and the lifespan of many of our community members short. And, I became an artist and an activist precisely to tell stories that were not being heard. As an artist, I know that stories change people, and people change systems and behavior.

Stories move faster than politics; in fact, stories shape our society. There is a dominant story in this world, and it's a story of extractive capitalism that accelerates the climate crisis. This dominant story, which is over 500 years old, says that there are certain human bodies, certain animal bodies, and certain ocean and forest bodies that can be exploited for the benefit of a privileged few. And that leads to a concentration of wealth and power. But we have the power to dissolve that dominant narrative. We are working in an industry that is creating global culture. And so it's urgent that we help shape a different story. If we are to find our way out of the climate crisis, we have to leverage the power of story, of culture, of art, of the imagination to elevate the stories of those who have been most impacted by the climate crisis: Black people, Indigenous people, disabled people, queer people, trans people, young people, elderly people. Because those who have been most impacted are the ones who have the solutions.

Reverend Lennox Yearwood, President and CEO, Hip Hop Caucus

This is not only a climate crisis, it's a climate crime. The fossil fuel industry is killing us for their greed. And so we need your narrative. We need your storytelling. We need it now because people think that the climate movement is a white-only movement in America. And that's a lie. That's right. It is a movement that impacts all of us in this world. And so we need you to do stories that are funny and have love and have sex appeal, have drama. We need you to do movies. We also need those who have resources in this room to put money behind it. But we need it right now, because as we are no longer just fighting for equality, we are fighting for existence. And the one thing that will remain will not be you, but it will be your films, your stories, your poetry, the next generation will see that. All power to the people.

Jeanell English, Executive Vice-President of Impact and Inclusion, Academy of Motion Picture Arts and Sciences

When there is just one of me at the table, I am expected to represent everyone. That single seat at the table actually divides the community, and I don't know about you all, but I am so much stronger when I have the diversity of my community sitting at the table with me. Don't be afraid of being a minority. Don't be afraid of community. Don't be afraid of culture. Don't just try to make money off of culture, but invest in being a part of the communities whose stories have been for too long exploited. Take your position of power and privilege and bring it out into the communities to truly understand the stories that need to be championed. Be fearless with that storytelling. And, for the executives that I sit with, I always ask: can I bring in another seat?

Favianna Rodriguez

Even in the film *Don't Look Up* (2021), which showed us that there's an appetite for this kind of storytelling, we did not see sufficient people of color. And so where there is a big gap, there's also a big opportunity. Our worldview today is extract, extract, extract and drill, drill, drill. It's a growth model – it's about we need more energy, we need more consumption, and we are going to dominate nature because we have to prioritize the economy, which of course, we know at a worldwide level is only benefiting a few. There are other worldviews. In many Indigenous worldviews, there is a stewardship of nature, not a domination of nature. And so Indigenous storytelling is a climate solution because it's presenting a different worldview. It's very simple. It's about healing our relationship to the natural world. We are connected to all that is alive, and we have to rewire our imaginations because this system has taught us that we are separate from it.

Culture is extremely powerful. It is how we get folks out to vote and mobilize. As an industry, we've been looking at race and gender, and of course we have a long way to go. But climate is teeny, teeny, teeny, tiny, and that is putting us on a losing track. And so when we talk about intersectionality, imagine climate trans stories with Latinas and black and Indigenous characters. That is the future I want to invite you all to talk about because that is how we are going to influence the political systems.

Reverend Lennox Yearwood, President and CEO, Hip Hop Caucus

We are in a crisis. But we are in a crisis that we can solve because we still have time. I don't care how you tell the story, I just need you to tell the story. Now or time runs out. The alternative is that we get used to wearing gas masks and wildfires.

Faviana Rodriguez

We as culture creators, we have a lot of power. We have people power. And when we unite that with earth power, we can take on this problem. And so, first of all, let's stand in our power and organize with each other. Create work groups, create associations, work with your unions to create climate initiatives, including BIPOC people in the leadership of these climate initiatives.

The tools now exist. The Good Energy playbook is a comprehensive tool, but we need to put those tools into action now, right? I'm on a lot of climate panels. I can't tell you how many times we actually can't find a showrunner who's telling BIPOC climate stories. [Apple+ TV series] *Extrapolations*, yes, breaking new ground. But we have a long way to go. The field right now is barren. That is a huge opportunity. So y'all who have climate story ideas, I can assure you there's going to be a moment when that is going to be popping. Work on your climate stories now. Get engaged in the climate movement.

Reverend Lennox Yearwood

You can start today. All power to the people.

Reframing and Supporting Indigenous Ways of Being and Storytelling

Despite representing 5% of the world's population, Indigenous people look after or steward 25% of the earth's surface and 80% of its biodiversity.[7,8] Therefore, there is a statistical and ethical imperative to reframe some of the stories that filmmakers have been making to include Indigenous communities telling their stories on screen. There are countless Native histories and stories of the land that have never been told on film or TV. Many of these stories include ideas of sustainability, caring for nature, and being good stewards of the earth. The idea of "land back," and healing the land or "rematriating" for example are conversations happening in the world but are not often mentioned on screen. Can you imagine an episode of a detective show, or a courtroom drama about that? Addressing climate change with traditional Indigenous practices and knowledge is an important part of a solution, too. Perhaps it's time to see more Indigenous elders as experts in movie stories. Unquestionably important is the need for **authenticity in stories, representation, and in casting**. For example, the casting of actual Indigenous people in *Reservation Dogs* (2021–2023), and shooting on the Muscogee Nation in Okmulgee, Oklahoma, instead of shooting on a Hollywood set with talent from Central Casting is hugely significant. The content gets better with authenticity and with community involvement.[9]

A USC report called "Native American Representation Across 1,600 Popular Films: The Lily Gladstone Effect" by Dr. Stacy L. Smith[10] examines Native representation across 1,600 films from 2007 to 2022. The study looks at every speaking or named character to see how many Native American roles appeared on screen. Dr. Smith found that "less than one-quarter of one percent (<0.25%) of all speaking roles went to Native American characters" across the 16 years studied. "Lily Gladstone's role in *Killers of the Flower Moon* is quite literally an anomaly in Hollywood," Smith said.[11]

Key lessons and action items from this study and other conversations around Indigenous peoples in film and TV are support programs to fund Native writers and filmmakers, audition and cast Native actors, maintain authenticity in casting and writing, and hire Indigenous people. As Taiko Waititi said at the Oscars in 2020 "Indigenous people are the original storytellers."

Can Film and TV Really Move the Needle?

Even successful, mainstream filmmakers who are trying to tell environmental stories acknowledge the difficulty of climate storytelling. James Cameron was quoted in *Variety* saying, "The thing you have to remember is that entertainment is market-driven. Frankly, [audiences] don't want to hear about climate change." Cameron, who has a passion for the environment and offers only vegetarian catering on his projects, remains doubtful about the impact of eco-themed movies. "I think you can insinuate these ideas into your storytelling. I've certainly done that with *Avatar*, but, frankly, *Avatar* came out 10 years ago. And in that time our population has grown by almost a billion people, and the effects of that alone on our environment and climate change are devastating. Does [climate storytelling] do that much good?"[12]

Producer, writer, and star of *Abbot Elementary* Quinta Brunson thinks that content *and* practice will move the needle. She explains that she tries out climate material on her own family, and finds that "being beat over the head with the message will make them turn the TV off. I get excited to find ways to sneak in all of my thoughts. For example, in the second episode of season two starts with 'Look how hot it is. We don't even have the infrastructure in the school to support how hot it is outside.' In the pilot of *Abbott*, it's Ava who says, 'Why is it January and hotter than a devil's booty hole?' That's the fun in it, though, to have Ava point it out so that my mom has a nice chuckle, but then goes, 'Yeah, *why is it* January and hotter than the devil's booty hole? Let me look that up.' I know it seems so stupid but I think that's really necessary for people who otherwise would not really be interested in looking into the climate."[13,14]

Franklin Leonard, founder of screenwriter resource The Black List and Roxane Gay, co-writer, World of Wakanda comic, discuss writing about climate issues in "The Big Picture: Representing Our Climate-Altered World On-Screen," a webcast co-sponsored by NRDC, Sundance, and Yea! Impact, 2023.[15]

Gay: "It's important that we include climate change and global warming in our art. But how do we acknowledge the realities of global warming, and that there are material consequences without making it sound like a sermon or lecture?

Leonard: Yes, exactly. How do we show the reality that we'll be living with if people don't get their act together?

Gay: The reality is that people don't see the gravity of something until they see how it might manifest in the extreme – which is why so many climate stories are set in dystopia. It's not all about disaster movies (which are deeply enjoyable). Those stories help, they work, but there are more subtle ways to reflect climate in our stories. Climate and the environment can be represented in small, everyday ways – just a mention of Hurricane Sandy for example, which affected a great many people, or Hurricane Katrina. These things matter in authentic storytelling.

Leonard: In the world of Wakanda, you are presenting a totally different kind of story – a world that lives as a self-sustaining egalitarian society that coexists with the natural world, how do you represent that?

Gay: The great thing about Wakanda creatively is that it's not necessarily an ideal society but it is a technologically advanced society, and it's also a society run by people who care about the world, who care about the planet, who care about natural resources, and who have found a way to embrace technology while also embracing the natural world. Nature can also be represented as an integral part of the world. In The World of Wakanda The environment is represented, they are using technology and natural resources wisely and in harmony with the natural world.

Gay and Leonard refer us to the podcast "*What Wakanda Can Teach Us About Climate Change*" for further explanation. But we don't need to live in Wakanda to have observations about the environment and climate.

Gay: As humans, we observe climate change and we see the news. We may not be experts in the science, but we are experts in our experience.

Leonard: And these stories don't exist in isolation – climate storytelling *is* class storytelling *is* talking about gender. You noted how women are disproportionately climate refugees.

The word is overused and misused, but this is exactly what **intersectionality** is. It's acknowledging that nothing exists in isolation, and I think that we are capable of telling stories that acknowledge this reality. By and large, it's not individuals who are causing climate change, and whether it's the 20-minute private jet flights, or the broader policies of global corporations and the disproportionately white men that lead them – the consequences of climate change are felt by people of the Global South and particularly by people of color and particularly women within that (the number is 80% of climate refugees who are female). That also feels like something that we are not seeing reflected on screen. You still have these disaster movies but they're about white guys navigating the disaster. Why?

Gay: Well, because we know who makes the decisions at movie studios, and in general: Studio Executives (white men). They prefer storytelling that reflects what *they* understand of the world and what interests *them*, and having sat in meetings with these men, they will straight up ask you to your face "why should I care?" when you want to tell a story about a black woman or a woman of color from some other race or ethnicity? It's so dispiriting to have accomplished a few things in your life and then have to justify storytelling about people who look like you, but that's the current climate that we live in – for all the progress that we've made. That's why we see so many disaster movies that focus on Dennis Quaid saving the day, or Bruce Willis saving the day or whatever. I mean these movies are enjoyable so it's not to say don't make them – but when we talk about who's actually affected by climate change, we can do better. And we should do better.

> Leonard: What does doing better look like? Is it as simple as swapping out the actors, or is it something more? Is it the disaster movie starring Viola Davis (which frankly I would like to see), is that enough? Or do the stories need to change along with who is the protagonist of them?
>
> Gay: Well, it's more than just changing the leads and the primary cast – though that's a step in the right direction. It's also about who's telling the story, who's directing the story, who's producing the story. These things matter.
>
> Leonard: A takeaway for everybody is that as storytellers we all have an opportunity and a responsibility to tell the world as it is. Through the stories that we tell, we all have a role to play in inspiring climate solutions for a better tomorrow. Nowhere is that more true than with the stories that we all tell each other about who we are and what is possible.

As consumers and students of media, what do you think about that conversation? Does that speak to your experience or observations of most stories on screen? What do you observe about stories that refers to climate change and the environment? Where are the problems as you see it?

Example/Exercise

Here is an example of an opening scene for a film that hasn't been made. What climate storytelling do you see in this example? What would you change?

FADE IN: EXT. PLANET EARTH – DAY

```
The ground is covered with a thick, green coat of prairie
grass under a great yawning blue sky. Sockeye salmon are
running in a stream and birds are perched in the trees.
Suddenly, a chainsaw screams out, sending the birds up
in a flurry. Two loggers are at work in the forest.

                    LOGGER 1
          Timber!

                    LOGGER 2
          Another dozen like that and I can pay my
          mortgage this month.

A great oak falls, ending its 100-year vigil. Oil der-
ricks are now visible behind where the tree once stood,
nodding in approval.
```

Let's say that this is the opening scene of a new scripted drama that you are co-writing. Writing is such a powerful art form – there are so many ways that we can make impactful changes to the content by only adjusting a few variables. Let's say for example that the slug line was more specific than the rather cheeky *Planet Earth* and was instead *Costa Rica* or *South Africa*. Now, in addition to the environmental subtext, we also hint at the echoes of extractive practices of Colonialism. That would be especially true if our characters had names like Sir Leopold Rhodes III or Isabella Pizzaro-Cortez. Or, perhaps one logger's next line could reveal that the two are First Nation people, practicing sustainable forestry – or that they are antilogging ecoterrorists. The point is that writing is such a powerful tool that we can make tremendous or very subtle changes by simply altering a few words.

Let's use that power in this example to make some smaller changes that don't alter the story so much as add environmentally conscious content to the color of the scene.

FADE IN: EXT. FOREST — DAY

```
The ground is covered with a thick, green coat of prai-
rie grass under a great yawning blue sky. A silent wind
turbine turns in the distance. Sockeye salmon are run-
ning in a stream and birds are perched in the trees. Sud-
denly, a chainsaw screams out, sending the birds up in a
flurry. Loggers MARIA and IVAN are at work in the forest.

                           MARIA
             Thank you, Great Spirit.
                           IVAN
             Sorry, tree.
```

A great oak falls, ending its 100-year vigil. Oil derricks are now visible behind where the tree once stood, nodding in approval. Ivan lifts a metal water bottle and pours some on the earth as a tribute before taking a drink himself.

What has changed? Not much, but the details are significant and they suggest some ecologically-minded behaviors that are normalized. The reusable water bottle, the respect for the great tree, the alternative energy source in the windmill, and even the fact that the loggers have names (instead of Logger 1 and Logger 2) humanizes the characters and makes them a little more developed, a little more complex perhaps.

Now it's your turn. Try out some of the exercises below.

Exercises/Practice

1 What else could you do to this scene to add to or change the climate storytelling? What if the setting were different – telephone poles in an urban environment instead of trees, or the characters are illegal marijuana farmers

on National Forest land, or they are on another planet? What do you see and hear? What could you say with the wardrobe or with casting choices? How do you think your changes impact the audience's perception of the climate issue and the story's emotional tone?
2 Look at the Good Energy Playbook for some ideas about writing with a climate lens. Write a short treatment for a brand new, original episode of your favorite TV show but with climate issues in it.
3 The "Do the Green Thing" blog has an article about screenwriters "ruining the planet." The article claims that "Our movie theatres are filled with stories that frame eco-irresponsibility – overconsumption, over-reliance on fossil fuels – as aspirational, cool or even just normal. At best, this gives we – the audience – tacit permission to let bad environmental behavior go unexamined."[16] What do you think? Discuss in class or as an online discussion. https://dothegreenthing.com/issue/how-screenwriters-are-ruining-the-planet/

In what ways can screenwriters unintentionally promote unsustainable behaviors? How can writers balance narrative integrity with environmental messaging?
4 Apply for a Climate Storytelling Fellowship: https://blcklst.com/programs/2024-nrdc-climate-storytelling-fellowship
5 YEA! Impact and the Hollywood Climate Summit have a YouTube channel with events and talks on climate change, screen storytelling, and activism. Analyze the strategies or narratives that are presented in these talks and presentations. What worked well? What could be improved? For bonus points, draft a follow-up question or a discussion topic that could be emailed to the speakers or posted in the online comments. Share it with your class or peer group.

Notes

1 NRDC site. https://www.nrdc.org/RewriteTheFuture
2 Good Energy site. https://www.goodenergystories.com/playbook
3 Soraya Giaccardi, Adam Rogers, and Erica L. Rosenthal. 2022, October. *A Glaring Absence The Climate Crisis Is Virtually Nonexistent In Scripted Entertainment.* Norman Lear Center Media Impact Project. https://learcenter.s3.us-west-1.amazonaws.com/GlaringAbsence_NormanLearCenter.pdf
4 See also chapter "Focus on Documentary."
5 Laura Dern; Cynthia Littleton. 2019, September 10. Is Hollywood Doing Enough to Fight the Climate Crisis? *Variety.*
6 "How Screenwriters Are Ruining the Planet." n.d. Do the Green Thing. https://dothegreenthing.com/issue/how-screenwriters-are-ruining-the-planet/.
7 S. T. Garnett, N. D. Burgess, J. E. Fa, Á. Fernández-Llamazares, Z. Molnár, C. J. Robinson, J. E. M. Watson, K. K. Zander, B. Austin, E. S. Brondizio, et al. 2019. *A spatial overview of the global importance of Indigenous lands for conservation.* Nature Sustainability, Vol. 1, pp. 369–374. https://doi.org/10.1038/s41893-018-0100-6
8 "Indigenous Peoples." n.d. World Bank. https://www.worldbank.org/en/topic/indigenouspeoples.

9 Hadadi, Roxana. 2023. "How 'Reservation Dogs' Built Okern in Okmulgee, Oklahoma." *Vulture*, September 28, 2023. https://www.vulture.com/article/how-reservation-dogs-built-okern-in-okmulgee-oklahoma.html.
10 Stacy L. Smith and The Annenberg Inclusion Initiative. 2023, October. *Native American Representation Across 1,600 Popular Films: The Lily Gladstone Effect.* https://www.assets.uscannenberg.org/docs/aii-native-american-rep-1600-popularfilms-20231017.pdf
11 Ibid
12 Cynthia Littleton. 2019, September 10. Is Hollywood Doing Enough to Fight the Climate Crisis? *Variety.*
13 We're All In: Why We Should Be Excited About the Hollywood Climate Movement.
14 Chuba, Kirsten. 2023. "Quinta Brunson, Daniels Talk Embracing Environmentalism on Screen and on Set: "We Have to Be Really Precise With What We'Re Doing"" *The Hollywood Reporter*, June 23, 2023. https://www.hollywoodreporter.com/news/general-news/quinta-brunson-danielsenvironmentalism-hollywood-climate-summit-1235521955/.
15 *"The Big Picture: Representing Our Climate-Altered World On-Screen," a webcast co-sponsored by NRDC, Sundance, and Yea! Impact, 2023,* https://youtubetranscript.com/?v=JMEke5-KbYc
16 "How Screenwriters Are Ruining the Planet." n.d. Do the Green Thing. https://dothegreenthing.com/issue/how-screenwriters-are-ruining-the-planet/.

7 Preproduction
The Plan

Preproduction is where we make our brilliant, cunning, and sneaky plan, like Wile E. Coyote at the drawing board or Dr. Olivia Octavius in the Spider-verse. Whether it's an improvised slingshot or a multidimensional supercollider, the plan is critical. That's where we begin to think about our footprint.

Most productions in the world do not have the same footprint or means of production that we see in Hollywood tentpole films. Your production plan will be different if you are shooting in a city like New York, Vancouver, Johannesburg, or Mumbai, just like it would be different for a farm in Iowa, Senegal, or rural Argentina. The point is that your plan should meet the local needs and environmental challenges of where you are. Buying a fancy solar recharging station might not be as effective locally as a clean-up at a nearby wildlife habitat or fishing hole, or planting a tree at your wrap party, or advocating for a local environmental cause. Part of your specific plan should address the pieces of the puzzle located where you are.

Making the Plan

Preproduction planning is hands-down the most important stage of production, and it's always the area that filmmakers wish they had spent more time on. Find your collaborators, assemble the team, establish regular production meetings, and make a sustainability plan part of your prep. In the same way that you make a financial plan to pay for the movie, and do a visual plan or lookbook for the cinematography of your project, you need to establish your sustainability strategy. Will you go for a Guinness World Record in sustainability? How much can you realistically tackle? Can you achieve a "green seal" for your credits? Which one? Is it going to be a huge battle just to get the team to recycle their aluminum cans and turn off the lights at night? What are your director's and producer's green goals? Maybe you want to halve the fossil fuel use of a similar production of the same type. Your goal might be to buy 30% less stuff or use only solar-generated energy. Laying down specific goals shared by the principal players will drive your action. You have the ability to make a difference; how much of a difference we make is what we

DOI: 10.4324/9781003425441-7

plan for in preproduction. One proven strategy to meet your goals is to bring someone onto your team as a Sustainability Coordinator.

Bringing on a Sustainability Coordinator

The person who does the legwork on your green filmmaking plan is your Sustainability Coordinator. On a big studio project for Disney or HBO, for example, the studio might have several people on the case: a Director of Sustainability, a Sustainability Coordinator, and/or an Eco PA. A Director of Sustainability role oversees the sustainability efforts across their slate, on the multitude of projects (TV shows, movies, etc.) that a studio might be working on simultaneously at any given time. Further, they might supervise an in-house department and dedicated Sustainability Coordinators on each show. A larger project might also have additional sustainability PAs; the company may have a Sustainability Internship. The staff and titles of people working on sustainability will be different for each project depending on the company, size, budget, country, resources, and environmental mission but all the major content producers, now address sustainable production on their shows in one way or another. One of the great success stories in green filmmaking is the rise of the sustainability expert in production.

For our purposes here, you might call this person a **Sustainability Coordinator,** but you can call them whatever you want to ... Green Film Coordinator, Eco-Rep, Eco Czar, Sustainability Overlord, Benevolent Eco-Princess, whatever makes sense for you and your team. Not every production has a sustainability person, of course, but it's a good idea to have a dedicated person to follow up on all the ways that the whole crew can participate in making the film "green." If you don't have the space or the budget to feed this extra mouth, consider upgrading a PA role to Sustainability Coordinator. They can still help with general PA tasks while also managing the set's sustainability practices – and may be more likely to work for free when receiving a better credit for their resume. Identify your sustainability person and get them involved early.

Thinking about sustainability early is not just a gimmick to make the film seem green from the start, it's also about making sustainability a recognized core value that you've built into the workflow of the whole project (see Figure 7.1). Having a sustainability person at the start of preproduction means that as department heads (also known as HODs) are brought on (DP, Production Designer, Editor, etc.), this person can help team members build sustainability into *their* process at the start too. For example, if your Sustainability Coordinator is on from jump, she can brainstorm with the cinematographer about green practices that might be applicable to the camera department. She could meet with the writers to see if there are eco-friendly actions, props, locations, or jokes that can be easily incorporated into the script. She can offer suggestions, answer questions, and discuss their ideas. Ideally, it's a collaborative process.

62 Preproduction

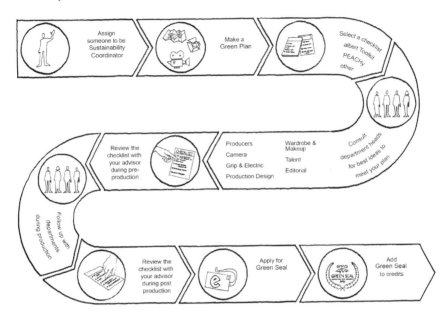

Figure 7.1 Make your green plan and workflow.

At the start of the project, have the Sustainability Coordinator sit down with the producers and director and create a list of your environmental goals. Checklists like the PEACHy or some of the other ones found in this book in Chapter 4 or in the supplemental digital materials online might help you to think up your goals. Maybe the screenwriter or director has a special interest in biking or gardening that can be incorporated into your goals. So, make a plan that people who bike to set get a special dessert, or a prize, or whatever. Maybe there is local mass transit that the producer wants to take advantage of, or new, energy-saving LED, quasar, or plasma lighting instruments that the DP wants to include. There could be a community partner to collaborate with during production – a local recycling initiative from a Scout troop, a local library talk about compost, a city park opening, or something else to tie the production into the community. Once you draft some simple, initial goals, you can create an e-memo or social media post to share with the crew and vendors to ask for their help in this initiative. When everyone is in on the plan it's incredible and inspiring to see how each individual can come up with different ways to support your goals.

This is the time for you to set up some policies and some boundaries too. For example, make sure that no one idles in their vehicle, commit to diverting at least 75% of your waste from landfills, use energy-efficient lighting as more than 50% of your lighting package, serve plant-based meals at least once a week, set a zero single-use plastic policy – on and off the screen. We'll talk about all these things, including on-screen behavior, in later chapters.

Preproduction is also when you'll need to investigate power needs. Does the building or house you're shooting in have enough power, or do you need to bring in a generator ("genny")? If mobile power is needed, can you use renewable diesel or a battery "generator" (sometimes called a "benny")? Can the local utility company provide a tie-in to the grid power? Is the grid power renewable? Tie-ins are usually possible but they take lead time, hence the importance of discussing them in early preproduction. If you're using mobile power, don't over-size it – calculate what you'll need. In Vancouver, you can get a discount on your film permit for using non-diesel power. There may be other benefits from being power-conscious where you are shooting.

On a student project, you might not have the time, money, and resources that a studio film, streaming episodic, or independent feature might have. There may only be 25 people on your set on its biggest day – or only five! But even a crew of just a few people can make a difference in your environmental footprint. Let's say you have a goal to save trees and paper and you know that you'll use one ream of paper to make hard copies of your script and some signage for craft service. First, default to digital distribution – make people opt-in for paper copies and use an app like StudioBinder or Scriptation to keep track of scripts and sides. Then, instead of buying standard bright white office paper, buy 100% recycled post-consumer content or "tree-free" paper. Now you've just cut down on your paper needs and met your "save trees" goal! If you have a goal, you can make a plan.

Regardless of the size of your crew, having a Sustainability Coordinator will really help you define and meet your environmental goals and will very likely make you more efficient with your time and resources. Think of that person as an efficiency expert. The earlier you talk about plans and goals with that person, the more efficient you will be.

I heard about a recent shoot where the Sustainability Coordinator was brought in on a TV show well after preproduction had moved to production. The result was that the systems were not set up for eco-success. The crew had already assembled their tools and a plan and weren't too happy about starting over again. Who could blame them? Why would they want to reinvent the wheel when it was already working (albeit inefficiently and decidedly not ecologically)? Can you imagine? They had their trucks, tents, workspaces, vendors, and everything ready to go when some new person comes in and tells them that they are doing it wrong. "What do you mean I can't have generators running all day in make-up and wardrobe? Well, sure there's nobody in there, but the vendor gave me a free generator – it's not costing me anything!" Making a change mid-stream is much harder than setting up a good plan before you get underway. Of course, there is no such thing as a perfect plan that never changes in film – maybe in some NASA missions, but on Earth things sometimes get messy. Sometimes we need to adjust the plan. When we've brought in our sustainability person early, then everyone has been working together and there is a teamwork mentality from

64 *Preproduction*

the start. Make it clear that green production is a collective effort and that every individual can help to solve the problems and meet the goals together.

This is the time to keep track of data too. Keep track of all the things that you do in terms of sustainability – the data will come in handy later, and you can also use it for school projects and marketing along the way. Make a report for your production class, an extra credit assignment, an article in the paper, or on social media for your department, school, or university. Take lots of "behind the scenes" (BTS) photos – they will be for good publicity, social, and marketing. Also, for getting your green seal, if you are going for one.

Setting Up the Office

Ooh, have we got an office? Depending on the scale of your production you might not have a full-on office space. But whether you are in an artist's studio, a shared office space, a garage, your car, or your dorm room, you have a workspace. Workspaces need supplies and vendors and have a workflow of their own. It doesn't take that much extra time to have someone (like your Sustainability Coordinator) help you look at your office use and establish a green workspace.

Consider what will come in and out of the office. Paper? Hard drives? Will you have a physical production binder or will it be digital (or both)? Can you buy supplies that are made from post-consumer recycled content? What vendors will you be using? Can you work with them to supply things like recycled paper or nontoxic cleaning supplies? Do your printers, computers, and other devices have power-saving features? If you are working on campus in a bullpen, production office, lounge, or library, you might be able to ask your department to switch to more energy-efficient lighting and appliances, or higher recycled-content supplies.

There are all kinds of daily tools and add-ons that you can bring to your office too – and more are becoming available all the time. Search engines Ecosia, Ekoru, and OceanHero are all designed to combat climate change through the support of planting trees, ocean clean-up, and ocean reforestation. Install your favorite on the computer that you use. Remember: even sending an email uses up to 0.074 microwatts of electricity.

We'll get into more in the chapter on the Production Department, but things like plumbed water, reusable dishes, double-sided printing, communal fridges, compost & recycling, and alternatives to pod coffee are all simple ways to decrease your footprint from the office.

Digital "Paperwork"

The dream of the "paperless society" that I remember hearing about in the 1970s and 1980s is not here yet. We still use paper, but it's getting easier to use less and less. Digital copies of scripts are common now, of course, and there are so many ways to make notes and comments to a digital script too. I make notes on scripts for my filmmaking students with "sticky note" type comment boxes in Preview or add comments in Adobe Acrobat or on a CMS like Desire to Learn or Canvas. Final Draft, Celtx, Scription, and Fountain all have paperless markup solutions too. Scriptation has some great functionality for notes, mark-up, break-down, and scribbles for ADs, scripties, actors, directors, and everyone else. Movie Magic has been an industry staple software since the late 1990s. Jungle Software and its Gorilla and Koala products are great for scheduling, breakdowns, call sheets, and the like too. Shot Designer and Previs Pro are good for floor plans and shot lists, and storyboarding. There are many great products out there.

For a while, one of the most bothersome problems in my own production practice had to do with getting documents like Location Agreements signed and sent to the appropriate parties. Printing a copy, then filling it out, signing it, scanning it, and emailing it to the next signer to print, sign, scan and return was not working for me. Too many steps and too much waste. Today, it's easy enough to fill in a digital copy of a blank form with Adobe Acrobat, Preview, Microsoft Word, or another PDF editor. Adding a legitimate legal signature can be a bit trickier (depending on your company's or school's policy) but the "fill and sign" features on the PDF editing applications are very handy, allowing you to virtually sign documents. Software like DocuSign, Adobe Acrobat Reader, and other e-sign tools are perfect for adding digital signatures with timestamps and authentication and all the things that make legal documents official. Production management websites like StudioBinder, Circus, and Dramatify allow you to do things like cast and crew contracts, kit rentals, and artwork releases completely digitally and in far less time since they can automate the process. Several offer student discounts or introductory offers. A "wet signature" (ink signature) is still sometimes requested from time to time by some permitting offices or administrative departments, but often a scan of a signed document will do just fine. Documents can be scanned to a file with a scanning app on your mobile device like Adobe Scan or the many other free and pay tools out there. With many of these production software companies offering bank-level encryption and password-protected storage that is safer than email, many people are moving away from scanned copies. Some of the tools even keep track of how many trees you saved by signing digitally, which is kind of fun to track too. Your school (or production company) may have accounts or software licenses for some of these tools already.

Working with Department Heads

As the department heads are brought on, the Sustainability Coordinator should set up a meeting with each one. Each department will have ways to contribute to the effort. Camera, Writing, Production Design, Sound,

Editorial, and the rest will be able to brainstorm different sustainable practices for their specific area. Ask for their ideas before giving them suggestions. Asking them shows that you value their ideas – and that will get them invested in the goals. The camera department might then offer that one particular battery pack is more efficient than others, Grip/Electric may have thoughts on power and lights, Craft Service will have much to contribute regarding food and food ware, and Make-Up will know product specifics practices for a smaller footprint. Asking for ideas will mean more tools to use, but it will also make everyone feel like they are contributing members of the team, not children being told how to behave. The last thing that you want to do is to create an us versus them dynamic that gets in the way of your collective goals.

On an independent or student project, the whole crew may be excited about ways to be more green. That's not always so on a paying gig. Maybe you have been (or will be) on a freelance job where crew members feel underpaid and don't have enough resources. The cast and crew may already resent producers who are skimping on salaries and buying cheap supplies. It's hard to tell *that* crew to conserve resources or get by with less. I can recall projects in my independent contractor career when crew members heard rumors that the producers were getting bonuses for saving money by underpaying for labor and quality materials. That kind of behavior can lead to safety problems – conserving resources or money is never worth risking someone's safety. Conversely, conserving resources for the *right* reasons often ends up saving money.

Similarly, efforts should start at the top and stay at the top. It's extremely frustrating when the crew is asked to do something that the executives aren't. Those pesky water bottles are a great example – you should never ask your crew to forgo the perceived convenience of a single-use water bottle when talent or execs are getting their favorite brand hand-delivered to their trailer doorstep.

There may be a need to create incentives in order to encourage sustainability. If helping the team earn a resume-noteworthy EMA Green Seal for Students, or a school Green Prize isn't enough, maybe (eco)swag at the beginning or end will help. A refillable water bottle with the school logo on it might provide inspiration, or you could plan a "green wrap party." Some department heads might be inspired to compete against each other – the department that documents the most green practices gets a prize. Ask your school bookstore or alumni office to donate a hat or hoodie with the school logo on it, or to give a gift certificate, a green pin, or something like that as a reward. The point is to make it a positive experience and get department heads to *want to* come up with ways to help.

If the conversation needs some inspiration, or ideas start to slow down, then bring out a tool like the GFSA PEACHy checklist or the GPG PEACH. Some other checklists and tools are referenced in this book and in the online digital materials.

Workflow – For Your Media AND for All Your Other Materials

What is your workflow going to look like? Are you shooting on film or digitally? Shooting film is fun, it looks great, and it's great discipline for efficient filmmaking habits, but the footprint is much larger. The chemical baths of developer, stop bath, fix, and all the chemical processes involved with making the emulsion and celluloid for the thousands of feet of filmstock and support materials are overwhelming. Making digital devices is not without waste, to be sure, but the recording medium is much cleaner. The environmental cost of copying and editing digital media is arguably far less wasteful, and easier than film. That said, there is a serious cost for digital too, which we will get into a bit later.[1]

What other workflows do we have in our filmmaking process? We are still pushing paper and pixels, and there are ways to improve those workflows too. We can probably save power and overhead costs by not working during "peak hours" (the afternoon and early evening, when more people come home and run their dishwashers, air conditioners, heaters, and giant TVs). The power companies charge higher rates for these hours because it is more difficult to meet demand. Maybe that's a good time for the office to take a break, take a nap, or take a hike. It's well-documented that a healthy and well-rested team performs more efficiently. What other workflows can you think of that you could adjust to reduce your carbon footprint?

Finding Green Vendors

The good news is that more and more businesses are interested in being responsible stewards of the earth and showing that they are thoughtful, ethical companies. There are many things that happen far away from our oversight in the production and distribution of all of our daily-use products. So, we need to do a little research. We need to be informed consumers.

We can bring refillable water bottles, but beyond that, it can be hard to tell what stuff is green and what is not. Some suppliers and stores that we use might make more of an effort than others. Which equipment manufacturers have gone green or use sustainable power sources? Take a look at the Green Production Guide's green vendor database or do a web search for eco-friendly products. A Google search for "eco-friendly businesses near me" on the west side of Los Angeles (where I live) revealed a health and beauty products store, a film production consultancy, and a market specializing in refilling containers. There are tons of places to choose from, and even grocery store chains and local shops have options. Fair-trade coffee in bulk, products without excessive plastic packaging, and biodegradable and compostable items are more available than ever. (Pro-tip: make sure you're working with a compost hauler who accepts your materials). Ask your local vendors to stock eco-friendly products too.

Lithium cobalt rechargeable batteries, for example, are in everything now: our laptops, our cars, our digital audio recorders, our cameras, our light panels, and our phones. Most lithium is mined in Bolivia, Argentina, Chile, and other places in or near indigenous land in a very wasteful and dirty way. Vast amounts of water are diverted to desert flats to bring the lithium up from the soil. Unfortunately, the water gets diverted from sources that indigenous people use for things like farming quinoa and other crops thus lowering the water table and making lands arid. Child labor and pregnant women are even used in some operations, which is unethical and unhealthy. Children in the Democratic Republic of Congo have gotten respiratory illnesses due to the dust in unregulated cobalt mines, not to mention the pollution due to runoff from wastewater and spoils from mines. The lithium, cobalt, and battery-powered products are shipped all over the world in vehicles that burn tons of fossil fuels.

The good news is that we can research the vendors that we use to see if some are using greener practices. The state of California is looking into mining lithium locally in dried lake beds, for example. For film students in the Los Angeles area, lithium batteries from California might be a preferable, more local resource that better fits their sustainability plan. Another bit of good news is that modern lithium batteries are close to 100% recyclable, unlike most other batteries. So, your recycling plan should be part of your production's resource workflow too.

Rechargeable batteries are just one of many countless products that we use every day. What is the environmental cost of some of the other products that we use? Can we mitigate those costs? Luckily many people are interested in our ecological footprint and progress is being made. Compostable plates and utensils are becoming commonplace. Fair-trade foodstuffs are now clearly labeled on packaging, as are postconsumer recycled products. There are more options than ever if you are willing to look for them.

Some new eco-friendly production studios are starting up like The Electric Owl Studios in Georgia, Portugal's Tage Studios project, or Alphaselect's proposed sustainable studio in the Malahat Nation on Vancouver Island. These are exciting and promising projects. New green companies like electric power station vendor Voltstack, and equipment mover Humble Cart are starting up each year with eager production folks looking on. Keep your eyes open for them.

The Footprint of Streaming Media

We tend to think about streaming media on our devices as a simple convenience without consequence. Binge-watching Netflix, following a YouTuber, or taking an online class from the convenience of my own home feels almost effortless and relatively harmless. After all, I'm not driving anywhere, I'm not contributing to paper waste. Computers, servers, hard drives, and data transmission all need power, however. And as anonymous as it feels to click away to the light of the blue screen, all those views, likes, and favorites use energy.

A recent publication of studies by researchers and professors at Simon Fraser University in Vancouver, The University of California – Irvine, and The University at Buffalo indicates a host of unintended and somewhat surprising consequences of streaming media. From the energy use of servers and transmitters to the electromagnetic radiation created in transmission, there is still an environmental cost to film distribution even though there is no physical film, film processing chemicals, or shipping of heavy film prints. A study from The Shift Project indicates that up to one percent of the world's carbon emissions may be coming from streaming media. The digital revolution has certainly offered up access and advantages to the global community, but it hasn't been without its consequences. Professors Marks, Hilderbrand, Livingston, and Oleksjczuk offer some useful research in this area.[2] Marks suggests that consumers and makers can stream less, select a lower resolution when streaming, or work with physical media or smaller file sizes. Lucas offers more ecologically friendly practices like reducing the amount you stream, lowering the resolution when you view, watching in groups, dimming your device, and lobbying your electricity provider to use renewable energy sources.

Production of all that streaming media uses energy too, of course. Some very good information will be relayed in this book from other important studies like the United Kingdom's Albert Annual Review, the United States' Close-Up report from the Sustainable Entertainment Alliance, the Producers' Guild, and others. I urge you to take a look at these interesting and important studies (see activity below).

E-Waste

Every day we use our computers, tablets, and phones, and in a short time replace them as soon as a new thing comes out. New devices are made with new connectors so that the old ones must be abandoned or adapted. What happened to all the first-generation Avid drives, DSLRs, firewire ports, and video camcorders of old? By and large, they went to the landfill. Some were reused and stripped for parts. Some were sent to "recycling" centers where they were often put in giant shipping containers and sent to developing nations where children and poor people tried to break them down for scrap or burn them to melt out metals from the circuit boards that can be sold. The pollution and toxic footprint of this "recycling" industry isn't very green either. We need to re-examine our relationship with new technology. Is "ending is better than mending," as Aldous Huxley's *Brave New World* puts it? Is our only choice to throw away old technology?

What if companies made things that were built to last? Or built to upgrade? Our constant search for products that are cheaper has left us with a legacy of things that break, wear out, and become obsolete quickly. The amount of waste created by this strategy can't possibly be worth the small cost savings that we enjoy when we purchase something. What can we do to change this? Can we buy technology that is built to be upgraded later – or built to be recycled? Thoughtful recycling of electronic waste (e-waste) is one of the easiest things we can do to help. Your ancient computer from 10 years ago may have components that someone can reuse. While you can't just dump it in a bin with your aluminum cans and glass bottles, you can recycle it. Look up recycling centers in your town or local region. There is often a city or county agency that collects e-waste and things like old paint or expired medicine. Goodwill Industries recycles e-waste in the United States from Arizona to Michigan to Washington, DC. Sometimes your city or local recycling center can pick it up from you, or sometimes they have collection points. I kind of enjoy the trip to the SAFE center near the Los Angeles Airport. At this facility, you drive up and open the trunk of your car while trained experts wearing PPE gather your old leaking batteries, obsolete chargers, and broken TVs. Search for "e-waste recycling near me" or for e-waste recycling guides from Consumer Reports, the Environmental Protection Agency (EPA), or your public library. Some civic groups, government agencies, and businesses keep lists of where to recycle goods on their sites as a community service. Businesses like Best Buy, Staples, and Curry's in the United Kingdom are also getting involved with electronics (WEEE) recycling.

Advocacy

Consider advocating for a local cause as a crew. Young creative people like you see the world differently than the "ruling elite." You can undoubtedly see some green causes that need champions in your area. It could be getting a recycling or compost bin nearby, it could be sending a letter to a local polluter, or to a vendor that uses too much plastic packaging. Maybe creating a petition to "dismantle capitalism" or "get out the vote" is important for you. Your movie can be a whole documentary about that issue. You already know what issues are important in your world. Make one of them a part of your plan.

Conclusion

The goals that you make in your preproduction plan will result in your cast and crew being better informed, making greener decisions, and reducing waste on set. Your plan will drive change. Your actions mean something.

Good preproduction always saves money, makes the film better – and allows for greener practices. Inevitable production problems are more easily controlled when we have been proactive and thoughtful in our preproduction. The same is true of our efficiency and our conservation of resources. How can we set up our basecamp and our whole Production Department to lay the foundation for sustainability? Our basic infrastructure in day-to-day production is going to lead our workflow and the efficiency of our sustainability practice. That is the topic of the next chapter.

> **Interview with Sustainability Coordinator and Consultant Mareike Pielot**
>
> Mareike Pielot is a certified green consultant based in Hamburg, Germany, who works with film and television productions to help them make their productions become sustainable, and earn a green seal to include in their credits (or anywhere else they want to share it). Being certified means that she has taken 120 hours of training (plus a test and presentation) for a certificate from the IHK Munich Certification Program.
>
> She is paid by the broadcasters, the production company, or the studio depending on the project. Her clients want to earn a green seal so they can show that they are sustainable. In some cases, the companies have a green mandate.
>
> Q: *How do you approach the team once you are hired? What do you say to the crew?*
> A: On a smaller film it's easier. You meet with the producers and department heads, and then each crew takes care of its own department.... It helps a lot that I have hands-on production experience because I know how a set works. Knowing who does what on a production means that I can talk to them in their language and listen to their ideas too. Other people with my job might just prefer to send emails to the department heads. In my experience, that's just not effective and gives the negative impression that an anonymous bureaucrat is giving orders....
>
> It's better when crew members and I feel like we are working on the same goal. For example, I had a case where one production had the idea of using rechargeable batteries instead of disposable ones for some of the gear. That was great, they were able to bring that idea to the conversation and so they felt that they were contributing to a green solution.
>
> Q: *How do you measure effectiveness?*
> A: Some of it is just keeping track of numbers – how many kilowatt hours were used, what kinds of meals were served, what materials were used in construction, etc. Using a set of guidelines, I write up the results and make a report. In some cases, my report is used to give the production a green seal, or other times it might be used to make a project eligible for funding.
>
> Sometimes my job involves using Environmental Psychology [a branch of Psychology that looks at the way that humans feel in relation to nature] to encourage people to have positive behaviors about sustainability in filmmaking. On my website, I ask: Are you ready to change the world? Well, I am.

Exercises

1 Go to the United Kingdom's sustainable production site wearealbert.org and explore the content. Read a few of the articles on being green at different stages of production, or look at the Albert annual report. What did you learn? What surprised you? Report back to your class or production.
2 There is a green filmmaking video course created by NYU, Smashcut Media, and Earth Angel called "Make a Film, Save the Planet" for filmmakers like you, and member schools of the Green Film School Alliance. The video course is available for free on the resources page of the Green Film School Alliance (GFSA) website. Register for the video course and watch one of the videos. Answer one of the study questions on the site.

Notes

1 MCFTA Democracy. 2023. *Sustainable Digitalisation: Ensuring a Sustainable Digital Future for UK Film and Television.* Minderoo Centre for Technology and Democracy. https://doi.org/10.17863/CAM.101504
2 Laura U. Marks, Joseph Clark, Jason Livingston, Denise Oleksijczuk, and Lucas Hilderbrand. 2020. Streaming media's environmental impact. *Media + Environment*, Vol. 2, No. 1. https://doi.org/10.1525/001c.17242

8 The Production Department

Ever heard of the Jovens Paradox?

It's the idea that as technology like solar panels or electric vehicles becomes more efficient and less expensive, there is a rebound effect where instead of energy use decreasing, it goes up. In addition, more power and resources are used to manufacture more products, because the cost is down and demand is up. In other words, suddenly every actor on the set wants a fancy solar-powered trailer, and the "planet is left footing the bill," says Jonathan Wang, producer of *Everything Everywhere All at Once*. Wang urges us to "use less stuff" and reject "this belief that we can endlessly consume at an infinite pace on a finite planet."

So, how can you set up your production to "use less stuff" instead of getting caught in the paradox? Let's look at the production department.

The production department is kind of the "office" of a film production. On a short film, documentary, or student production, the production department might just be one producer, wherever they happen to be working that day. The entire office might consist of the producer's laptop, phone, and whatever they have in their backpack. On a larger production, there may be a producer, production manager, first and second AD, coordinator, office PA (production assistant), locations person, accountant, and more. Whoever makes up your production department, you are going to need to set up an office or mobile workspace. Setting up the office in a sustainable way sets the tone for the whole shoot and postproduction.

Use Less Paper (and Make Sure It's Recycled)

First of all, ask yourself if you really need to print something – the greenest approach to paper is not to use it at all. If you do need a printout, check that you are set up for double-sided printing and that the paper you purchase is Forest Stewardship Council (FSC) certified and/or has a high post-consumer recycled content.[1] FSC-certified products have a tree logo with a little check mark next to it; some office supply stores are now putting green check marks next to eco-friendly products on their website – but you should still check the label. Some sides, schedules, and other production paperwork can be printed

DOI: 10.4324/9781003425441-8

in mini-versions to save paper by selecting a "four to a page" layout in the printer settings.

Keep Your Script Digital

Paperless solutions like Final Draft, Celtx, Fade In, and StudioBinder are some of the most popular script-writing programs. The formatting tools are invaluable, and exporting to a PDF file makes for easy paperless distribution. Scriptation is a great product for the script user side, since it allows you to mark up, write on, draw on, and add notes to a digital copy – and then transfer your notes if/when you're given a new or revised version of the script. No more wastepaper baskets full of obsolete versions and no more office PAs collating endless script pages.

Digitize Forms

In production, we love forms. Well, we may not all *love* them, but we do use them often. In the past, some career producers felt like paper-pushers with all the liability waivers, permits, contracts, and start-up paperwork they needed to generate, get signed, and send on to the next signer. Think of all the couriers and production assistants employed over the years to drive, bike, run, and walk all over the place to get signatures and deliver paper envelopes to their recipients. Fortunately, in the digital age, we have lots of options for a digital workflow with PDFs, emails, and electronic signatures, as we looked at in the Preproduction chapter. No system is perfect, but there are some great paperless tools out there for your forms.

Adobe Acrobat is one of the premiere tools for PDF (Portable Document Format) creation and editing. As Adobe's website puts it, this file format "gives people an easy, reliable way to present and exchange documents – regardless of the software, hardware, or operating systems being used by anyone who views the document."[2] If you don't have experience creating or editing PDF forms, learn how. There are tutorials on YouTube, LinkedIn Learning/Lynda.com, Adobe, Apple, Canva, Docusign, and lots of other places online. You don't need to use Adobe products to work with PDFs. Adobe Acrobat works really well for editing and signing PDFs, but there are also lots of other tools out there that work too.

DocuSign is another great option for electronic signatures and forms. Some campuses and workplaces may have a subscription to the service, but just as with Adobe, signers don't necessarily need to have an account to electronically sign a document. The cool thing about these software and web-based solutions is that as a producer, you can flag where you need people to enter information (addresses, contact information, etc.) and where you need an initial or a signature. DocuSign and some other tools allow you to send the form to one signer and then to the next, and the next, electronically in the proper sequence, in a way that can be tracked so that nothing gets lost. No forms are getting rained on, goofed up in the fax machine, eaten by a dog, or spilled on. Instead, forms are transparently tracked by signers and signees and done in a legal and secure way that can't be forged. Docu-Sign has a cool feature that shows you how many trees and other resources you've saved too.

Paper documents can also be signed with a "wet signature" and "scanned" by your phone with the Adobe Scan App before being emailed to the next recipient. Preview, Adobe Fill and Sign, Canva, Sejda, and lots of other tools are available for editing your PDFs and filling out PDF forms as well. For some forms, you might need to use an application that keeps track of various meta-data, including a verified, authenticated email address, for legal reasons. Registered Adobe accounts and DocuSign accounts are good bets for that.

Buy Eco-Friendlier Devices and Computers

We can't have a production department without laptops, phones, tablets, and other devices. Going back to the days of paper, strip-board scheduling, and chalkboards is pretty much unthinkable. (Although that's a film I'd love to see. Who's up for a film project that ends with "no computers were used in the production of this film" in the end credits?) Our devices are not without their environmental cost. Some are manufactured in factories that don't adhere to the most basic guidelines regarding pollution, not to mention labor laws. Exploitation of people and natural resources in the tech industry is a growing concern. The UN's 17 Goals for Sustainable Development outline the interconnected practices that "recognize that ending poverty and other deprivations must go hand-in-hand with strategies that improve health and education, reduce inequality, and spur economic growth – all while tackling climate change and working to preserve our oceans and forests."[3] We can be mindful of what devices we buy and the practices that those companies use. One source is EPEAT (the Electronic Product Environmental Assessment Tool), which rates computers and devices on their sustainability.

Lots of computers and other devices have "energy saving," "battery saving," or "eco" modes that exchange maximum processor speeds and display modes for energy efficiency. You can also save some energy and battery life by simply turning down the brightness of your screen. Dimming your display won't save the rainforest overnight, but if you don't need maximum brightness 100% of the time, why use the energy? There are also browsers with an energy saver mode that you can turn on in the browser settings.

Over the years, a number of eco-search engines have appeared. Ecosia, OceanHero, Ekoru, GiveWater, and Rapusia all use a portion of their ad revenue to contribute to environmental causes.[4] Ecosia's mission is to plant trees; according to their website, their revenue supports planting one tree for every 45 searches.[5] OceanHero combats ocean pollution and plastic waste. Some search engines donate to social causes and other environmental issues.

There are also phone cases and phone chargers that are marketed as eco-friendly. They may be made of 50–100% recycled materials or sustainable materials like bamboo, but buyer beware; some of these products are more about greenwashing than effective green practices.

Recycle and Reuse Signs

You'll almost certainly be making or purchasing signs of one kind or another for your production. You may need a "Quiet please, recording in progress" for a documentary, or a "Your entry and presence on the premises constitute your consent to be photographed, filmed…" sign. You are likely to need a sign for parking and/or for the production office, with arrows pointing in the proper direction. Try to make any signs reusable and with recycled materials. Reuse a cardboard box, for example, and/or print out a few nice, clean signs, guilt-free, if you are going to reuse them. It's okay to use paper occasionally, especially if you will be using it again.

Your production company, studio, or school may want to consider printing out a few of these signs on durable, recycled material to be available for checkout. Ask your school's production coordinator or equipment center about implementing this. It's really the same practice as checking out safety items like traffic cones, safety goggles, and first aid kits – it's all about setting up best practices for future behavior. Maybe you can create a "sustainability in film kit" or "zero-waste kit" for your school or studio that has reusable plates and utensils, signage, and other things for a greener set. Fishtown Films in PA has become famous for producing films with only enough trash left to fit into a 16-oz jar.

The Green Production Guide (greenproductionguide.com) has a free toolkit available for download that includes some helpful signs and resources too. There is a starter memo for producers like you to get you going and a Best Practices Infographics for the production office. While you are there, take a look at the infographics for the stage, construction, and on location too. This will really help to inform your plan as you set up the next stages of production. The downloadable toolkit has some on-point signs about plastic use, catering, reusable water containers, and other things.

Carpool

Many of us love our cars. We love them for transportation, for a portable office, for dates, for on-the-go meals, and even for naps. So, sharing your car can feel like sharing your bedroom or your fortress of solitude. Nevertheless, fuel use is the largest portion of our carbon footprint. If you're lucky enough to have a private vehicle, carpool, or use public transportation sometimes to help make up for it.

Having a carpool can be fun too. You can even make a competition out of it. For example, one of the companies I used to work for, New Deal Studios, started a competitive carpool initiative. It was a busy time for the company as they expanded to work on two major Hollywood feature films along with all the other projects and original material they were working on. A chart was drawn up with everyone's name on one axis and the things that you could get points for on another – including carpooling, riding your bike to work, and walking. It was a big success, it made people feel good, and it helped with the parking situation since the parking lot was being used for some major set construction, prop fabrication, and custom painting. There were prizes for weekly winners and more prizes at the end of the production. It was fun and morale was high. Gamifying works.

Shop Locally for Production Supplies and Expendables

Where are you sourcing your materials? Are you ordering from an online vendor that wastes resources on packaging? Are you efficient with your purchases? Are you buying multiple versions of the same prop, knowing that you can return whatever you don't use?

Your film project might be small enough that the producer is the person who does the shopping. A bigger production office might have a purchaser or coordinators doing research about sourcing and then getting approval for purchases from a producer. Sourcing your purchases from green vendors and local vendors is key. The Green Production Guide and Albert both have a list of green vendors. The lists may include vendors in your area. Your local chamber of commerce or town hall may have a list of sustainable vendors too.

Shopping locally makes a difference, especially when you get there via bus or another green form of transportation and bring your own bag. Your local family-owned hardware store, general store, or pharmacy is a good first stop, but you can't buy gaffer's tape or a BNC connector or surveillance earpiece at 7–11. If your area has a local film board, film office, or film directory, check it for nearby expendables vendors. Sometimes this office is connected with a local board of tourism.

Go Solar

Charge devices in an eco-friendly manner by harnessing the power of the sun. Solar chargers and solar charging battery units are a great way to effectively and sustainably charge devices and free up an outlet on location for a light, a piece of safety gear, or the coffee pot.

Is your backpack your office? Consider one of the solar backpacks on the market. The attached solar panel can charge an internal battery while you are walking around or sitting in the sun. The battery then charges your phone, laptop, camera batteries, walkie-talkies, whatever. There are several models on the market, so do your research: Some have panels with higher wattage output than others, some are manufactured domestically, some work in indirect sunlight, and some are made out of recycled materials. You may also want to look at other portable, durable solar panel products (foldable panels, briefcases, mountables, etc.) to add to your kit.

Can you use solar in your workflow? There are production companies and studios trying out solar trailers, solar units, and zero-emission sustainable facilities. Check with your power utility to see if you can specify a preference for using sustainable power. Many power companies will gladly switch you to green power – for a small fee.

Skip the Bottled Water

Some offices have water delivered in big plastic bottles that go upside down on the water cooler. It can feel fun to have the special mountain spring mineral water delivered, and it may even sound healthier. But consider all the extra resource costs involved to pump thousands of liters of water out of the spring or reservoir where nature puts it and bottle it in plastic containers. Petroleum generates the electricity used to pump the water and produce the plastic bottles used for storage. Then more fuel is used to transport the water to where it is distributed or sold and finally delivered to the office.

Fortunately, the use of all those extra resources can be avoided by simply using the tap. Almost all tap water in developed nations is safe to drink.[6] If you want to filter it to remove chemicals and/or improve the taste, sink filtration devices are one option. For drinking water, there are a variety of filtered water jugs and dispensers available in plastic, glass, and ceramic.[7,8]

Finally, consider buying reusable water bottles instead of bottled water for your crew. A custom logo or stickers from your film, school, or department are great for team-building, and they look great in the behind-the-scenes photos!

Use Real Dishes and Cutlery

Just like you would in your dorm, house, or apartment, bring in dishes and silverware. If you don't have enough to spare to bring them from home, buy some cheap from a thrift store. Bring along some dish soap and you can wash and reuse your coffee cups and lunch plates for the whole project – saving money on disposable plates and cutlery and reducing your contribution to the landfill. Easy.

Brew Your Own Coffee by the Pot

Another easily avoidable offense in offices all over the world is the dreaded single-use disposable plastic coffee pod. Coffee snobs everywhere might roll their eyes, but pod users like the idea of saving time, effort, and clean-up with this "modern convenience." Unfortunately, this convenience is not efficient – it's wasteful, it costs more, and often doesn't taste as good as making drip coffee. The other advantage of brewing coffee a pot at a time is that you can compost the used grounds. Most paper filters can be composted too. Or choose a coffee maker that doesn't need paper filters and instead uses a metal mesh basket, which will also save you money.

Consider Expenses from a Green Perspective

For a low-budget film, you probably don't have an accounting department per se, but there are accounting tools that the producer may want to keep on the radar. There are tools by albert, EcoProd, there is PEAR, and others. At UCLA, for example, a group of students is creating a cost and environmental accounting tool that looks at sustainable practices not just in terms of monetary cost benefit, but also their effect on the environment. Sustainability consulting company Green Spark Group has a sustainable production office course and a circular economy course that offers training in this discipline for those who want to go deeper. You can even get a certificate to show future clients or future employers.

Keeping good records is good accounting and good producing. It will also give you data to use when it comes time to calculate your environmental footprint. Keeping track of things like fuel purchased, plastic water bottles versus aluminum, and amounts of sustainable materials acquired is really the only way to figure out how well you did versus other films that tried sustainable practices.

But how can we tell if there are additional consequences from the exhaust from our vehicles or the power plant that made our electricity? Those things are harder to figure out. To calculate the "dark budget" of a film's environmental footprint, we could turn to a carbon calculator like albert's or like PEACH+, but even these powerful green filmmaking tools can't do a full life-cycle analysis of each purchase in each line item of a film's budget. (More on that later.)

Document It

Keep track of everything that you do sustainability-wise. The actions are important, but so is the data. You can leverage your findings later into a report for a class, an extra-credit project, or a paper. Summaries of unique projects like a sustainability study are perfect features for your social media posts, or for the dept, college, school, or GFSA social media. Do BTS (Behind the Scenes) documentation. It makes for good publicity articles and social media marketing.

Use Less

Sometimes the best solution is to simply get by with less stuff. If you buy a gigantic case of recycled printer paper or a cool solar phone charger and never use it, that's obviously a waste. The most basic rules of thumb for a sustainable basecamp and office are pretty obvious: be conscious of what you buy, how much you use, and what you do with your trash.

Sort Trash, Recycling, and Compost

Let's talk trash. Of course, you will want to *reduce* and *reuse*, but you'll also want to set up systems for recycling, composting, and landfill trash in your production office. Some of what you are able to do on this front has to do with what is available in your area, so you may need to do some research on your city or county website regarding the recycling and composting options available to you.

At the very least, you can get two trash bins: one for recycling and one for landfill. Blue is a good color for your recycling bin, and simple labeling is a must. There are some excellent free printable signs available on the Green Production Guide and the Green Film School Alliance websites (Figures 8.1 and 8.2).

Figure 8.1 Some organizations like the Green Production Guide have free, downloadable signage for your set.

Figure 8.2 A downloadable sign from the Green Film School Alliance.

In some cities, glass, metal, paper, cardboard, and certain plastics can be recycled in a mixed bin. In Japan and some other countries, you may see a bin for trash that can be burned. Some other areas don't take plastic, or only take aluminum, or require separating different colors of glass. Cardboard may be recyclable in your area, but oily, dirty cardboard pizza boxes probably aren't. However, they could be compostable – check out the options where you live. Young movie people eat a lot of pizza!

In any case, be sure that whatever you put in a recycling bin is clean and free of contaminants. Rinse out glass jars and metal food cans before you toss them in the bin. Some grocery stores that had been recycling plastic bags stopped doing it because of one major contamination problem: people left their receipts in the bags.[9] Anything left in the bags would contaminate the batch, but those plastic-y wax-y thermal receipts can't be recycled with regular paper either since they contain toxic BPH. So, think before you toss.

Does your building, campus, or city recycle? They might even have area-specific premade signs that show what is recyclable and what is compostable. If there is no recycling in your area, you might be able to bring your bottles and cans to a recycling center; they may even give you money for certain materials. Alternatively, there may also be recycling and composting services that come to your location and pick up from you for a fee. If you are shooting on campus, your school administration may even foot the bill because they're excited about starting up a recycling or composting practice. You can be a leader on the cutting edge of change!

Recycle e-Waste and Toxic Waste

We've gone over trash, recycling, and composting, but what about things like old light bulbs, printer cartridges, or broken computer chargers? Don't throw them in the landfill. That stuff can be recycled too. Set aside a bin or cardboard box and write "Toxics and E-Waste" on it. Batteries, old paint, broken printers, busted phone cables, expired medicine, old glue bottles, and the like can all go in there. It might take you a Google search or two, but there is likely a toxics drop-off point, a hazardous waste disposal, or e-waste center in your area. At many such places, you can drop off items for free if you live or work in the area. (See also Chapter 18 for more ideas about what to do with things at wrap.)

Choose Green Cleaning Products

Many of the products sold in the supermarket or in big box stores will get the job done well for a reasonable price but contain toxic chemicals. You would be surprised at the number of common household cleaning products that contain carcinogens and chemicals that are toxic to the environment. Choose low-toxin, low-carcinogen products and biodegradable sponges, rags and wipes.

Clean Up … Cleaner

The production office sets the tone for your whole film. Keep things neat, and clean up in the office when you're done. You'll do that on set too, but it all starts at the top. Good cleanup is good environmental stewardship, part of your filmmaking best practices, and also just common courtesy.

Exercises/Homework

1 Take a look at the toolkits on the Green Production Guide or Albert. Can you use some of the signage (ex: signs encouraging people to "bring your reusable water bottle," "what to compost," "best practices," etc.)? What else can you adapt or use for your next project? What ideas do you have of your own?
2 Suppose you are the producer or the AD of the project. What are your duties on the production? Which duties overlap with sustainability in the production? Which responsibilities affect both safety and sustainability?

Notes

1 B. Carter. 2019. Which Eco-Friendly Paper Is Best – Recycled or FSC Certified? https://www.ecoandbeyond.co/articles/eco-friendly-paper/; https://us.fsc.org/en-us/market/paper-printing; https://environmentalpaper.org/
2 Adobe website marketing materials. https://www.adobe.com/acrobat/about-adobe-pdf.html
3 Department of Economic and Social Affairs. 2015. *Sustainable Development Goals*. https://sdgs.un.org/goals
4 Chomsky, Raf. 2024. "5 Eco Friendly Search Engines That Save the Environment." Sustainable Review. January 29, 2024. https://sustainablereview.com/5-eco-friendly-search-engines-that-save-the-environment/. Southern, Matt G. 2023. "Eco-Friendly Search Engines: Making a Difference One Search at a Time." *Search Engine Journal*, April 22, 2023. https://www.searchenginejournal.com/eco-friendly-search-engines-making-a-difference-one-search-at-a-time/485193/.
5 Ecosia website. www.ecosia.org
6 Al Jazeera Staff. 22 Mar 2022. https://www.aljazeera.com/news/2022/3/22/infographic-which-countries-have-the-safest-drinking-water-interactive
7 J. Bowyer, H. Groot, and K. Fernholdtz. 2018. *The Environmental Impacts of Tap vs. Bottled Water*. https://www.mwra.com/monthly/wscac/2018/113018-DovetailConsumeResp1Water.pdf
8 Oregon Department of Environmental Quality (DEQ). 2009. *Life Cycle Assessments of Drinking Water Systems*. https://www.oregon.gov/deq/FilterDocs/wprLCycleAssessDW.pdf
9 *Earth 911*. 2022, March 16. How to recycle plastic bags. *Earth 911*. https://www.earth911.com/recycling-guide/how-to-recycle-plastic-bags/

9 Production Design, Art, Construction, Props, and Set Decoration

"The dumpsters just line up at the end of the show, and there's no talking about it because it's time to get off the soundstage,"[1] said veteran art director Karen Steward in a recent interview on National Public Radio's *Morning Edition*. Steward has been working toward creating more sustainable sets for 20 years.

Although companies such as EcoSets, recycledsets.com, and Film Biz Recycling reuse and recycle sets and props donated by studios, many Hollywood-area warehouses that would store old sets have downsized or shut down in recent years thanks to the increasing value of LA real estate. Producer Jonathan Wang suggests that filmmakers plan for reducing their environmental impact in the same way that they planned for shooting during the pandemic – by allocating 4% or 5% of their budget to cover things like health and safety officers and testing. As he noted in the *Morning Edition* story, "we adapted to the emergency on set. And we are currently in [another] emergency, burning through resources faster than we renew them."[2] Use and re-use of sets, props, art, and construction materials is a big part of the solution. In this chapter, we explore some of these alternatives to traditional production work.

Setting the Stage

Production Design (PD) is the art and craft of establishing the film's look or aesthetic through its set, props, color, shape, line, and everything else that creates a visual environment. It is also a very important part of character development. Students of directing may appreciate the way that Mary Lou Belli and Bethany Rooney put it in their book, *Directors Tell the Story*, "Everything that is in the frame that is not human is part of the production design."[3] Therefore, when designing and building the story world, we can make a difference by thinking about everything nonhuman in the frame, what it's made of, how to reuse as many of those things as possible, and being careful about throwing stuff away.

PD is a vital extension of storytelling and character development. For example, the script may call for a table for a character to put her keys on

DOI: 10.4324/9781003425441-9

PD, Art, Construction, Props, and Set Decoration 85

when she comes home from work. For the most part, a table is a table, right? But every frame of our movie is an opportunity to inject more story, more detail about our character, and more authenticity into our film. So, what kind of table is it? Is it a precious antique? Something wobbly but charmingly made by a relative? Is it a cheap, mass-produced thing or made from sustainable bamboo? Those short minutes of screentime are precious, and we must use every little bit of physical and temporal space that we have to deliver story information. Maybe our character is concerned about some of the same climate issues that we see in our own lives. The keys could land on the table next to a bus pass, a reusable water bottle, an organic trail mix, and a metal straw. Just as our writing and development can include environmentally related content, so can our PD. What design elements, vehicles, chairs, textures, and colors, tell you most about the character? Is there something that the character lives with that has to do with the environment or the climate crisis?

The production designer (or art director) conceptualizes and creates the world of the story in collaboration with the director and cinematographer. In a Hollywood production, there are usually other folks to lead the set construction, prop acquisition, and set decoration. On a small scripted narrative project, a student film, or some documentaries, this might all be one person – sometimes called the Art Department, Production Design, or PD. For purposes of this discussion, let's imagine that we have people in the positions of PD, construction, props, and set decoration. (Although wardrobe and makeup are in the Art Department too, not to mention greensperson and animal wrangler, we'll limit the discussion for the time being.)

How can we bring meaning and sustainability to the Art department, one of the potentially most toxic departments of all, given its tendency to use and then trash large quantities of construction materials? We can do it both on-screen, with elements of our mise-en-scene and character development, and off-screen, in the way that we work.

What's in the Background?

The backgrounds for all the expert interviews in a documentary like *13th* (2016), *An Inconvenient Truth* (2006), or *Body Parts* (2023) are carefully chosen or staged to say something about the person speaking or the content of the film. A scientist being interviewed might typically have a wall full of framed degrees behind them or be in a lab with fancy equipment. In *My Octopus Teacher* (2020), for example, diver and filmmaker Craig Foster is filmed talking about his octopus friend in his home office, where we see evidence of his collection of data and growing personal passion about mollusks and octopuses.

What else could be in the frame of your own film that would acknowledge the realities of the human/nature relationship or climate change? Framed art with an eco-theme? A refillable coffee mug? Recycling signage? One resource to consider: If you're looking for art or eco-posters for a set wall, the nonprofit group Global Inheritance has a great collection of free downloadable posters. The Global Inheritance POSTed Studio bills itself as a place where individuals (sometimes kids) "design poster concepts around social or environmental issues that matter to them. The concepts are then transformed by professional designers and made available to share with the rest of the world."[4]

If you are designing a scene or space, could you design with nature in mind? Maybe that means situating plants or animals in your mise-en-scene or shooting outdoors. Could you position humans as a part of the natural world somehow, instead of against it?

Hopefully, the everyday in our near future will look more sustainable. Showing solar panels or wind turbines in a shot helps normalize renewable energy. Consider shots of people interacting with nature – on a hike, biking, even canoeing across a lake. On-screen behaviors affect off-screen behaviors – just ask advertisers, who pay thousands for product placement in a big movie.

Jack Fisk is the production designer of *Killers of the Flower Moon* (2023) directed by Martin Scorsese. He has worked with Alejandro González Iñárritu, David Lynch, Terrance Malik, and his wife Sissy Spacek. A *New York Times* article[5] describes Fisk's work as being akin to painting, with the goal of creating believability and realism, even on a low budget. The designer creates an immersive world not only for the camera, but also for the actors and all the other collaborators too, inviting everyone working on set to become a part of the performance via the construction, color selection, and set decoration. The process might involve attention to a quiet beauty; a slow, methodical look at nature, light, time, and weather; and the characters' messy, layered surroundings. Part of each character's internal and external landscape has to be their interaction with the natural world and their environment. So, the question is: How can you as a designer, as a filmmaker, convey your characters' relationship to the environment? And if concern for the planet is a part of the reality that your characters experience, why exclude it?

Materials

If your school or studio has a sustainability department or office, it's a great place to start looking for partners in your efforts. Sustainability coordinators might want to reach out and befriend someone in that department (or the school's purchasing department), at the very start of pre-production.

Don't over-buy. Buy what you need, and use up what you have. Ever cleaned out a relative's old workshop or garage? Think of all the materials, compounds, paints, and detritus that accumulate over time. I helped clean up an old shed a few summers ago and was amazed to discover ancient marvel mystery oil, lead-based paint, tar paper, liquid wrench, liquid weld, liquid nails, powdered cleansers, coffee cans filled with assorted lug nuts, and a half-dozen bottles of dried-up glue. It was a toxic fume-fest, waiting to spontaneously combust. What do you do with 35 pounds of rusted roofing nails, anyway? Lots of this needed to be taken to a local toxic waste drop-off site. This could be your set if you're not careful.

What materials will you need to create your story world? Buy materials that are environmentally conscious and look for nontoxic, eco-friendly resources. Instead of particle board made from composite wood and toxic glue, use reclaimed wood, sustainable bamboo, plyboo (bamboo plywood), or certified sustainable lumber. Use simple, natural products and materials. Being environmentally conscious in your sourcing or shopping is not that difficult, but it does require effort. Don't just automatically hop on Amazon and order the first thing in your search results. There may be a local shop whose staff can give you expert recommendations on materials that are less toxic. There may be a merchant that you didn't know about that caters to clients who are looking for the same types of things that you are. Advisors and online vendors like Green Building Supply, Green Building Advisor, My Chemical Free House, might be good resources for your research. There is already an established market for nontoxic products for people with chemical sensitivity and other concerns.

In a paper for the *FilmForum 2022 XXIX Udine International Film and Media Studies Conference on Sustainability in Film*, I included some suggestions about lumber:

> Look into sustainable lumber certified by the Forest Stewardship Council (FSC), the Programme for the Endorsement of Forest Certification (PEFC) or an equivalent organization in your area. Certified materials are labeled with the logo of these organizations and are in line with internationally recognized sustainability practices. For example, the PEFC mission specifically refers to and contributes to the UN sustainable development goals.[6] Many lumber shops carry these products, although the cost is markedly higher, which can be a problem for filmmakers on a budget. Since many schools and institutions now have sustainability mandates, students may be able to ask their institution's purchasing department or the facilities management department to partner with them to achieve a sustainability goal.[7]

When building, make things to be reused, disassembled, or recycled. Making a kitchen set? Can you make it so that it's easily transformed into something else, like a small restaurant or office space? Can the counter be easily redressed for another scene in the film or for someone else's movie? Every reuse saves resources.

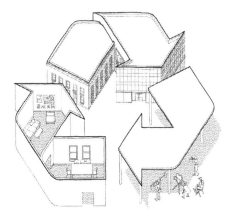

Figure 9.1 Sets can be built out of recycled materials, and built to be reused.

Don't build it to be indestructible or to barely get through the day – build it to be reused but also so it can be easily disassembled or broken down into components for storage or repurposing. Instead of synthetic glue and nails, use nontoxic wood glue like Titebond or Elmer's, and use nuts and bolts or removable fasteners. Making it lightweight means it uses less material and is cheaper to transport if you need to move it.

Look for low-VOC paints and other products. VOC stands for volatile organic compounds. The European Environmental Agency defines a VOC as "organic chemical compounds that under normal conditions are gaseous or can vaporize and enter the atmosphere. VOCs include such compounds as methane, benzene, xylene, propane, and butane."[8] You can find low-VOC paints, solvents, cleaning supplies, and building materials now.

Consider whether there is someplace nearby that can use this set when you are finished with it. Is there a school that could use the workbenches you made? Can you donate that countertop or rolling shelving to a daycare or senior center when you are finished using it? We'll address this subject again in the "wrap" section.

Million Dollar Idea: Eco-Foam – Start a New Business with Your Engineering and Chemistry Friends

Styrene and other plastic-based foam materials are cheap, lightweight materials that are great for carving custom props, models, custom cliff faces, statues, buildings, mountains, and other features. They are also made from toxic materials that will essentially never biodegrade. Some companies are beginning to make plastic-like products out of seaweed and other organic compounds. Could we someday see seaweed-based biodegradable foam for custom building or even for insulation in construction? Maybe you and/or friends in other majors and specializations will crack the code and make a much-needed product. It might make a killer surfboard core too (see Appendix A for more ideas).

Free

There is so much out there that you can get for free! "FreeCycling" and "Buy Nothing" groups in your area are great resources. Borrow things from friends, family, and neighbors! Some art department people have even been known to find great stuff from the dumpster at the mall. But even with gloves and work boots you really should avoid anything that could give you tetanus. Be safe. Free stuff is all around you. Most of the time, all you need to do is ask politely.

Renting

If possible, get used sets, props, and flats from a local theater company, or production company, or from a business that rents and sells used flats and set pieces like EcoSets in the Los Angeles area, recycledsets.com, or Film Biz Recycling on the East Coast. Larger cities will also have prop houses that you can rent some amazing things from. Renting from Sharegrid and other online resources can be economical and greener than building from scratch if you have a budget.

Thrift stores, garage sales, and secondhand stores are great for cheap props, and bonus, you are reusing something rather than consuming something new. Some cities also have prop rental houses if you have the budget for it. Like many other students and directors of low-budget projects, you will likely be borrowing props from friends and family too – another eco-friendly practice.

Live Plants

I've got one word for you, Benjamin. One word. Are you listening? One word: plants. Sure, the old guy in *The Graduate* (1967) said "plastics" to a young Dustin Hoffman, but plants are way better. Live plants are great props. They clean the air, add atmosphere to a set, and generally make people feel good. Live plants make a place feel alive. Did you ever see *Between Two Ferns with Zach Galifianakis* (2008–2019)? It's a good example of live plants as a pivotal part of the set design – through eight seasons and a movie, the ferns are central characters.

In his book *Biophilia* (1984), biologist Edward O. Wilson suggests that a connection to plants may be deeply rooted in our biology. In fact, studies show that plants reduce stress, boost moods, make us feel peaceful, and increase creativity.[9–11] Some plants even actually reduce toxins in the air. NASA did an experiment to see which plants would be the best at cleaning the air in a space station. Some of the winners were mother-in-law's tongue (aka snake plant – *Sansevieria trifasciata laurentii*), English ivy (*Hedera helix*), Peace lily (Spathiphyllum "Mauna Loa"), and Chinese evergreen (*Aglaonema modestum*).[12] Of course, it takes a lot of plants to add up to a dramatic air quality change, but every little bit helps. Whatever plants you incorporate in your shoot, take them home when you're finished with them, or donate them to a local hospital, school, or senior center.

Clean Up and Wrap

Old sets, props, and construction materials can be recycled and reused. The major studios and all kinds of production companies make an effort to donate, reuse, and recycle.

As you build your set, think about what you will do with everything when you are finished with it (see also Chapter 18 on Wrap). Mixed construction waste is a huge problem and tough to dispose of properly. Some of the trickiest stuff to get rid of is paint, adhesives, solvents, and other toxics; if you can't find anyone to use them, they will need to be dropped off at a hazardous waste disposal site.

Students may be able to use subsidized city toxic waste sites to get rid of some things at no cost, but where I live, businesses are not allowed to.

If you're starting a production company of your own, consider that you might need to pay for certain waste disposal and research outlets like Goodwill or Homeboy Recycling in Los Angeles to take your used electronics, textiles, and other surplus. Check your local options.

Exercise

1 Imagine you are the production designer for films like the Oscar winners *Everything, Everywhere, All at Once*; *CODA*; *Parasite*; *Oppenheimer*; or *Nomadland*. How does your production design include the characters' relationship with or views about the natural world? List and describe some ways you will represent that on screen.

Notes

1 Karen Steward in a recent interview on National Public Radio's *Morning Edition*. https://www.npr.org/transcripts/1228136040
2 Ibid.
3 Mary Lou Belli and Bethany Rooney. 2016. *Directors Tell the Story*. Routledge Press.
4 "Global Inheritance." n.d. https://www.globalinheritance.org/programs/posted-studio
5 Noah Gallagher Shannon. 2023, October 22. The Genius Behind Hollywood's Most Indelible Sets. *The Sunday Read, New York Times, "The Daily" Podcast*. https://www.nytimes.com/2023/10/22/podcasts/the-daily/fisk-killers-of-the-flower-moon.html
6 Programme for the Endorsement of Forest Certification. Sustainable Development Goals. https://www.pefc.org/what-we-do/sustainable-development-goals
7 K. Hayward. 2024, November. Sustainability in production and the green film school alliance. In *FilmForum 2022 XXIX Udine International Film and Media Studies Conference – (Un)bearable Lightness of Media (cfp 2022), Critical Approaches to "Sustainability" in Film and Audiovisual Production*. Mimesis. Circulation and Preservation, Udine, Italy.
8 "Glossary." n.d. European Environment Agency. www.eea.europa.eu/help/glossary
9 Das, Lala Tanmoy. 2023. "What Science Tells Us About the Mood-boosting Effects of Indoor Plants." *Washington Post*, December 12, 2023. https://www.washingtonpost.com/wellness/2022/06/06/how-houseplants-can-boost-your-mood/.

10 Sill Staff. n.d. "The Benefits of Houseplants." The Sill. https://www.thesill.com/blog/why-you-need-plants-in-your-life.
11 S. Gritzka, T. E. MacIntyre, D. Dörfel, J. L. Baker-Blanc, G. Calogiuri. 2020, April 28. The effects of workplace nature-based interventions on the mental health and well-being of employees: A systematic review. *Frontiers in Psychiatry*, Vol. 11, p. 323. https://doi.org/10.3389/fpsyt.2020.00323. PMID: 32411026; PMCID: PMC7198870.
12 B. C. Wolverton. 1989. nasa.gov/api/citations/19930073077 https://ntrs.nasa.gov/citations/19930073077

10 Camera, Grip, and Electric

The camera department and the grip and electric department are the two most iconic parts of a film shoot. After all, they are two-thirds of "lights, camera, action!" These two departments work closely together, and on a student film shoot, documentary, or independent shoot, they might be interchangeable. Occasionally, they might even be just one single person (although that'd be a lot for one person to do!). On many films, they are discrete, separate departments, but for this chapter, I'm grouping them together because the territory that they cover overlaps when it comes to their environmental impact.

Since the sprocket days of film, much has changed in the camera, grip, and electric departments. Shooting digitally means no toxic film-processing chemicals, but there is still a footprint from energy use and expendables. Sustainability questions still arise, like what kind of lights to use, how to power the set, and what to do with plastics and e-waste when we upgrade equipment. The purpose of this chapter is to look at all the ways that the camera, grip, and electric departments can influence a film's sustainability and make a positive difference.

Safety First for People and Environment

It must be mentioned that there is also a dangerous bravado that can come over the camera and G&E team members when it comes to doing "whatever it takes to get the shot." The good ones know that there is never a time to sacrifice safety for a shot. Being sensitive about resources, and the health and welfare of the environment doesn't always rank as urgent as personal safety, but it's related. And sometimes what's bad for people on set is also bad for the planet. For example, there have been multiple instances of film workers falling ill from carbon monoxide poisoning from using generators without proper ventilation; carbon monoxide emissions also contribute to the greenhouse effect.[1,2] The "juices" inside of that leaking AA battery aren't too good for you either. So: "safety first, safety always" – which may also help the environment.

DOI: 10.4324/9781003425441-10

Situating the Story

Content is King (... or Queen if we're in a Matriarchy). The method and technique of your shoot must come from the story and themes of your content. Commercials, public service announcements, talk shows, documentaries, and narratives all exist in a world that we create. The content drives where we are shooting, and what we are shooting. As you consider all the visual, and photographic things that affect content like light, time, location, movement, color, and the rest, don't forget to situate your content within the natural world. Do we see some Nature in this story? Will we see plants and trees or animals in the frame when we open that door? What about the sun, moon, or the constellations? It's easier than you might think to forget about Nature and the outside world when you're shooting in a studio. All film projects still exist in a story world with Nature and an environment – it's not the *only* thing to consider as you make your visual plan and frame your shots, but don't forget to consider it.

Exteriors and Natural Light

Where are you shooting? Can you choose to shoot in natural light? If you are shooting an interview for a documentary, or some b-roll of a subject, can you shoot it outside or by a window? There may be artistic reasons why you don't want to do this – but if it works for the concept, consider the possibility. This isn't a new idea – In the pre-studio days, cinematographers and filmmakers created their own studio spaces to take advantage of the light of the sun (like Méliès' glass house with its diffused light, or Dickson's Black Mariah studio that could rotate to follow the sun).[3] Shooting in daylight means that you will need fewer lights, and therefore use less electricity. Maybe the café scene can be moved from indoors to out on the patio, or by a window. Less power use, and fewer lights, stands, and cables also mean saving money on gear rental, diesel generator use, and space in a truck to move it all. That will make the producing team happy too. This is a decision that a producer or 1st AD might suggest as a method of saving money or time in the production day – but it's the cinematographer who will make the creative recommendation on that (after consulting with the G&E team). Usually, the script is our bible, but changes can be made if the director feels that it works with the story. Sometimes shooting outside will just not be possible due to audio issues, weather, or passers-by. Outdoor lighting is hard because that giant daylight-balanced solar spot in the sky keeps moving. Changing angles of light, brightness, and color of light make it challenging – but not impossible. If you can shoot outside, the reduction to your overall footprint can be considerable.

If we are shooting an exterior or using daylight that is spilling indoors, there are all kinds of tools that can help with that. Bounce light using flex fills, white cards, and bounce boards will give you soft light from the sun as long as it's sunny. If you have the ability, a nice 12′ × 12′ silk in a frame above your scene will change harsh and difficult direct sunlight into forgiving soft light that won't move around like the sun does. Shiny boards and mirrors can give you hard light for backlight and other things as long as you have the patience to adjust them with the sun. "Negative fill" (something black that essentially absorbs light) can be created with Duvetyne, black flags, and some flex fills. A big, solid black of some kind can help you to create contrast and shadow on the downstage side (camera side) of your subject – right where we want it. The sun also makes a great backlight or a nice gigantic fill on an overcast day.

Creative Green Content

What are we shooting? The first question is always: how can I place the camera and frame the shot to further the themes and content of the film? Cinematographers are also constantly considering a million ethical things like is my camera placement or framing unflattering to my subject in some way? Is my camera height looking up at a male character and down at a female character? Is the camera's presence changing, affecting, or unjustly messing with the content? I suggest that we also ask ourselves: Can we put some green content in the frame? In Chapter 1, we looked at the way that nature and humans are often placed in opposition in the stories and content of movies and TV. Do we need to follow that antagonistic, Colonial, extractive, old model every time? In our day-to-day life, humans are more a *part of* nature than we are *in opposition* to it. How can we reflect that in our cinematography? It could be as simple as including a tree in your shot. Too simplistic? Maybe. But a recent examination of several thousand articles and over 200 studies showed that trees can help with everything from mental health, stress reduction, physical healing, heat exposure, air pollution, active living, and moods.[4,5] Even just looking at a tree or an image of something in nature can be beneficial. Why not include some nature in your movie?

   Let's say that a script you are shooting has a slug line or scene heading like: EXT – OFFICE BUILDING – DAY. You could easily have landscaping or trees in the shot, or you could frame them out. Leave them in your frame – why not? Similarly, you can bring in live plants to the interviews or dialog scenes you're shooting to create texture or depth to our shots, or leave them un-greened. Just as our writers are looking into the practice of Climate Storytelling (see Chapter 6) for new ideas and inspiration, there is a huge opportunity for cinematography to include climate content and the natural world in their practice too. Think of the forest in Akiro Kurosawa's classic *Rashomon* (1950), photographed by Kazuo Miyagawa. It's practically a principle character. Terrence Malick's *The Tree of Life* (2011) or *The Thin Red Line* (1998) and others are full of lovely cutaways of grass blowing in the wind, or other elements of nature.

Camera, Grip, and Electric 95

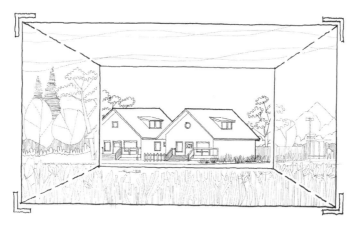

Figure 10.1 Sometimes, creating a story-based composition that includes nature-positive or eco-positive elements is as simple as zooming out. Going wider in this establishing shot includes more context around this setting: a house surrounded by trees, there's a bus stop nearby with solar panels on top. This home is also a part of a visually interesting nature-scape.

In David Ingram's book *Green Screen: Environmentalism and Hollywood Cinema* he analyzes the way that cinematography describes setting, specifically in the wilderness. A great deal of effort is placed on what human elements to exclude in the frame to make the wilderness seem more pristine.[6] The goal in that case is to position the camera and its rectangle viewfinder in the best position to create an ideal representation of nature.

In an issue of American Cinematographer, Director of Photography Sophie Darlington (*Nature* and *Our Planet*) says "It is all about eliciting emotion.... It's about being able to make people feel emotionally involved with nature. Loads of people stopped eating octopus because of *My Octopus Teacher* (2020), even though the film doesn't ever say anything about that. Beauty is the sharpest tool in the box."

"We have been guilty of 'chocolate boxing' nature," says Darlington "Commissioners didn't want to screen the conservation themes, but we have to stop pretending that nature is in a great state. I did three shoots this year and came away desperate every time. We are in the midst of a biodiversity and climate crisis, and we have to speak out."

Tania Escobar, a Mexican cinematographer based in Brazil, says, "Every time you're out there, you see how rapidly things are changing and how biodiversity is impacted. You see trash everywhere, plastic everywhere. I did a shoot in the Amazon in November, and we saw fires burning everywhere all the time."[7]

Nature, the spiritual, and the sublime are what *Landscape and the Moving Image* Author Catherine Elwes suggests inspire us when looking at landscapes. She subscribes to "'the art of looking'; how our 'ways of seeing' the world frame our relationship to the non-human, organic manifold that surrounds us." She reasons: "we are tied to nature, not only by our entwined material existence but also by our interior emotional landscapes that are stirred by any encounter with the sight, smell, and sounds of rivers, mountains and trees."[8] In other words, nature is literally awesome. So why not include it in your shot?

Digital versus Film

Are you shooting on film or are you shooting digitally? Shooting on film requires the manufacture of the film stock, all the toxic chemicals in the "soup" that we run it through in order to make a negative and prints. The photochemical process is pretty toxic, resource-dependent, and heavy on energy use. Not to mention the disposal of all those smelly chemicals. It is generally agreed upon that shooting digitally is much cleaner and greener than shooting film. There are fewer film lab workers inhaling carcinogenic fumes and less pollution from accidental chemical spills, but there is a fallacy that digital technology is a totally green technology. It is not. Far from it.

Just think of all those old lenses, plastic hand grips, hard drives, LCD screens, cables, connectors, digital tapes, circuits, and tons of plastic that have gone to the landfill since the dawn of the digital age. The energy use from servers and streaming media has increased exponentially in recent years (see streaming media in Chapter 17 on editing and Chapter 7 on preproduction). The minerals, chemicals, and special materials that are manufactured or extracted to create our brand new FLIR-LIDAR-LED-mark-II gadget have a cost to the environment.

In contrast, one old-school photo negative and paper print can live on a shelf or in a drawer for a hundred years with no footprint. The same digital master and final file in cloud storage lives in some noisy, hot, air-conditioned Amazon server farm in the Arizona desert drawing more and more power off the grid every day. The sustainable myth of digital is inaccurate. Digital isn't always better than analog, just different. *The Digital Dilemma,*[9] a report from the AMPAS Science and Technology Council elaborates on this problem.[10]

When you are choosing your digital tools, only use the gear that meets the needs of the project. Do you really need to shoot 6k with an Alexa or RED? The least expensive, best workflow might be your phone. If you are renting gear, then are there camera, grip, and lighting rental houses or manufacturers out there that are more green than others? (There's a research paper idea for someone!).

Energy-Efficient Lighting

There are all kinds of different lighting technologies used in the movies: tungsten, HMI, LED, fluorescent, plasma, and others. They each have different color profiles, which produce different looks and skin tones on your subjects. They use power differently too.

In 1900–1950s, most movie lights were carbon-arc lights. They were bright, noisy, and fussy, they emitted smoke and used a ton of electricity. By the 1940s, tungsten lights were more and more popular. Tungsten is the little metal filament in a traditional, incandescent light bulb that glows when electricity flows through it. It's got a nice, bright output of full-spectrum, orange-ish-white (3,200°K) light, but they get pretty hot after they've been on for a while. They look great though.

Fluorescent tubes and compact fluorescents use less energy and have very lightweight fixtures, but they have toxic mercury in them and technically require toxic waste protocols to dispose of them. Often Kino-Flos are sleeved in a plastic tube so that they stay contained if/when they break. They have a limited spectrum too.

HMIs are around four times more energy efficient than tungstens but can flicker, create heat, and have some spikes in their color profile.

Plasma lights never caught on despite their improved energy efficiency, low heat signature, and long-life span of the bulb. Hive plasma lights are still out there but they are few and far between.

On a set today you see a lot of LED (light emitting diodes) instruments, which are much more energy efficient, and come in many varieties. Newer, professional units are much better than they used to be in terms of their color spectrum, they're lightweight and can get very bright too. They aren't all perfect for every situation, but are becoming the popular light of choice, especially for the energy-conscious.

The Sun is still full-spectrum, bright, and totally free.

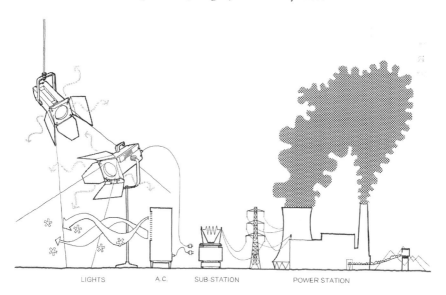

Figure 10.2 Inefficient lights create heat, which necessitates air conditioning (AC), which pulls more power from the grid and uses more fossil fuels, causing more global warming. How can we break the cycle?

Lighting instruments convert electrical energy into light, but some energy is also lost as heat. Tungsten lights are not as efficient at that conversion as LEDs – about 80% converts to heat and only 20% to light; it's roughly the reverse for LEDs. LEDs use about half the electricity of most other lights, and they can run 40–50 times longer. So why not ditch the tungsten and use all LEDs? Well, you could. Some DPs prefer the look of tungsten light for certain applications, however. Tungsten light better represents the full spectrum of white light – from red to violet, thus more accurately representing the colors of skin tones, your set, your wardrobe, etc. Different LEDs, fluorescents, and other lights have different characteristic curves too, some look better than others in certain situations. And, as you may have noticed, some fluorescents and LEDs have problems with flicker too.

So which light is best? That's up to the DP, the gaffer, and the vision of the director. However, a good Sustainability Coordinator will check in with each department (including Camera and G&E) to advocate for the director's sustainability goals. This is where it's so important to include the expert advice of the department heads. Maybe the DP needs tungsten lights for certain situations and wants to use fluorescents or plasma lights for others. Maybe the gaffer and key grip have a cool idea for bouncing sunlight into a space instead of using electric lights. DPs, Gaffers, Key Grip, and Best Boy may all have some expert and innovative ideas for your green initiative.

"Energy efficiency is a priority for sustainable production" declares a Sustainable Entertainment Alliance (SEA) report. "In recent years, the rapid advancement and widespread adoption of LED lighting for production has significantly reduced electrical demand on set while also revolutionizing the creative process. Additional energy-efficient equipment, ... could further reduce the environmental impacts of production while serving necessary functions."[11]

One simple practice that you should already be doing is to save or **dim the lights** between takes or setups. Obviously, you don't want to turn off the lights while people are walking around, creating a safety hazard – dim the channel on the lighting board at breaks if you're in a studio or theater space. Ballasts on some lights have a dimming feature or on/off switch too, so you can "save the lights."

Power

According to another SEA study in 2021, fuel and utilities are the largest generators of emissions on productions in North America.[12] Albert reports have come to similar conclusions about UK productions. Try to decrease your carbon footprint and avoid diesel and gas generators – they are loud, smelly, and polluting. A big truck-mounted 400–1,200 amp diesel generator could burn as much fuel in one 12-hour day as you might use to drive across Canada.[13] There are a number of simple ways to avoid using fossil fuel generators.

Use **house power** whenever possible. Plugging into the location's power is much cleaner than using a generator, and there are no chemical batteries involved. Save your batteries for when you really need them. Ask your gaffer where you can plug into the wall. If you are the gaffer, you hopefully went on the location scout and learned all the places where you can plug in to house power and where you cannot. **Tying into the grid** means using an experienced electrician to set up a direct line from the electric grid that you can use for your shoot. It's a bit more involved than simply plugging into the wall, but it does take advantage of the economies of scale involved with using city power over burning fossil fuel in your generator. One alternative to fossil fuel generators is a generator that uses **alternative fuels** like bio-diesel or even hydrogen. These fuels are far cleaner and can reduce the amount of carbon emissions by 65% or more. Biodiesel is available in many cities at specialized fuel stations. In Los Angeles, there are many fuel stations that sell biodiesel, and you can even make your own fuel from oil fryers if you know how. According to the US Department of Energy, all diesel generators can operate using biodiesel,[14] but some engines recommend specific blends, so check the manufacturer's recommendations before dumping the deep fryer oil in your gas tank.

Independent filmmakers may be more likely to use **battery packs** or **power stations** as a more sustainable power alternative to generators. They are essentially giant batteries that look a bit like a generator and they come in different sizes depending on your need. Rechargeable gold mount batteries, Sony-style batteries for LED panels, camera batteries, laptops, and phones can easily be charged with these clean, quiet power stations. They are very portable (some even have wheels) and are easily charged from the grid the day before you go to your location. Most are also easy to charge from an efficient or renewable source like solar panels, or even a portable wind turbine. Heavy-duty, rechargeable studio-grade units like Electrix from GripTrix, SaltE Dog, Voltstack, Ecoflow, Humble Cart, and Valid can be rented in some cities, while Goal Zero, Nature's Generator, or Jackery battery units can be purchased at outfitters like REI, Bass Pro Shops, Dick's Sporting Goods, Cotswold, Home Depot, or Walmart. Look at the instructions for whichever unit you choose – to fully charge a unit from the wall socket could take anywhere between 4 and 24 hours. If you plan on recharging with solar panels, it can take even longer. Solar recharging in the field might be a way to extend the life of your battery pack, but it probably won't be enough for a full recharge depending on your use and the weather conditions. Check the manual of your unit and do a test as part of your preproduction.

What we want to aim for is a circular system for energy production. A **circular system** could generate power for our lights and equipment, with a byproduct of something that could then be reclaimed, or converted into additional fuel for the generator, thus making an efficient cycle. Circular systems can capture, reclaim, and save as much as 80% of the energy used.

As a proof of concept, solar activist group SolarPunks took on the challenge to power an American Film Institute (AFI) shoot for two weeks in 2022.[15] "We were able to fully replace the loud noise and strong stench of diesel generators with electric generators that allowed us avoid fossil fuel usage & minimize carbon emissions. The generators were fueled by photons generated from our (48-kW photovoltaic panel array) creative community microgrid...." Power was stored in Voltstack 30-k electric power stations. "We worked closely with the team to design an efficiently distributed energy plan with enough headroom based on their shoot schedule and gear list. We were also able to accommodate one extra day of filming at another location." Pretty cool experiment.

Portable Electric (the vendor who manufactures the Voltstack "electric generator") writes about sustainable sets of the future in an article on its site[16] which explains some of the benefits of their battery power stations. Loud diesel generators have stinky exhaust which neighbors complain about when you're on location. Getting rid of that and eliminating the miles of cable run to put the generator away from all the microphones is a huge saving of resources, money, and hassle. But they are not the only supplier of e-generators out there.

Germany-based Green Film Shooting lists several examples of alternative power solutions on its website. Mobilespace, for example, is offering the hybrid solution EcoBaze as an eco-friendly alternative power supply for production. The diesel truck has a euro 6 emission standard and a big battery for powering basecamp and other needs. They also offer a number of electric power stations.

The Sustainable Entertainment Society in Canada has some thoughtful articles on green energy on its blog.[17] Take a look for more information about clean energy advocacy, mandates, incentives for clean energy, and much more.

Clean Energy on Set Is Here

Clean power was on display at the recent "Clean Mobile Power Initiative's LA Cleantech Demo."[18] Lena Welch from NextEarth Consultancy helped put the event together. "It was highly successful, really educational, and normalizing: this is not the *future*, this is *now*. It was glaring that a solar basecamp is completely possible. We didn't have one fossil fuel generator or external power plug for the whole event." The electric, lighting, and cinematographers' unions were there, along with 20 industry suppliers and 70 pieces of cleantech equipment that are currently available in the LA market. There were power stations, clean vehicles, solar trailers, and green power from hydrogen, lithium, and sodium. "The sodium battery power station Salt-E Dog was really cool. It's a bigger battery, and it has a bit less power, but the ergonomics are good: it's taller, so no bending over, and it's lighter." Promotional material refers to it as the industry's first 9-kilowatt-hour sustainable power supply which uses salt-based power cells. Sodium is a much more prevalent material than lithium, or cobalt, or the lead-acid found in many battery units, and it's 100% recyclable too.

With all of these new battery units and all the new technology there is always some good and some bad. Welch explains that "the unknown is what we are trying to find out – we won't know what will go wrong until it is in practice. It won't go wrong until we need it to go right. An LED volume for example is great but all the unknown still needs to be uncovered. And in some cases, we just don't have enough data yet." She adds that "the way that clean energy is becoming more prevalent is part of it too. California has it, Canada has it even better, but you are only as good as your grid. So, an LED volume in Canada could be better than somewhere else." But we won't know until we know, so we have to try multiple paths at once to solve the clean energy problem.

As inspiration, Welch recommends the Bill Gates book *How to Avoid a Climate Disaster – The Solutions We Have and the Breakthroughs We Need*.

"Essentially, Gates argues that we need to solve the climate disaster by any means necessary," she says. "In other words, every action that can be taken needs to be taken immediately. We're looking at a ticking time bomb. Sometimes, it's about doing things imperfectly to see what works. The perfect can't be the enemy of the good."

Reuse, Recycle

Donate leftover expendables (gaffer's tape, gels, etc.) to other films in production after yours. Don't forget those documentary film projects too. Gels, diffusions, cut lengths of rope, half-used tape rolls, and all kinds of mostly used-up stuff is very welcomed by budget filmmakers. For about 30 years, the Expendables Recycler in the Los Angeles area has been a great place to buy used expendables at a discounted price and to sell back slightly used materials after production to recoup some cash. At the time of this writing, the store owners are looking at retirement and are temporarily closed. Maybe some young entrepreneurial film person reading this will take up the mantle or consider a similar business to fill the void in the marketplace.

Clean Up – Leave No Trace

Just like when you are camping, or cleaning up from a kid's birthday party, or a messy crime scene, leave nothing behind. No evidence of your having been there. Leave the place better than you found it (see also Chapter 18).

Tips for Expendables and Materials Use

- **No foam core or bead board** for your bounce lighting – Eliminate the use of polystyrene materials made from petroleum and chemicals. They will never fully decompose and styrene products take up huge chunks of our landfills already. Use show-card, flex fills, or metal frames (like a 6 × 6 with muslin, or a combo frame). They can be recycled, repaired, reused, or repurposed when you are finished with them.
- **Reuse your cloth tape** – ACs do it all the time with labels for slates, t-marks, camera tape, gaffers tape, etc. If you can use it twice, you've doubled its life. More than twice and you're an eco-hero.
- Get some **reusable T-marks** – T-marks are the tape marks (in the shape of a "T"), put on the floor to show where an actor begins ("one"), or lands ("two") in the scene. Film Sticks makes rubber Ts that can be reused, and Kupo has reusable bean bag Ts with little metal balls inside. You can also make your own reusable T-marks with different colored tape covering a metal t-plate or t-strap from the hardware store.
- Use **microfiber lens cloths** instead of single-use lens tissue when possible. They're washable so you can reuse them. Have a bunch of them on hand.
- **Save your black wrap and Duvetyne scraps** – even small ones can be useful for blocking light leaks, covering viewfinders, killing reflections on a matte box, etc.
- **Be kind to your gear.** Those video and audio cables will give you more re-use if you coil them properly (over/under). All of your gear will last longer if you treat it with respect.
- You can buy a simple kill-a-watt **electricity meter** (or one by Emporia, Sense, or Eyedro) and use it to measure just about any electricity use on set or in crafty.[19] Knowing how much juice you use will help you to figure out where and how to conserve.
- Instead of single-use canned air, try a **canless handheld air unit**, or try an air compressor, a bulb blower, or a rechargeable air duster/blower. Portable electric units can be around $100, so maybe your school or company can try one out in the equipment prep room to see if it measures up to your use.

Practical Field Work

1 Daylight challenge: Using only reflected sunlight, try to achieve lighting ratios of 2:1, 4:1, 8:1 (more?). You can use show card, flex fills, mirrors, shiny boards, or any other type of bounce. Get unconventional and use a wall or the side of a white truck as a giant bounce card.
2 Indoor challenge: How many different ways can you use one light as two sources? For example, a key or back light that is also used to bounce as fill light; or back cross keys as a way to do more with each light.

Exercises

1 Shoot, edit, and share a video project using electrical energy that you have personally collected and generated with solar power. This project can most easily be produced on a smart phone, which is designed to be a very energy-efficient camera and editing device. You will need a 7W (or more) solar panel and battery pack. Keep in mind that you may need to charge in direct sunlight for much of the day. Take a picture of your solar setup after your phone has been charged so that the image you capture is itself sustainably produced. Film and edit a short sequence and share it. Bonus: Do the math. How much electricity did you use?
   This exercise is courtesy of Temple University Professor Michael Kuetemeyer.[20]
2 Imagine you had a challenge to shoot a short film off the grid in the wild with only a biodiesel van with one tank of fuel. You can bring solar panels, power banks, turbines, and/or hand-crank generators. What gear would you bring? What lights would you bring? How could you use the sun and reflectors to enhance your use of daylight?
3 *Math problem* – if we had an electric power station or battery bank with 3,000 Watt-hours capacity, and we want to run four 100-Watt lights on a night location shoot, how long can we run the lights before depleting our power unit? *Hint: Watthour = Watts × Hours, A: 3,000 Watthours = 400 Watt × n hours = 7.5 hours.*

Notes

1 Penney, David, Vernon Benignus, Stylianos Kephalopoulos, Dimitrios Kotzias, Michael Kleinman, and Agnes Verrier. 2010. "Carbon Monoxide." WHO Guidelines for Indoor Air Quality: Selected Pollutants - NCBI Bookshelf. 2010. https://www.ncbi.nlm.nih.gov/books/NBK138710/.
2 "10 Treated for Carbon Monoxide on Innocent Lilies Sequel Set." 2014. Anime News Network. June 16, 2014. https://www.animenewsnetwork.com/news/2014-06-16/10-treated-for-carbon-monoxide-on-innocent-lilies-sequel-set/.75603.
3 Brian R. Jacobson. 2015. *Studios Before the System: Architecture, Technology, and the Emergence of Cinematic Space.* Columbia University Press.
4 Kathleen L. Wolf, Sharon T. Lam, Jennifer K. McKeen, Gregory R. A. Richardson, Matilda van den Bosch, and Adrina C. Bardekjian. 2020. Urban trees and human health: A scoping review. *International Journal of Environmental Research and Public Health*, Vol. 17, No. 12, p. 4371. https://doi.org/10.3390/ijerph17124371
5 The Little Known Physician and Mental Health Benefits of Urban Trees. https://yaleclimateconnections.org/2023/02/the-little-known-physical-and-mental-health-benefits-of-urban-trees/
6 David Ingram. 2004. *Green Screen: Environmentalism and Hollywood Cinema.* University of Exeter Press.
7 Terry McCarthy. 2022, September 20. *Documenting Nature: Cinematography in the Wild: Filmmakers Share Their Perspectives on Capturing the Natural World.* American Cinematographer. https://theasc.com/articles/documenting-nature
8 *Landscape and the Moving Image*, Introduction, p. 5.

9. Milt Shefter, Andy Maltz, 2007, "The Digital Dilemma," Academy of Motion Picture Arts and Sciences, http://www.theodoropoulos.info/attachments/076_pdf-stc_digital_dilemma.pdf
10. "The Digital Dilemma I Oscars.org I Academy of Motion Picture Arts and Sciences." 2024. Oscars.Org I Academy of Motion Picture Arts and Sciences. April 15, 2024. https://www.oscars.org/science-technology/sci-tech-projects/digital-dilemma.
11. Sustainable Entertainment Alliance. 2021, March. *Close-Up: Carbon Emissions of Film and Television Production.*
12. Sustainable Entertainment Alliance, SPA. 2022, July. *Close Up Look in North America, Regional Analysis of Film and Television Carbon Emissions.*
13. *Film and Digital Times*, 2023, June, No. 121.
14. "Alternative Fuels Data Center: How Do Diesel Vehicles Work Using Biodiesel?" n.d. https://afdc.energy.gov/vehicles/how-do-biodiesel-cars-work.
15. "American Film Institute — SOLARPUNKS." n.d. SOLARPUNKS. https://www.solarpunks.club/projects/afi.
16. Dsouza, Meryl. 2024. "Sustainable Sets – Electric Generators in Film." Portable Electric. May 7, 2024. https://portable-electric.com/sustainable-sets-the-future-of-power-in-film/.
17. "The Sustainable Production Forum I Greening Film and Television I Green Energy in Arts and Culture I Sustainable Production Practices I Sustainable Entertainment Vancouver I Green Vendors I Green Filmmaking I Environmentally-Friendly Movie Sets." 2024. SES. March 19, 2024. https://www.sustainableproductionforum.com/spf-blog/.
18. RMI. 2024. "Clean Mobile Power Initiative's LA Cleantech Demo 2023." https://www.youtube.com/watch?v=LDM9VOv6MYg.
19. PCMag. 2023. "Power-Hungry PC? Here's How Much Electricity Your Computer Consumes." PCMAG. September 20, 2023. https://www.pcmag.com/how-to/power-hungry-pc-how-much-electricity-computer-consumes.
20. Temple University Prof. Michael Kuetemeyer includes several sustainable projects in his Film & Media Arts 5242 Videography class.

11 Actors, Talent, and Casting

Don't forget about the power and ability of your talent. Actors, performers, voice-over artists, and other talent have a difficult job. Some young crew members forget about the abilities and creative power of their talent. Actors are not furniture, lights, or cameras, to be set up and turned on with the flick of a switch – they're collaborators. Some of them may also want to participate in the area of sustainability. Don't overlook that – be sure to include them as allies and partners in your sustainability plan. If you *are* the talent: don't forget that you have agency, ability, and ideas to share with the team. When you are hired, ask if there is a sustainability plan or a sustainability coordinator on the production. Just asking might be the cue to production to start up a green initiative. Offer to help them out with sustainability if you're up for it – or give them this book.

Figure 11.1 Actors or talent have the agency and ability to contribute to the sustainability plan.

DOI: 10.4324/9781003425441-11

In the United Kingdom, the British Actors' Equity Association (the actors union also known as Equity) has a 'Green Rider' campaign that actors are signing on to. For actors who are at the point in their careers where they feel comfortable doing it, a rider is a clause in your contract where you can ask for specific things like a private luxury trailer, or only red M&Ms. Instead of requesting something extravagant, some actors are asking instead for a consideration for the environment.

The *Last of Us*'s star Bella Ramsey said: "Equity's Green Rider is a practical route to positive change in the film and television industry in regard to sustainability. We can make all the films in the world about climate change but unless we are environmentally conscious in the process of making them, our efforts are superficial. The media has historically inspired change, so I'm excited about the introduction of this Green Rider and the conversations it will incite."[1]

The US actors' guild SAG-AFTRA has a Green Council Initiative founded by its president Fran Drescher to promote eco-responsibility in entertainment. The initiative is targeting the reduction of single-use plastic on set, and on screen with the goal to influence behavior, much like the "Buckle Up Hollywood!" campaign worked to promote seat belt use in the 1990s.

Advocacy

People listen when a famous actor like Jamie Lee Curtis says "we are f^@king the world" at a Comicon appearance to promote her graphic novel *Mother Nature*. Or when Rosario Dawson, actor and producer of the regenerative farming documentary *Common Ground* (2023) says "We only have one planet."[2] "We have to do something to stop this! …put pressure on companies and the government because sweeping change is necessary."[3] Jane Fonda has mentioned in at least one public appearance, "I think it's helpful for us all to realize that there'd be no climate crisis if there was no racism." Referencing the oil companies, she notes, "They choose communities of color, they choose indigenous communities, they choose communities of poor people who don't have the political power to fight back."[4] Celebrities with a voice can sometimes take on an issue like climate change or fossil fuel companies. But, being the talent isn't all about taking up a cause. Working hard on the job in front of you is the immediate priority, and it doesn't have to involve any public statements. There is already so much work to be done to prepare for a part. Most early career and student film actors are not in a position to demand big changes – but they can still inspire change by being an example and by starting a conversation about it. For example, talent can endeavor to be paperless.

As Paperless as Possible

Talent can decide to not print scripts as they practice their lines and do their prep work and mark-ups. As noted in earlier chapters, producers, directors, and actors alike should strive to be paperless. That means that your scripts and sides should be electronic – PDFs on a tablet, a phone, or a laptop. Software like Scriptation was invented to help people mark up, line, break down, and scribble on electronic scripts or PDF files, and then transfer those notes to another file if a new draft of the script comes out. If someone offers a paper copy of something, don't shame them, you can say something like "Thank you. Could you do me a favor? For the next document, could you please send me the file, I'm trying to go paperless."

Having said that, if that is just not your thing and you prefer to mark up a paper copy by hand – that's fine. Just make sure to use recycled paper – preferably 70–100% recycled content. There are some people on set who just really need a paper script with their pencil and highlighter scribbles and sticky notes all over it. That's ok, especially if you are a principal cast member, the director, or script supervisor. Consider this question later though: What are you going to do with the paper script when you are eventually finished with it? Keep it or recycle it probably. What are you going to do with the device you downloaded the PDF on to when you are done with it? Try to recycle it, hopefully, but with mixed success rates probably (see "E-waste" in The Production Dept and in Post-Production chapters).

Distance Casting and Casting Concerns

There was a day when all auditions were held in person with the director or casting director. Post-COVID-19 pandemic and lockdown, online, streaming, Zoom auditions, and "self-tapes" (where actors are given a prompt or sides to read and record themselves) are now common. The convenience factor is huge. No driving, no traffic, no parking, no parking tickets, and a considerable amount of time–and energy– is saved. It's not the same as meeting in person – not for the talent, and not for the production team. In so many ways it's not as good. But it's here to stay it seems. The production team and talent should be as professional and respectful as they can in their online manners – this is a professional meeting, not social media. In terms of sustainability, the reduction of tailpipe emissions from even a handful of actors driving to one project's auditions is significant. Being online means no paper used to print scripts, headshots, or resumes, and no plastic water bottles to offer either. There is still a footprint involved with streaming media, but its impact is hopefully much smaller than the real-life alternative.

The casting team and casting folks should consider representation and climate justice concerns too (see Intersections in Production chapter). Including a diverse cast and crew makes the world of your story and the world of its production more authentic, and also offers the opportunity for complete conversations about every kind of problem-solving that comes up in production. Remember that inauthentic and even racist practices of the past are part of what got us into the mess we're in. It should be pretty clear by now that there are enough talented Indigenous people to play Indigenous roles, enough disabled, brown, and queer people to play those roles, and that our cast and crew should look like the rest of the world we live in.

Casting local actors can have an effect on your footprint too. Flying in actors or having them drive from far away will be a huge portion of your fossil fuel use. Only a small percentage of global citizens fly at all, but it's the frequent flyers who have a much larger carbon footprint.

BYO (Bring Your Own...)

It's a good idea to bring your own stuff. A refillable water bottle is a must, of course. Consider also bringing reusable lunch utensils. Many natural foods stores and camping supply places have sets of a bamboo fork, knife, and spoon with a metal straw all in a cute little package. You could even bring your camping "mess kit" (sold in camping stores often as a self-contained bowl, plate, mug, and spork). Or just bring a fork and plate from your kitchen cupboard. Maybe you could be the sustainability leader who inspires the whole cast and crew to bring their own utensils and plates.

Wardrobe may be something you are asked to bring too, especially if it is a low-budget project. Bring a few options. If you don't already have what you need in your closet, try sourcing wardrobe from a thrift store or vintage shop. Lots of movies and shows, including *Everything, Everywhere, All at Once,* and *Reservation Dogs*, used clothing from resale shops. See the wardrobe and makeup chapter (see Chapter 13) for more ideas and information.

Be a Part of the Solution

Filmmaking is a collaborative process as we all know, and so is the environmental effort. Nothing will happen if no one participates. Cast, actors, and talent of all stripes can be an important part of the solution to save the environment on our planet.

Exercise/Homework

1 The Sustainable Production Toolkit for Theater and the Broadway Green Alliance also have solutions for actors, talent, and theater people. What commonalities do you see in these tools? If you were asked to do a revision to one of the checklist tools mentioned in this book, what would you add or change? Is there anything that's been overlooked or misstated?

Notes

1 Edie sustainability group. https://www.edie.net/actors-back-film-industry-green-rider-initiative/
2 Cogan, Marin. 2020. "Rosario Dawson Is Fighting the Good Fight." *ELLE*, April 1, 2020. https://www.elle.com/culture/celebrities/a31752677/rosario-dawson-interview-conservation/.
3 Elle. 2020, April 01. "Rosario Dawson is fighting the good fight: Her childhood primed her for the sustainable life. Now she's channeling her unique history into environmental action."
4 Hollywood Reporter and Hollywood Climate Summit 2023.

12 Food

Catering and Craft Services

Happy crew members are good collaborators, while empty bellies are just a few short steps away from rebellion. When it comes to low- and no-budget productions, food can easily be the biggest line-item expenditure, and for good reason: people are volunteering their time, most of your gear is free from school or friends, and it's a shoestring budget. And the cardinal rule is that people who are working for free need good food. Sometimes a nice, hot cup of coffee and a cookie is all the motivation that a person needs to get through the last hour of cleanup or the first hour of an early day. So, the person in charge of the food can really make or break your project. Good food can be expensive, but it doesn't need to be. The same is true for sustainable or eco-conscious food choices for your set – you can do it on a budget.

When we talk about food on set, we're generally talking about *catering* and *craft services*. **Craft services** is the go-to area where you'll find coffee, snacks, water, and bites to eat throughout the shoot day; sometimes it's just a table with some snacks laid out, but on a larger production, there is someone there all-day making coffee, bringing out new items, or even making fresh snacks to deliver to the hard-working crew. **Catering** is a sit-down lunch or dinner that is brought in for a meal break. Both can be wasteful or disappointing if done poorly – and both can make a big difference if done well. In this chapter, we'll talk about best practices for feeding your crew to keep them happy – and your production green.

Reusable Water Bottles

When *Abbot Elementary*'s Quinta Brunson wanted to cut plastic water bottles from the set, she took a step back first, acknowledging,

> I know who probably uses plastic bottles the most, and it's our below-the-line crew members. These are the people who are carrying things and doing the hard jobs. And I was like, "How do you guys feel if we switch to like these really f^@king fancy water bottles, you can refill them, and I'll buy them," and then that was a change that got to happen from our below-the-line up. And I think that just really makes a huge difference.[1]

DOI: 10.4324/9781003425441-12

Even if you can't afford to buy your crew reusable water bottles, you can ask them to bring their own. Get a big orange Igloo or Rubbermaid 5-gallon water cooler to refill water bottles with – or if you want to avoid plastic altogether, get a stainless steel or ceramic dispenser instead. Asking the crew ahead of time to bring reusable water bottles may be obvious, but it's also important. Not only does it save the resources to make and transport the bottles, but it also sets expectations for the production's sustainability before anyone even steps on the set.

If you really, really want to provide packaged drinking water, there are a number of canned options to choose from instead of buying plastic bottles. Brands like Proud Source, Path, and Liquid Death come in aluminum cans, which are 100% recyclable. And unlike plastic, aluminum is a material that can be re-recycled.[2] Some of these aluminum water containers are 100% reusable too.

Don't buy single-use plastic water bottles, and try to avoid plastic packaging on set in general as much as possible. The Plastic Pollution Coalition reminds us that plastics can be found everywhere, from the oceans to fresh waterways, to the soil, the air, and even in space.

> Plastic contains harmful chemicals and never benignly degrades; ... plastic items and particles easily travel across the planet, threatening the health of wild animals, plants, humans, and the interconnected ecosystems we rely on to survive. Instead of being recycled, most plastics are sent to landfills, illegal dumps, or escape into the natural environment; are incinerated; or are shipped to developing nations unequipped to handle this waste.... Plastic pollution is an environmental and social justice issue which disproportionately impacts Black, Brown, and Indigenous (BIPOC), and rural and low-income communities.[3]

Buy Organic, Local Produce

Buying organic does cost a little extra, but organic produce is better for your health and better for the environment.[4,5] In fact, according to a review of studies of organic versus conventional food, "organic foods have been shown to have lower levels of toxic metabolites, including heavy metals such as cadmium, and synthetic fertilizer and pesticide residues. Consumption of organic foods may also reduce exposure to antibiotic-resistant bacteria."[6] In addition, some studies have shown that organic foods contain more nutrients and Omega 3s.[7]

Growing organic produce also avoids soil erosion, biodiversity loss, and water pollution from synthetic fertilizers and pesticides involved with conventional farming methods.[8]

Finally, buying local, seasonal produce reduces the amount of fossil fuel used to deliver your produce, which might otherwise come from another state or country. Shop at your local farmers market or look for local produce signs at your grocery store.

Go Vegetarian

Commit to at least one meatless meal during your shoot and have vegetarian or vegan options for other meals. It's not difficult to find or make delicious veggie food that everyone will like – and skipping the meat will save you considerable cash.

The meat industry is a big polluter, and using land to graze cattle yields far less nutritional food product per acre than growing fruit and vegetable crops. In fact, the livestock industry is an "important contributor to global climate change, contributing between 12% and 18% of total greenhouse gas emissions."[9]

Have a "Meatless Monday" (or Thursday or Saturday). You may even want to commit to lunch from a vegan restaurant or bring in your own vegan food (think rice and beans, avocado toast, or hummus, pita, and baby carrots) that day. If vegetarian and vegan food doesn't sound like a meal to you, don't worry: there are actually lots and lots of good vegetarian options in the world. Indian and Ethiopian food is very commonly vegetarian, and Mediterranean, Vietnamese, Mexican, Thai, Italian, Halal, Kosher, and Japanese cuisine includes lots of vegetarian dishes. Don't forget good ol' American grilled cheese sandwiches, tomato soup, mac 'n' cheese, and apple pie!

Single-Use Dishes and Utensils

Remember, there is an efficient technology out there that is better than single-use or even multiple-use disposable utensils and dishes. Imagine a dish more durable than polystyrene plates, more reusable than multi-use aluminum plates, and less expensive than repurchasing compostable plates. It's called a regular plate. Yep, you can just use regular plates and wash them. Like people do every day at home.

Buy a bamboo drying rack, a sponge, and some eco-friendly dish soap and let people wash their own dishes. Or, ask collaborators to bring camping mess kits. Maybe you even want to spring for some as crew gifts. It's not that difficult to rinse off your plate and coffee mug, and you can leave it in the craft services area until your next use. Disposable plates and cups might save you time washing up, but it means more trash to deal with at the end of the day – and you'll just need to buy more disposables for your next shoot.[10] In fact, each year about 40 billion plastic utensils are wasted. According to a 2016 study from the Overbrook Foundation, 561 billion disposable food-service items are used a year in the United States, becoming a total of 4.9 million tons of waste.[11] That's a lot of plastic forks and polystyrene plates.

If you prefer not to use your own or the cast and crew's dishes and want a multi-use option, buy aluminum cups. Have everyone write their name on the cups in Sharpie so they can be reused, and then after the three-day (or five-day or whatever) shoot is over, they can be recycled.

Choose Compostable over Polystyrene

If you can't reuse, compost! Polystyrene (sometimes erroneously called by the construction materials brand name Styrofoam) cups and plates are the Worst Offenders in the category of nonbiodegradable, lightweight, easily windblown, single-use plastics. A single polystyrene cup can last over 500 years in a landfill, according to a 2016 paper from Washington University in St. Louis.[12] Even after it's "broken down," it's still there as tiny, nanoplastics. If you must have single-use plates and cups, get compostable ones. Compostable plates and cups are made of organic materials like corn-resin and starch and will break down in a compost bin, just like an apple core or leftover pizza crust. Some may not compost as well in a backyard compost pile, though. Read the fine print and instructions written on the box of the brands available in your area.

In general, using compostables diverts trash away from the landfills, which reduces waste and greenhouse gas production. Organic material in a landfill produces more methane than in a compost heap. But when it's composted, it also results in nutrient-rich compost that can be used to grow more plants!

Making Composting Sexy

Think of the example of seatbelt use on screen. Buckling up on-screen and in public service announcements encouraged viewers to do the same at a time when people weren't habitually using seatbelts – just like smoking on screen encouraged viewers to smoke in the 1940s. Maybe we can do the same for compost: make composting sexy.

There are many ways to compost, but a simple composting bin, hand-crank barrel, or yard composter may be the best way to go for easy use. Food waste can be minimized but rarely avoided altogether. Compost food waste at a local garden, in municipal composting projects, or encourage your school to start a composting program or to use a composting vendor.

Composting really isn't that difficult once you get into the habit of it. Separating compostables is another habit to acquire, like recycling – but it's not a big deal once you get used to it. If you are managing your composter or compost pile out back, you will need to turn it once a week or so with a shovel or pitchfork.[13] Urban dwellers may be better off with a composting service or with a city-supported program. At least nine US states are beginning to allow food scraps and compost in the curbside yard waste bins now, which is great. In fact, California and New York both now have mandatory composting for food scraps.

An electric kitchen composter (like Lomi, or FoodCycler, or Mill) could be an interesting way to make composting a part of your crew's conversation by taking food waste from the set and turning it into compost that people can take home with them for their gardens. The output from these units is pretty agreeable (dried grounds or pods depending on the appliance you buy). Technically, it's not compost until it has steeped in all the natural bacteria and earthy stuff that nature does to make dirt. There is some disagreement about whether electric kitchen "composting" units are greenwashing or are actually effective for household food waste,[14] but as an educational tool, this could be the perfect application, especially for a larger crew or for a school. Try it out and share your results!

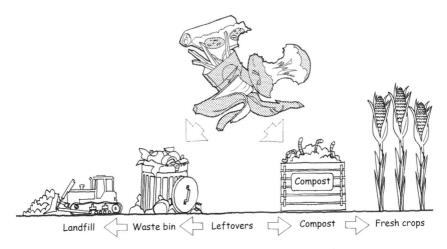

Figure 12.1 Food waste that is composted turns into nutrient-rich food for plants, but when compostable waste sits in a landfill, it is more likely to release the greenhouse gas methane into the atmosphere, a byproduct of anaerobic decomposition.

Coffee and Tea

The most important meal of the day for some. Many crew members may not be able to make proper decisions without a good cup of coffee or tea.

Look for fair trade organic coffee and tea. Fair trade means that the workers are getting a fair wage, there is no child or slave labor in the workflow, and basic social, economic, and environmental standards are upheld.[15] Organic coffee is grown without synthetic pesticides that are harmful to the environment and to humans. Shade-grown and bird-friendly tend to be sourced from farms that are not deforesting land to create high-yield fields with few to no trees.

Reusable metal mesh or hemp filters reduce waste, especially if you compost the grounds. Be sure to measure the amount of water and coffee or tea properly to avoid waste and to optimize the efficiency of your brewing device. A French press or reusable metal mesh filter will avoid added waste from paper filters. However, if you compost your filter along with your grounds after use, you're moving in the right direction.

Single-use pods have so much extra packaging and plastic that they just can't be recommended for an eco-conscious set.

Recycling Bins

Recycling is more and more common these days, but there is a wide variation of what can and cannot be recycled from place to place. Put up signs on your trash, recycling, and composting bins so people are not confused about where to put things. For example, if someone walks in with an empty paper coffee cup with a plastic lid, can they recycle the cup? Or is it trash? What about the plastic lid? Is the cardboard sleeve recyclable where you are? Once you've found out the rules yourself, make or print out signs. Whatever you do be sure to make the recycling and composting rules very clear. One carefully sorted bin of clean, recyclable cardboard can be contaminated if someone dumps an old latte all over it.

Signage

Premade signs can be found on the Green Production Guide (GPG) website,[16] or on the Green Film School Alliance (GFSA) sites.[17] The Green Production Guide has a whole toolkit available for free download at greenproductionguide.com that includes some helpful signage about reusable water bottles, best practices, recycling, trash, and the like. There is even a "choose re-usable plates and utensils" sign and a really great infographic for green catering tips. Green Film Shooting has a cute "ABCs of Sustainability" poster on its website that would look great at craft services too. The Green Film School Alliance has recycling signs for download too. Other helpful signage can be found on the tools and resources sections of the albert, Reel Green, EcoProd, and AdGreen sites, to name a few.[18] Better yet, make your own homemade signs from used cardboard boxes and cut-out letters. Whether printing or making, save your signs for the next shoot or donate to someone who will. Some schools and production companies have started to make "zero waste kits" for checkout with reused signage included.

Donate Extra Food to a Local Charity

Give extra food to the food insecure in your area. There are many shelters, food pantries, and charities that will accept food donations. Some will take leftovers; some will only take sealed, packaged items. Your sustainability coordinator can do some research to see what the options are in your area. Or keep it hyperlocal and give extra food to your crew and cast.

Every Day Action (EDA, www.youreverydayaction.org) is a nonprofit organization created by Hillary Cohen and Samantha Luu, two Directors Guild of America assistant directors. After years of working on productions where good food got thrown out for no good reason instead of going to homeless and needy families, they decided to take action. They found legislative standing and liability releases to protect all parties involved and began to collect donated food from productions and various companies to distribute to the food insecure. They even employ out-of-work PAs to do the deliveries.

A Word About Food Safety and Health Protocols

The COVID-19 pandemic left us with a legacy of tons of individually wrapped and packaged items on set. The packaging is depressing to throw away, and it's almost never recyclable or compostable. Flu and cold seasons come and go. We want to be hygienic and safe with food but use common sense too. Instead of relying on individual packaging, serve snack items in a big bowl with a serving spoon, ladle, or cup to scoop into reusable, washable containers. Look into a food safety class in your area, and see what sustainability practices you can bring to the lessons you learn.

Bulletin Boards and Calls to Action

Everyone comes to craft services – it's a central hub. Take advantage of the "water cooler effect" and share fun facts about sustainability there. Put up a bulletin board so people can sign up for stuff (e.g., carpooling or help with recycling). Maybe offer a freecycle day or swap. Put up a climate change-related poll or a petition or other call to action.

The Green Production Guide has a free toolkit for download that includes some good resources for this. There are infographics on best practices for the stage, construction, and on-location tips too. There are also great signs to post near your craft service like "Choose re-usable plates and utensils…. More than 100 million plastic utensils are used by Americans each day." Bring in that environmental newsletter or magazine that came to your mailbox last week. Have a couple of books handy for people to look at too. While you're at it, put out some flowering live plants for people to enjoy. It's all ethical food for the soul.

Notes

1 Kirsten Chuba. 2023, June 22. Quinta Brunson, Daniels talk embracing environmentalism on screen and on set: "we have to be really precise with what we're doing" Brunson, Jane Fonda and the "Everything Everywhere All at Once" team all took part in the 2023 Hollywood Climate Summit on Thursday. *Hollywood Reporter.*
2 K. Hayward. 2022, November. "Sustainability in production and the green film school alliance." In *FilmForum 2022 XXIX Udine International Film and Media Studies Conference – (Un)Bearable Lightness of Media (cfp 2022), Critical Approaches to "Sustainability" in Film and Audiovisual Production.* Circulation and Preservation, Udine, Italy.
3 Plastic Polllution Coalition. 2024. "Plastic Pollution Facts | Plastic Pollution Coalition." Plastic Pollution Coalition. March 24, 2024. https://www.plasticpollutioncoalition.org/learn/plastic-pollution-facts.
4 "Likely human health benefits associated with organic food production." A. Mie, H. R. Andersen, S. Gunnarsson, et al. 2017. Human health implications of

organic food and organic agriculture: A comprehensive review. *Environmental Health*, Vol. 16, p. 111. https://doi.org/10.1186/s12940-017-0315-4
5 S. Dabbert. 2006. Measuring and communicating the environmental benefits of organic food production. *Crop Management*. https://doi.org/10.1094/CM-2006-0921-13-R
6 Vanessa Vigar, et al. 2019. A systematic review of organic versus conventional food consumption: Is there a measurable benefit on human health? *Nutrients*, Vol. 12, No. 1, p. 7. https://doi.org/10.3390/nu12010007
7 "Organic Foods: Are They Safer? More Nutritious?" 2022. Mayo Clinic. April 22, 2022. https://www.mayoclinic.org/healthy-lifestyle/nutrition-and-healthy-eating/in-depth/organic-food/art-20043880.
8 Anuradha Varanasi. 2019, October 22. *State of the Planet*. Columbia Climate School.
9 N. González, M. Marquès, M. Nadal, and J. L. Domingo. 2020. Meat consumption: Which are the current global risks? A review of recent (2010–2020) evidences. *Food Research International*, Vol. 137, p. 109341. https://doi.org/10.1016/j.foodres.2020.109341. Epub 2020 May 29. Erratum in: *Food Res Int*. 2020 Nov;137:109620. PMID: 33233049; PMCID: PMC7256495.
10 Tenenbaum, Laura. 2019. "Plastic Cutlery Is Terrible for the Environment and We Don't Need to Have It Delivered." *Forbes*, July 16, 2019. https://www.forbes.com/sites/lauratenenbaum/2019/07/16/plastic-cutlery-is-terrible-for-the-environment-and-we-dont-need-to-have-it-delivered/.
11 Ellie Moss and Rich Grousset. 2020, February. "The mismatched costs and benefits of U.S. foodservice disposables and what to do about them. The Dirty Truth about Disposable Foodware. The Overbrook Foundation. https://static1.squarespace.com/static/5f218f677f1fdb38f06cebcb/t/5f282d24acbc6f5e2a38560c/1596468523446/Overbrook+Report.pdf
12 Manu Chandra, Colin Kohn, Jennifer Pawlitz, and Grant Powell. 2016, November 22. Washington University in St. Louis – Real cost of styrofoam. In *St. Louis Earth Day Saint Louis University MGT 6006-02: Strategy and Practice Experiential Learning Project*.
13 Beck, Andrea. 2024. "How to Compost: Feeding Your Plants and Reducing Waste." Better Homes & Gardens. April 4, 2024. https://www.bhg.com/gardening/yard/compost/how-to-compost/.
14 Rosie Spinks. 2023, November 19. The problem with those kitchen composting machines – Spoiler: For starters, what they produce is not compost. *Sierra Club Magazine*. https://www.sierraclub.org/Sierra/composting-machines-food-kitchen-waste
15 Anoushka Carter, "Ethical Coffee & Coffee Beans | Ethical Consumer." 2024. Ethical Consumer. February 8, 2024. https://www.ethicalconsumer.org/food-drink/shopping-guide/ethical-coffee-coffee-beans.
16 "Resource Library – Green Production Guide." n.d. Green Production Guide. https://greenproductionguide.com/communications-fact-sheets/.
17 "Production Tools." n.d. www.greenfilmschoolalliance.com. https://sites.google.com/view/greenfilmschoolalliance/production-tools.
18 "The Resources Guide for Production Companies." n.d. https://www.wearead-green.org/guides/the-resources-guide-for-production-companies; "Tools - Creative BC." 2024. Creative BC. June 26, 2024. https://creativebc.com/reel-green/tools/.

13 Wardrobe, Hair, and Makeup

After four weeks of rehearsals for *The Wizard of Oz* (1939), the actor initially cast as the Tin Man developed cramps and shortness of breath so severe he was sure he was dying. Although he eventually recovered, he had to be hospitalized for a month to treat a lung infection caused by the aluminum dust in the toxic silver makeup he wore for the movie.[1]

Although such a strong reaction is rare, the incident illustrates the importance of making eco-friendlier choices when it comes to makeup, hair, and wardrobe – both for your cast and for the planet. These departments are often the first stop for cast and extras beginning their day on your production, so start the day out right with sustainable on-set practices.

With a limited budget, wardrobe, hair, and makeup often don't get the attention that they deserve. If money, resources, and crew were infinite, many filmmakers would have a trailer and a whole staff for each area. As it is, however, talent is often left to bring their own wardrobe and do their own hair and makeup. Let's assume that you are somewhere in between, working on your modest documentary, multicamera studio production, experimental film, or scripted narrative project. How can you be environmentally responsible and still get the maximum impact for wardrobe, hair, and makeup?

Wardrobe

The wardrobe department can learn a lot from the sustainability struggles of the clothing industry. If you are looking for a documentary film to inspire and educate you on the subject of sustainability and fashion, take a look at *Fashion Reimagined* (2022). The film follows renowned English designer Amy Powney on a quest to create a less impactful line of clothing. Fashion is not a field known for environmentalism. In fact, according to the film:

- If the worldwide fashion industry was a country, it would be number three in carbon emissions behind China and the United States.
- Hundred billion garments are produced every 12 months and 60% of them wind up in a landfill before they're one year old.[2]

DOI: 10.4324/9781003425441-13

Wardrobe, Hair, and Makeup 119

Of course, the wardrobe department on a film is not the same as the fashion industry as a whole, but there is overlap, and understanding the pitfalls of the garment industry can lead to more informed, sustainable choices on set. Here are some specific suggestions.

Go with Secondhand

According to costume designer Sinéad Kidao, who worked on the film *Little Women* (2019) and the Netflix series *Black Mirror* (2011–), "On any given project, [costume designers] buy or make more clothes than the average person will own in a lifetime."[3]

But there is another way: Choose used items and give new life to old pieces. Sourcing costume items from secondhand stores or even from cast members themselves bypasses the need for new clothing production, which involves resource-intensive processes. You can also get free wardrobe pieces from your local Buy Nothing Facebook group or app; these groups allow users to request items, and other members of the group can meet the request by loaning or giving you the item.

Figure 13.1 Shop at secondhand stores: it'll save money and it's reusing existing stuff instead of relying on new manufacturing.

Establish a Collective Wardrobe

Does your school or film group have a community wardrobe? Encouraging sharing among productions can extend the lifespan of costumes and minimize the need for new purchases. Establishing a collaborative network where different productions can borrow and lend costumes fosters resource efficiency and reduces your film's overall environmental impact.

Wash Clothes with Eco-Safer Products

If you borrowed clothing for the shoot, you'll want to wash it before returning it. Switching to biodegradable, nontoxic laundry products helps minimize water pollution and reduces the introduction of harmful chemicals to the environment.[4] Look for eco-friendly detergent or dehydrated detergent that comes in minimal recycled cardboard packaging, at your local supermarket. Or make your own sustainable, nontoxic, inexpensive laundry detergent from two parts borax, two parts castile soap (you can buy it as soap flakes or a concentrated liquid, or grate a bar of it), and one part washing soda, all of which you can find in the supermarket detergent aisle. Add one to two tablespoons of the mixture per load.[5]

Skip the Dry Cleaning

Many delicates, such as a silk blouse or wool sweater, can be hand washed in cold water with castile soap (such as Dr. Bronner's) instead of dry cleaned. However, if you need to clean a dry-clean-only item such as a suit or formal gown, you'll need to take it to a cleaner. If you can find a cleaner that does professional wet-cleaning, that's your best bet, but if not, choose one that offers organic cleaning. Organic cleaners aren't regulated and may use DF-2000, which is considered a neurotoxin, but if that's your only option in your area, it's still better than traditional dry cleaning, which relies on tetrachloroethylene (aka perc), a dangerous chemical and probable carcinogen.[6]

Makeup and Hair

Are your stars ready for their closeup? Not until they've had their hair and makeup done. But that doesn't mean you have to assemble an arsenal of beauty products full of chemicals. Here are some greener options to try instead.

Choose Minimalist Hairstyling and Makeup

Simply using less product, whether you're asking actors to bring their own or providing them yourself, can make a big difference. Adopting a less-is-more approach to cosmetics and styling products cuts down on the consumption of resources; in addition, embracing natural hair textures reduces the demand for energy-intensive equipment like blow dryers and straightening irons.

Go for Nontoxic Beauty Products

If you're buying cosmetics and styling products for your shoot, prioritize eco-friendly products free from harmful chemicals and sold in minimal, recycled packaging. Many people assume that the US government tests beauty products for safety, but that is not the case. In fact, personal care products currently on the market contain over 10,000 chemical ingredients, some of which are known carcinogens and developmental toxins.[7]

However, brands like Honest Beauty[8] and Well People[9] (which can be found in some drugstores, specialty beauty stores, and Target) offer nontoxic alternatives to old-school beauty brands. All cosmetics are required by law to list their ingredients on the packaging, so you can see what you're putting on your face, though that requires some familiarity with chemicals with long, hard-to-pronounce names.[10] One shortcut: Check out the Environmental Working Group's Skin Deep Cosmetics Database, which rates products based on ecotoxicity, health hazards, and/or contamination concerns,[11] online at ewg.org/skindeep. Or you can download the EWG's Healthy Living app on your phone, which lets you scan product UPC codes as you shop.

Special Effects Makeup

If you're using special effects makeup rather than mass-market cosmetics, you'll need to check out the ingredients yourself rather than looking at ratings. Here are the dirtiest dozen ingredients to avoid:[12]

- Formaldehyde
- Paraformaldehyde, a type of formaldehyde
- Methylene glycol, a type of formaldehyde
- Quaternium 15, which releases formaldehyde
- Mercury
- Dibutyl and diethylhexyl phthalates
- Isobutyl and isopropyl parabens
- PFAS, long-chain per- and polyfluoroalkyl substances
- *m*- and *o*-phenylenediamine

You can also try making your own special effects makeup rather than buying it. For example, a classic recipe for fake blood involves mixing chocolate syrup and corn syrup with red food coloring;[13] if you really want to go green, use concentrated beet juice in place of the food coloring.

122   *Wardrobe, Hair, and Makeup*

Look for Greener Packaging and Applicators

Choosing products with minimal packaging reduces contributions to landfills and cuts back on the use of plastics. Some brands offer makeup and hair brushes made from sustainable materials, such as bamboo. However, keep in mind that you will likely need to use disposable cosmetics applicators to avoid cross-contamination if you're planning to apply makeup on multiple people, so look for biodegradable, compostable options such as swabs made from bamboo rather than plastic.

Keep It Matte

Most shimmery makeup contains mica powder made from nonrenewable silicate minerals.[14] Although mica is not considered a danger to those wearing it, mica mining often depends on child labor in developing countries and has been linked with respiratory problems in miners.[15] Some brands have switched to synthetic mica, which is manufactured rather than mined, and is a better option if you really want your stars to shine.[16] Other kinds of makeup get their sparkle from glitter, which is really just a more festive word for microplastics (aka: avoid).[17]

Skip the Aerosol Hairspray

Aerosol hairsprays (not to mention aerosol deodorants, sunscreens, etc.) contain chemicals that are bad for the environment. In fact, aerosols have even been linked to changing rainfall patterns, reducing rainfall in developing nations where it's needed for food production.[18] Pump sprays are better for the planet (and better for the health of your cast and crew, as they don't expose your actors to potentially harmful chemicals). In other words, choosing non-aerosol beauty products helps reduce emissions and waste, which benefits the planet and promotes a healthier work environment.

Use Up What You Have

The advertising and packaging for cosmetics and hair products promise instant glamor, so it's easy to find yourself filling a shopping cart with fabulous new products that seem to guarantee a camera-ready cast. However, the eco-friendlier route is to finish what you've already got before loading up on new products.

For more helpful tips, check out albert's hair and makeup *guide* on its production handbook site.[19]

Set Up a Truly Green Room

Create a greener "green room" – a hang-out spot in or near makeup, hair, and wardrobe that inspires cast and crew to think about sustainability.

People will be spending time here, so this is a great opportunity for signs and literature to set the stage for your green production.

Hang signs that are available through the Green Production Guide. Have books (like this one!) available for interested people to read. You might also set out a copy of Greta Thunberg's *The Climate Book*, the Sierra Club magazine, and/or a composting guide. People may be curious about your sustainability mission, so having resources available makes sense. Add live plants to make your green room greener and improve air quality.

Wardrobe, hair, and makeup play a big part in your film's look and feel – and its environmental impact. Committing to eco-friendlier options is often cheaper as well as better for your crew and the planet.

Exercises

1. Research Wands for Wildlife, a nonprofit that recycles mascara brushes to help professional animal rehabilitators care for sick and injured animals. How effective is the group? What are the possible pitfalls involved?
2. There are many do-it-yourself guides for making your own low-impact hair, makeup, and wardrobe products and items. Research and make a list of ten DIY hair, makeup, and wardrobe ideas. Is DIY always a solution that saves money and reduces environmental harm? Why or why not?
3. Take a look at this article from the newsletter *Heated*: "The beauty industry is a climate disaster," by Emily Atkin: heated.world/p/the-beauty-industry-is-a-climate. Is there something in this article that you hadn't thought about before? What surprises you or doesn't surprise you? What parallels can you make with how makeup is used in the film industry?

Notes

1. Mikkelson, David. 1997. "Was Buddy Ebsen the Original 'Wizard of Oz' Tin Man?" Snopes. July 25, 1997. https://www.snopes.com/fact-check/buddy-ebsen/.
2. Richard Kestenbaum. 2023, October 2. If you care about sustainability and fashion: This is your film. *Forbes Magazine*.
3. Admin-Alchemy. 2019. "Sinéad Kidao - Albert." Albert. August 19, 2019. https://wearealbert.org/2019/07/22/sinead-kidao/; https://eco-age.com/resources/sourcing-sustainable-costume-with-costume-directory-sinead-kidao/
4. Nidhi Gupta and Seema Sekhri. 2014. Impact of laundry detergents on environment – A review. *Journal of Asian Regional Association for Home Economics*, Vol. 21, No. 4, pp. 149–158.
5. Linnea. 2023. "Sustainable Home Swaps 101: How to Make Your Own Laundry Detergent." *EcoWatch*, January 7, 2023. https://www.ecowatch.com/make-your-own-laundry-detergent.html.
6. "Is 'Organic' Dry Cleaning Really Organic?" n.d. Sierra Club. https://www.sierraclub.org/sierra/2019-2-march-april/ask-mr-green/organic-dry-cleaning-really-organic.
7. "About ‖ Skin Deep® Cosmetics Database ‖ EWG." n.d. EWG. https://www.ewg.org/skindeep/learn_more/about/.
8. "Search Results ‖ Skin Deep® Cosmetics Database ‖ EWG." n.d. EWG. https://www.ewg.org/skindeep/search/?search=honest+beauty.

9 "Search Results ‖ Skin Deep® Cosmetics Database | EWG." n.d. EWG. https://www.ewg.org/skindeep/search/?search=well+people.
10 Nutrition, Center for Food Safety and Applied. 2024. "'Trade Secret' Ingredients." U.S. Food And Drug Administration. March 26, 2024. https://www.fda.gov/cosmetics/cosmetics-labeling/trade-secret-ingredients.
11 "Understanding Skin Deep® Ratings ‖ Skin Deep® Cosmetics Database | EWG." n.d. EWG. https://www.ewg.org/skindeep/understanding_skin_deep_ratings/.
12 "The Toxic Twelve Chemicals and Contaminants in Cosmetics." n.d. Environmental Working Group. https://www.ewg.org/the-toxic-twelve-chemicals-and-contaminants-in-cosmetics.
13 ProductionPro. 2022. "5 Stage Blood Recipes for Your Show." ProductionPro. April 7, 2022. https://production.pro/blog/5-stage-blood-recipes-for-your-show.
14 Coley, Holly J. 2022. "What Is Mica Powder? Uses in the Beauty Industry and Sustainability Concerns." Treehugger. January 19, 2022. https://www.treehugger.com/what-is-mica-powder-5216422.
15 "The Problem With Mica | Ethical Consumer." 2023. Ethical Consumer. December 12, 2023. https://www.ethicalconsumer.org/health-beauty/problem-mica.
16 Coley, Holly J. 2022. "What Is Mica Powder? Uses in the Beauty Industry and Sustainability Concerns." Treehugger. January 19, 2022. https://www.treehugger.com/what-is-mica-powder-5216422.
17 Reeve-Parker, Nicole. 2023. "A Microplastic in Disguise: Why Glitter Is Problematic - UW Combined Fund Drive." UW Combined Fund Drive. September 6, 2023. https://hr.uw.edu/cfd/2023/06/27/glitter/.
18 *Climate Change: Vital Signs of the Planet*. 2020. "Just 5 Questions: Aerosols," December 23, 2020. https://climate.nasa.gov/news/215/just-5-questions-aerosols/.
19 "Hair + Make-up - Albert." 2019. Albert. August 19, 2019. https://wearealbert.org/production-handbook/in-your-role/hair-make-up/.

14 Transportation

According to a Sustainable Entertainment Alliance 2021 Carbon Emissions Report, far and away the biggest contributor to carbon emissions on film and television projects is fuel use.[1] In fact, fuel for transportation and diesel fuel for generators made up almost half of the carbon emissions on the productions contributing to the 2021 study. Documentary and other creative non-fiction productions may use less fossil fuel in generators to create power for lights and other equipment, but data from nonscripted productions indicates that air travel accounts for the largest portion of their carbon emissions. We've talked about using bio-diesel in generators in the chapter on camera, grip and electric, and bringing in electric power stations/generators on set. What else can we do to reduce fuel use and make transportation more efficient in filmmaking?

Electric, Hybrid, and Alternative Fuel Vehicles

Interestingly, some of the very first automobiles ran on ethanol, steam, and electricity. In 1893, German mechanical engineer Rudolf Diesel invented a compression engine that ran on peanut oil, Henry Ford's wife, Clara, drove an electric vehicle."[2]

Vehicles powered by something other than gasoline are not a new concept, but they are gaining traction in the marketplace. A 2023 BloombergNEF report shows that global electric vehicle sales grew more than fivefold from 2018 to 2022.[3] A 2023 Cox Automotive study[4] found that in the US, 51% of vehicle shoppers indicated they were considering an electric vehicle, and, that same year, 1.2 million electric vehicles were sold just in the United States alone.

Cars powered by gasoline pollute the air with nitrogen dioxide, carbon monoxide, hydrocarbons, benzene, and formaldehyde.[5] Fortunately, today you can drive a car that runs on biodiesel, hydrogen, electricity, or compressed natural gas (aka "fossil gas") instead. Some of us are lucky enough to live in an area that offers an electric car charging infrastructure or hydrogen fueling stations.

DOI: 10.4324/9781003425441-14

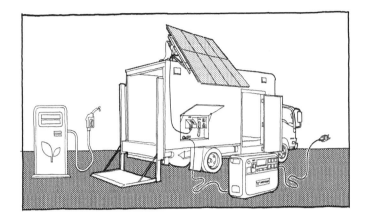

Figure 14.1 Alternate fuel transportation and power on set are already here and ready to expand to help your productions.

If your grip truck is diesel, you may not realize that it is already running on up to 5% biodiesel[6] (B-5), because all diesel gas sold in the United States contains some portion of biodiesel; in fact, some commercial vehicles run on diesel with biodiesel levels as high as 20% (B-20).[7] Biodiesel is made from modified vegetable oil (usually soybean oil, palm oil, or canola oil, but used restaurant fryer oil can also be converted).[8] Unfortunately, you can't just pour used French fry grease in your engine – that would wreck it – but biodiesel is greener than petroleum-based diesel for your diesel truck, car, and generators. More biodiesel means less hydrocarbon, carbon monoxide, sulfates, and particulate emissions.[9]

According to the US Department of Energy, "all diesel vehicles, whether classified as biodiesel or conventional diesel, are one and the same. They have the same internal combustion engine and components. Although all diesel vehicles can operate using biodiesel, some original equipment manufacturers (OEMs) do not approve the use of higher level blends of biodiesel. Before using biodiesel, be sure to check your OEM engine warranty to ensure that higher level blends of this alternative fuel are approved."[10] So unless your manual says not to, you can choose higher biodiesel blends at the pump.

Consider partnering with a community group focused on fuel-efficient cars. There are lots of community groups out there like the Electric Vehicle Association of Southern California or the B20 Club of Indiana with pickups or station wagons running on reused fast-food deep fryer oil. Local alt-fuel car clubs and service organizations might even be up for the challenge of helping your production as part of a service project or social media campaign. Can you imagine getting a club of biodiesel hobbyists to be your transportation crew?

In summary, Treehugger breaks down the basics of biodiesel to these three items: "diesel engine originally designed to run on vegetable oil; no modification needed to run a diesel engine on biodiesel; heating mechanism needs to be added to run engine on SVO"[11] (straight vegetable oil). Waste vegetable oil (used fryer oil) can be converted into biodiesel for your truck or generator, but it's not a project for beginners. They also note that "too often, rain forests are burned to plant crops for fuel" (biodiesel), like palm oil or soybean oil.

Renting a Vehicle

Film productions (including student productions) often rent vehicles. If you rent a car or truck, consider an electric, hybrid, or alternate fuel vehicle – or borrow one for your film. Green car rental companies are sprouting up all over, and many of the big car rental companies now offer green vehicle solutions.

Filmmakers often use inexpensive trucks for moving around heavy, bulky film gear, but as one of my students recently said while we were reviewing green solutions: "There are no electric U-Hauls, and we aren't going to use a horse-drawn wagon." However, the film services and transportation company Saniset Fleet,[12] which is based in Los Angeles, rents electric and solar production vehicles. Like U-Haul, Budget, and other vehicle rental companies, Saniset Fleet is a great option for renting vehicles for your production – but unlike other companies, they offer electric vehicles (EVs). If you're shooting in LA and it's in your budget. Saniset and other specialty services like it also offer electric battery generators/power stations and other low-emission electric infrastructure solutions. (See Chapter 10 for more on power solutions.) In Germany, Mobile Space has a fleet of green film vehicles, offering more sustainable solutions for transport, power, trailers, solar solutions, and more. More and more companies are bringing low-emission work vehicles to the marketplace every year. Next time you rent a production vehicle, ask if the vendor has EV or alternate fuel solutions.

Mass Transit

People who live in New York, London, Paris, Tokyo, Chicago, San Francisco, Washington D.C., and other metropolitan areas don't think twice about taking mass transit to work, including on a film set. I live in the Los Angeles area, where we have a nice rail transit system, but I have never taken it to work on a film project. If you have a train or bus in your area, think about it as you plan your locations. What transit lines are your locations close to?

Bibesh Roy, head of the International Academy of Film and Media in Bangladesh, used the train for company moves in a 2023 filmmaking workshop focused on sustainability. One Eco Film workshop project called *From Surma* attempted to think about the environment at every step of the process from content to transportation. Considering the locations and resources, renting production vehicles (much less low-emission vehicles) just wasn't in the cards. The team shot several short films during the workshop and made green production a priority. Moving from location to location, the team simply took the train.

Bicycles

Why not be the production that has everyone commuting on their bikes? Has anyone ever done that? Be the first in your area. Maybe you can partner with a local biking activist group (there are many) to promote cycling usage and safety. Wear helmets, use hand signals, and connect with your film instructors about insurance and liability. The big film studios are famous for having bicycles (and electric golf carts) on the lot so that people can navigate the large campuses in shorter times. Film critic Steven Rea has an amazing collection of photographs of celebrities riding bikes that he shares in his book "*Hollywood Rides a Bike*" (2012) and website ridesabike.com. Take a look for great photos of Bogie and Bacall riding past stage 19, or Jimmy Stewart and Grace Kelly sharing a bicycle in between set-ups on *Rear Window*.

Whether for personal use or on set, it can make sense to have a bike with a cargo rack and/or trailer for quick errands. Some bikes have baskets in the front, and some have racks or a bucket in the back. Cargo bikes are also available as rechargeable e-bikes, with power and power-assisted pedaling for big loads. E-bikes can make it tempting for people to ride too fast, or forget to pedal at all, so keep safety in mind and remember the big picture.

Best Practices with Your Gasoline Vehicles

Not everyone has access to a fancy low-emission vehicle. Is Arnold Schwarzenegger's electric Mercedes SUV way out of reach for you? Is Beyonce's Tesla too much for your budget? There are still plenty of things that you can do to use less fuel in the beat-up 1998 Toyota Corolla that you bought cheap from your cousin.

When scheduling the countless errands that you and your crew will be doing to get through production, try not to make single-trip errands for just one item. Combine your runs; it's good time management and good resource management. Do all the ordering, research, and rental agreements on one day from the production office (your dorm or wherever) and then save the errands to do all in one trip to save time and fuel and reduce your footprint (or send your Production Assistant who's driving the hybrid Prius.)

When you are loading the truck or waiting to pull up to the rental house loading dock, turn off your engine. Idling your car or truck was once a common practice in the dirty days of cheap gas. There is no reason to leave the vehicle running – with the possible exception of the few minutes that you might need to operate the electric lift gate.

Offer incentives to people who use mass transit or carpool (see Chapter 8). Never underestimate the power of a fabulous (even if very inexpensive) prize. Competition and gamification make things fun. Invent a good mileage incentive – instead of paying a "wear and tear" cost per mile, pay a bonus for fuel efficiency or best mileage.

A Virtual Company Move

The use of visual effects like green screens, miniatures, or new technologies such as Virtual Production is revolutionizing the way that we film stories. One beautiful thing about shooting in a virtual world is that it eliminates the "company move." A company move is when the whole production team moves the crew, cast, equipment, and supplies via truck, plane, or other fuel-powered craft to a new location. For a science fiction project like a *Star Wars* series, this can take the team to Morocco, Iceland, or Mexico – which can require a huge use of fossil fuel and every other resource you can imagine.

So visual effects and virtual production can save us the huge fossil fuel expenditure involved with flying, driving, and hauling everyone and everything to a distant location. It has another cost, though, as we'll see in the next chapter.

Lydia Pilcher

Producer, Teacher, and member of the Clean Energy Working Group
Pilcher Teaches cultural strategy for impact at NYU Tisch School of the Arts, and Climate Change: Storytelling Arts, Zeitgeist, and our Future at Columbia University's School of the Arts

> I am working with an Inter-Guild and Union Clean Energy Working Group on the issue of power and fossil fuel use in production. As members of different unions and guilds, we are all involved in a massive use of fossil fuels to power and fuel our productions. Data has revealed that this is the cause of over half of the carbon emissions in our work in the entertainment industry. As the world transitions to clean energy, on our sets we promote the standardization of systems for making a smart power distribution and transport plan on each production, including the use of renewable diesel, right-sizing diesel generators, utilizing hybrid and electric generators & vehicles and, whenever possible, tying into the grid.
>
> Well-planned power distribution and utilizing clean energy options can often eliminate a diesel generator. Pair smaller diesel generators with battery packs that power video village, craft service, DIT, sound, and smaller sets. Use solar trailers when available. At night, power working trucks and catering with battery sources.
>
> These are some of the strategies we're recommending for energy use and transportation.

There are no two ways about it, transportation is a huge part of the film production business – and a huge part of its footprint. However, armed with some of the ideas laid out in this chapter, and more that you may invent, you can make your way toward lower fossil fuel emissions and more use of clean energy in your film productions.

Notes

1. Sustainable Entertainment Alliance 2021 Carbon Emissions Report.
2. On display at the Henry Ford Museum on American Innovation in Dearborn, Michigan. https://content.time.com/time/specials/2007/article/0,28804,1669723_1669725_1669734,00.html
3. "EVO Report 2024 | BloombergNEF | Bloomberg Finance LP." 2024. BloombergNEF. June 12, 2024. https://about.bnef.com/electric-vehicle-outlook/.
4. Cox Automotive Study. 2023, June. *Path to EV Adoption: Consumer and Dealer Perspectives*.
5. "Reducing Car Pollution - Washington State Department of Ecology." n.d. https://ecology.wa.gov/issues-and-local-projects/education-training/what-you-can-do/reducing-car-pollution.
6. Lyden, Sean. 2006. "Truck Fuel Pros & Cons: Biodiesel Vs. Diesel." © 2024 Work Truck Magazine, Bobit Business Media. All Rights Reserved. May 1, 2006. https://www.worktruckonline.com/145401/what-are-the-pros-and-cons-of-biodiesel-vs-diesel.
7. Research, Hearst Autos. 2020. "Biodiesel Vs. Diesel: Everything You Need to Know." *Car And Driver*, April 22, 2020. https://www.caranddriver.com/research/a31883731/biodiesel-vs-diesel/.
8. Ibid.
9. Lyden, Sean. 2006. "Truck Fuel Pros & Cons: Biodiesel vs. Diesel." © 2024 Work Truck Magazine, Bobit Business Media. All Rights Reserved. May 1, 2006. https://www.worktruckonline.com/145401/what-are-the-pros-and-cons-of-biodiesel-vs-diesel.
10. "Alternative Fuels Data Center: How Do Diesel Vehicles Work Using Biodiesel?" n.d. https://afdc.energy.gov/vehicles/how-do-biodiesel-cars-work.
11. Vadim, Vanessa. 2017. "Do You Have to Modify a Diesel Engine to Run It on Vegetable Oil?" Treehugger. June 5, 2017. https://www.treehugger.com/do-you-have-to-modify-a-diesel-engine-to-run-it-on-vegetable-oil-4864172.
12. "Saniset Fleet | Advanced Clean Fleet Compliance | Los Angeles, CA, USA." n.d. Saniset Fleet. https://www.sanisetfleet.com/.

15 Effects

Here are some things that the movies didn't do: blow up the Hoover Dam, melt the Eiffel Tower, sink Venice under the Mediterranean Sea, fill an elevator with blood and dump it into the lobby of a historic hotel, shoot Tom Cruise, shoot James Cagney,[1] or destroy Tokyo Tower. Doing those things for real would have created a lot of clean-up work – and not been very environmentally friendly. Fortunately, the movie magic wizards had the very good sense to make those spectacular (and sometimes silly) cinematic spectacles as visual effects.

Special effects (also called practical effects) are the physical effects that you do on set, like fog, smoke, rain, pyrotechnics, dust, wind, miniatures, and all the rigs that you might set up to achieve an in-camera effect. Visual effects are process shots (mainly digital) that might involve compositing various elements together, like green screen, background plates, CG, practical elements, and other digital manipulation. Visual effects are sometimes thought of as postproduction, but really, they are usually produced concurrently with first-unit preproduction, production, and post.

Unfortunately, effects aren't always very eco-friendly; the snow in *The Wizard of Oz* (1939), for example, was made of asbestos.[2] Fortunately, there are better alternatives available today – but of course, the greenest (not to mention safest, cheapest, and easiest) alternative is no effects at all. Do you really need, say, snow and wind in the shot, or can you shoot your characters shivering and warming their hands in front of a fireplace to get a similar effect?

Still, there will be times that you really *do* want digital and/or special effects. For those times, here are some greener guidelines.

Visual Effects

Even digital effects have a big footprint, despite there being no debris to pick up afterward. The amount of energy that it takes to run a server or a render farm on a VFX-heavy project is huge. Heard of the vast amounts of power required for Bitcoin mining? This is very similar. Streaming video, too, is a big energy consumer in that all those computers, hard drives, servers, fiber-optic

DOI: 10.4324/9781003425441-15

132   *Effects*

relays, and monitors need power.³ There are no longer physical strips of film being processed with harmful chemicals and running through optical printers to create analog composites, but we shouldn't think that there is no footprint to VFX production. The energy consumed and the amount of e-waste (obsolete and broken computer components going to the trash, or hopefully recycled) is significant. (More on this cost in Chapter 17 on Post-Production.)

Special Effects

Special effects often use toxic materials for smoke, dust, particles, and special construction, not to mention the hazards of water and fire. The number one concern over any other is *safety*. It will be much safer (not to mention greener) to do most of these things as digital effects. Please, no open flames, always use Personal Protective Equipment (PPE), and follow all the safety guidelines given by your insurance company and your school, *no matter what*. Good filmmakers protect themselves and their people. Period.

Now, assuming that safety is buttoned down, try to use nontoxic alternatives for your special effects materials. Look at the labels when you purchase liquid latex and glow-in-the-dark paint and choose a nontoxic or low VOC (volatile organic compounds) variety. Do you need to use plastic snowflakes that will get into all the landscaping, or can you use organic flour for your fake snow? Could you use biodegradable glitter instead of the old-fashioned sparkly plastic kind?

If you have clearance to use smoke in your location, what is your smoke fluid made of? In the olden days, there were incidents of people's lungs and vision being damaged by oil-based smoke fluid.⁴ Your fog juice or smoke liquid should be water-based⁵ and contain no chemical scents or flavors.

If you are doing some kind of rain effect, or cloud tank, or water gag – especially if you're shooting somewhere with water restrictions or that is experiencing a drought – remember that clean water is a finite resource, and proceed accordingly. In fact, does the scene really need to be in the rain at all?

Check Yourself

The PEACHy green filmmaking tool asks filmmakers these questions about effects:

a Was the effects team able to avoid burning toxic materials such as plastic, rubber, diesel fuel, etc. and use propane instead of liquid fuel for fire effects?
b Did you only use water-based smoke fluids?
c When utilizing wind and rain effects, was care taken so as not to damage any sensitive or pristine environment and did you protect the environment before an effect and clean up afterward? Firefighting equipment, clean-up equipment, and a spill kit must be on hand.

d   Did you limit the amount of hazardous materials purchased, used, and stored on location?
e   Did you use digital VFX when possible instead of practical?

This last item may need further consideration. Which has a bigger footprint, digital Yoda or puppet Yoda? A puppet creature uses materials like latex, a metal armature, animatronic components, wires, servos, and more, while a digital one uses a virtual armature, skin, I/O controls, and lots of energy for servers, rendering, and computer components. Both methods allow for a certain amount of reuse. Making the comparison between practical, digital, and something like virtual production (VP) requires a more detailed life-cycle assessment (LCA).

Life-Cycle Assessments

Birgit Heidsiek from *Green Film Shooting*, a magazine dedicated to sustainability in film, offers the simple example of the life cycle of a snack. "We need to look at the whole chain. For each item that a production might buy from a vendor (a carrot as a snack for a crew member, for example), there is packaging, there is fuel consumed in the supply chain to get that item from the farm to storage, to the market, to you. Is it organic? What are the environmental effects of making or growing that item? Do the farmers use responsible labor practices? So, it's complex." If we want to take it further, we can look at the water used to wash the carrot, the recycling or discarding of the packaging, the composting of the green leafy bits, or any leftover part of the carrot. All of those processes are a part of the footprint of that carrot.

The Environmental Impact of Filmmaking (EIF) project is looking at the LCAs of props, costumes, and some digital elements in the *Star Wars* series as examples of how we might use this type of assessment to evaluate and compare the sustainability of different methods for getting an effects shot.

Siti Syuhaida Mohamed Yunus, EIF Project Research Associate describes it this way: "A **life cycle assessment (LCA)** is the systematic analysis of a product or service's potential environmental impacts. It typically involves calculating carbon emissions at different stages of a product's build and use, for example, cradle-to-gate, which covers production to consumer delivery, or cradle-to-grave, which measures from manufacture to disposal."

Increasing numbers of researchers are interested in comparing LCA data on the impact of physical versus digital or VP.[6] As the industry continues on the path of making sets, props, and creatures made from pixels instead of physical materials, LCAs are essential to understanding the costs and benefits of that approach. For example, the *Star Wars* series *The Mandalorian* is known for shooting in a digital volume with LED screen walls. With backgrounds and other elements created and manipulated in a virtual world with Unity or Unreal Engine, the hope is that the environmental footprint of the project can be minimal. After all, there is no need to fly cast, crew, and equipment to Tunisia or Iceland, thus minimizing fossil fuel consumption and emissions. No styrofoam, paints, glues, plastics, lumber, or other materials are used to build virtual props and sets either.

So shooting green screen or shooting with VP in an LED volume like the Stagecraft LED panel system that LucasFilm and ILM use on *The Mandalorian* seems like it will be the way to make the scene work for many productions. But (like the carrot) in order to do a full LCA, we really must look at the footprint of the tools of the means of production too – the cradle-to-grave environmental cost of building and operating the LED stage.

Sure enough, a study from a UCLA practicum comparing the life-cycle analyses of physical and VPs of scenes from three popular television series concluded that "The results show that virtual production has reduced CO_2 emissions compared to traditional filming methods across the board."[7] However, some work from the EIF Project indicates that it may not be that simple in the case of some VPs and their LCA.[8] These are all early studies, and there is much more data and analysis to come.

It's difficult to calculate the invisible costs of technology-dependent productions. Data regarding energy use and purchasing can be relatively easy to come by, but it's harder to answer questions like: What is the impact of mining or sourcing the copper, manganese, lithium, gallium arsenide, silicon, fiberglass, and cobalt needed to make digital equipment? How long will the technology last? Can you recycle the equipment once you're done with it?

There is also a human cost. What are the ethical practices of these mining operations? Do they provide safety equipment to the workers? Do they pay a fair wage? Do they employ children or pregnant women as workers? How much clean water do they use in the process?

Is it the Jevons Paradox again? Relying on digital effects avoids the damaging effects of transportation and building physical props, but does it justify the potentially wasteful practices and costs incurred in the creation of the tools we use? What about e-waste? If one part of the workflow is cleaner, but another much more wasteful, have we made a net gain? Or does new technology make the whole workflow much cleaner now overall? What if the creation of more efficient technology leads to much more production and therefore a net increase in waste and pollution? It's a complicated machine.

One thing is certain, though: if we don't try to reduce pollution, waste, and fossil fuel use, then the problem gets worse. So, creating cleaner processes and keeping real data on each step of the process are vital.

Cleaning Up

"Leave no trace" is what Scouts say after a camping trip or activity. Or maybe you've heard "take only pictures, leave only footprints." Film sets generate trash, it's true, but clean up after yourself and don't be a polluter. Scheduling time for everyone in the crew to clean up is part of being a good effects person/filmmaker/AD/producer/artist/human being. This one is hard to stick to when you are running behind and you're about to lose the location – but you have to do it. Just like in kindergarten, we clean up our toys – the physical ones and the virtual ones.

Exercise

1 If you were asked to do an LCA (life-cycle analysis) study of how a film production or specific area of the filmmaking process affects the environment, what would you write about? How would you collect data? What challenges or unique opportunities could your study present?

Notes

1 Actually, they did shoot real bullets at him in *The Public Enemy* (1931), since blanks and squibs were thought to be too expensive or impractical as an on-set effect.
2 Davis, Heidi. 2013. "Snow Job: How Hollywood Fakes Winter on Film." *Popular Mechanics*, February 9, 2013. https://www.popularmechanics.com/culture/movies/g1092/snow-job-how-hollywood-fakes-winter-on-film/?slide=2.
3 Laura U. Marks, Joseph Clark, Jason Livingston, Denise Oleksijczuk, and Lucas Hilderbrand. 2020. Streaming media's environmental impact. *Media + Environment*. https://doi.org/10.1525/001c.17242
4 Kay Teschke, Yat Chow, Chris Netten, Sunil Varughese, Susan Kennedy, and Michael Brauer. 2005. Exposures to atmospheric effects in the entertainment industry. *Journal of Occupational and Environmental Hygiene*, Vol. 2, pp. 277–284. https://doi.org/10.1080/15459620590952215
5 Roger Armbrust, 2019, "Study Shows Smoke and Fog Harm Actors" Backstage Magazine. https://www.backstage.com/magazine/article/study-shows-smoke-fog-harm-actors-21854/
6 Environmental Impact of Film Making. 2024. "Filmmaking Life Cycle Assessments: What, How & Why – Environmental Impact of Film Making." *Environmental Impact of Film Making* (blog). April 17, 2024. https://eifproject.com/life-cycle-assessments-what-how-and-why/.
7 *Virtual vs. Conventional Production for Film and Television: A Comparative Life Cycle Assessment.* www.ioes.ucla.edu/wp-content/uploads/2023/06/UCLA-IoES-Practicum-SPA-Virtual-Production-Final-Report-2023.pdf
8 "The Environmental Impact of Filmmaking." 2024. Research at the Open University. May 22, 2024. https://research.open.ac.uk/societal-challenges/sustainability/environmental-impact-filmmaking.

16 Sustainable Sound Practices in Film Production

What does sustainability sound like? What does green filmmaking sound like? Why does this book keep asking me questions? Good questions. We hear you. The answer is that every department, including sound, has a role to play in sustainability. In this chapter, we will explore how the sound department makes its mark by focusing on the use of rechargeable batteries, e-waste, the psychological benefits of nature sounds, some of Michel Chion's theoretical concepts, and other best practices in the audio departments.

Psychological Benefits of Nature Sounds in Sound Design

In many of the chapters of this book, we are looking at on-set practices. Sound recording is an on-set practice, but it is in the service of the overall *sound design* (or artistic sound strategy for the film) – something that we often think of as a postproduction practice that happens much later. In order to record the best and most appropriate sound on set, we actually need to consider the strategy of the sound design during our production phase too. As sound guru Randy Thorn says "Design the film with sound in mind."[1] Begin with the end in mind and have an emotional map of your sound strategy and its psychological storytelling plan.

Psychoacoustics is the branch of psychology concerned with the perception of sound and its physiological effects. Incorporating nature sounds into sound design not only enhances the cinematic experience but also has psychological benefits that can align with your film's worldview and sustainability goals. Nature sounds, such as chirping birds, rustling leaves, and flowing water, connect audiences with the environment, fostering a sense of empathy and even a responsibility towards nature. The hope is that this emotional connection can inspire individuals to adopt more sustainable practices in their daily lives, and there is some evidence to suggest that this is so.

Research conducted by the University of California, Berkeley, indicates that exposure to nature sounds reduces stress and increases feelings of well-being. When viewers are immersed in films that feature nature-inspired soundscapes, they experience a form of sonic therapy, elevating their mood and promoting a connection to the natural world.[2,3] Thus, by incorporating

DOI: 10.4324/9781003425441-16

nature sounds into their films' sound design, filmmakers not only create an engaging auditory experience but also contribute to a more environmentally conscious audience.

Figure 16.1 Record nature sounds.

Michel Chion, a French film theorist and composer, wrote about the different ways that sound can transport listeners through various mental and emotional landscapes. By incorporating nature sounds, sound designers can guide the audience on an auditory promenade that reconnects them with nature. Such is the case with Terance Malick's *The Thin Red Line* (1998), which takes moments to pause the narrative to look at or listen to nature – the peaceful sound of wind through the grass as a contrast to the sounds of war.[4]

Chion's concepts are also evident in a film like *32 Sounds* (2023), an immersive documentary by Sam Green. The film is clearly intentional with its sound design, much of which consists of rich nature soundscapes, immersing the audience in the natural world. The auditory journey leads viewers through a series of scenes accompanied by rich nature sounds, with the aim of fostering a deeper connection to the environment and promoting a sense of environmental kinship. Sound good?

Sound recordists and designers may want to experiment with what's called "acousmatic listening" – the practice of listening to sounds without visual context.[5] Maybe you already record sound this way sometimes – with your eyes closed. Building a soundscape underneath a dark screen is the same kind of experience for the viewer. Acousmatic listening allows audiences to focus solely on sound, theoretically opening a window to a heightened sensory experience. This concept fits with pro-environmental efforts by encouraging audiences to appreciate the richness and diversity of the natural world through sound, inviting viewers – or rather, listeners! – to detach from the visual, connect deeply with soundscapes that evoke nature, and encourage them to consider their impact on the planet. Try it out in your sound design, see if it changes your work or your outlook.

By way of a comparison, consider the "natural world" represented in *Avatar*'s Pandora, or the nature-scapes in *Strange World*'s Pando. Both have computer-animated, fantasy versions of *Nature*, and both have the verisimilitude of a lush, natural world. Looking more closely at the processes used to create a technically beautiful soundscape of natural sounds, we see that ironically, they are created and exhibited in an energy-consuming, e-waste generating, matrix of plastic servers, and radiating electromagnetic fields. What do you think about that contradiction?

Power and Rechargeable Batteries

The sound department utilizes all kinds of cool electronic devices, such as wireless microphones, recorders, amplifiers, computers, and headphones. Historically, disposable alkaline batteries have been the go-to power source for many of these devices, contributing to electronic waste and toxins leaching into the soil and water table. Each year, Americans throw away more than 3 billion batteries, totaling 180,000 tons of hazardous waste.[6] That's a lot of nickel, cadmium, mercury, lead, and other stuff just stewing and brewing in the landfill. Instead of using batteries, if possible, sound mixers, and recordists should simply plug gear into the wall and use "house power" (from the grid) instead. If you can't plug in, then use rechargeable batteries.

Rechargeable batteries, such as lithium-ion, nickel–metal hydride (NiMH), and even sodium batteries[7] offer numerous benefits. First (and maybe obviously), they reduce waste by minimizing the need for single-use disposable alkaline batteries. According to the Environmental Protection Agency (EPA), rechargeable batteries can replace hundreds of disposable batteries over their lifespan, resulting in fewer batteries ending up in landfills. Additionally, rechargeable batteries often have a higher energy capacity, reducing the need for constant battery replacements. This can translate into cost savings for film productions, as well as fewer resources used in battery manufacturing and disposal.

In a report called "Going Green and Saving Green," sustainability in production expert Emilie O'Brien and PGA Green cite this testimonial from Thomas Varga, the sound mixer on *Gods Behaving Badly* (2013): "We decided to try rechargeable batteries for all of our Comtek listening devices [used on set]. Not only did we prevent 520 batteries from entering a landfill, but we also saved the production company hundreds of dollars. This is an exciting new change to the way my department will operate, and I am looking forward to helping film companies leave less of a footprint."[8]

So, if we are making the argument to our producer, or boss, or the experienced sound department engineer who doesn't like rechargeable batteries because they were a problem in the past, here are some bullet points:

- Reduced waste: Disposable batteries contribute to pollution due to their toxic components, including cadmium, lead, and mercury. Rechargeable batteries help minimize this waste by extending their lifespan through multiple-charge cycles. Properly recycling batteries is crucial in this effort too.

- Cost efficiency: While the initial investment in rechargeable batteries might be higher than conventional, the long-term cost savings are substantial. Rechargeable batteries can be reused for hundreds of cycles, reducing the need for frequent replacements.
- Energy savings: Manufacturing rechargeable batteries may require more energy than producing disposable ones, but if you reuse them enough, rechargeable batteries contribute to lower overall energy consumption, and a smaller footprint of the sound department.[9]
- Convenience: Having a ready supply of charged batteries is crucial. Rechargeable batteries can be charged overnight, ensuring a constant power source without the need to constantly purchase disposable batteries. You have to make it convenient, though – have lots of extra batteries charging. If a mic goes down you don't want anyone blaming the eco-friendly substandard batteries that you chose.

Research and purchase the highest mWh (milliwatt-hours) rechargeable batteries you can find and afford. The charge, or capacity of a rechargeable battery, is measured in milliamps per hour (mAh), which refers to the amount of charge it can hold and deliver at a certain current over time. The higher the capacity, the greater the amount of energy the battery provides.[10] Lithium batteries have the highest energy density of any other battery cell, meaning they store more energy. There are plenty of rechargeable AA batteries with 2,000+ mWh of charge that can be recharged 1,000 times or more – a good target for your comparison shopping.[11]

Look for manufacturers who are sourcing responsibly too. Some lithium mines rely on unethical or questionable practices – careless use of water, poor labor practices, etc. The Nevada Thacker Pass Lithium Mine, for example, proposes to operate on a site that is sacred to local indigenous peoples (see also lithium mining in the preproduction section).[12] *Ethical Consumer* has a rechargeable battery guide that rates manufacturers based on use of recycled content, conflict-free materials, use of plastic, and other criteria. Their guide concludes that it cannot recommend any disposable batteries, but gives GP and Varta brand rechargeable batteries their highest ratings (38/100), and Amazon and Duracell the lowest.[13]

My own class of intermediate, junior filmmakers at California State University Long Beach experimented in 2022 with switching to rechargeable batteries for their audio gear. They were surprised at how easy the transition was, and how many batteries they saved that semester. They wrote up a presentation about all the sustainable practices they tried that year, which earned them a prize at the campus sustainability fair.

Recycling E-Waste

The sound department's commitment to sustainability extends beyond the choice of batteries to the responsible disposal of electronic waste (e-waste).

Many recording devices, including their batteries, contain hazardous materials that can harm the environment if improperly discarded. To mitigate this impact, sound technicians should make sure that used batteries and e-waste are recycled properly.[14]

The Electronic Recycling Act of 2003 requires manufacturers to establish recycling programs for electronic devices, including rechargeable batteries.[15] Organizations like Call2Recycle and Battery Council International provide resources to locate battery drop-off locations for recycling.[16,17] Finding new ways to recycle these materials will also be important in the future – theoretically, anything can be recycled if there is a process in place and a market for it.

More Sustainable Audio Production Practices

Using digital audio distribution methods reduces the need for physical copies such as USB drives or the tapes and CDs of the olden days. This will also help by minimizing packaging waste and transportation emissions. However, digital and cloud methods are not a panacea – there is still a footprint.

One way to reduce power use and waste generation is to simply plan efficient shoots during preproduction. Coordinate with the production team to create efficient shooting schedules for the sound and camera departments. Consolidating shooting locations and scenes reduces transportation emissions and minimizes the overall carbon footprint of the production.

- What else can sound departments do to save energy? A few ideas: Invest in energy-efficient equipment that consumes less power, and collaborate with other departments to share gear to reduce the need for duplicate devices (power tools, soldering irons, refrigerators, etc.), saving resources and energy.
- Practice smart power management. Plug into house power when possible. Turn off equipment when not in use. Power down wireless microphones, headphones, and other devices during breaks or when they are not actively needed on set.
- Consider being an advocate for an environmental cause. Is there a sound-related issue that you might like to champion or raise awareness for? Maybe it's noise pollution in an urban area near you, maybe it's bringing audio recordings of naturescapes to people who are not physically able to get out in nature. Perhaps it's something else. Post a flyer at craft services, or make your call to action a part of your social media. What ideas do you have for the ways that audio can contribute to a green cause?

The sound department has much to contribute to the sustainability efforts of film production. By trying some of these practices, sound technicians can play a crucial role in reducing the environmental impact of filmmaking.

Exercise

1 Sit quietly in an urban location and then a location in nature. Write down everything that you hear. How do these two spaces make you feel? Next, write down all the sounds you'd need to record and then layer in Protools in order to recreate those soundscapes. Could you manipulate your soundscapes further to introduce additional nuance regarding sustainability or a message about the natural world?

Notes

1 *Designing a Movie for Sound.* http://filmsound.org/
2 University of California, Berkeley. *Calming Nature Sounds Show Promise in Stress Reduction.* https://news.berkeley.edu/2017/04/19/calming-nature-sounds-show-promise-in-stress-reduction/
3 *The Hypersonic Effect – Prof. Honda – "The Sound of Nature."* https://www.bbc.co.uk/programmes/m001kh53
4 Michel Chion. 2004. *The Thin Red Line (Bfi Modern Classics).* British Film Institute.
5 Michel Chion. 1994. The three listening modes. *Audio-Vision: Sound on Screen.* Columbia University Press.
6 Planet, Heal. 2023. "#11 Batteries—HEAL THE PLANET." HEAL THE PLANET. August 15, 2023. https://healtheplanet.com/100-ways-to-heal-the-planet/batteries.
7 Crownhart, Casey. 2023. "How Sodium Could Change the Game for Batteries." *MIT Technology Review*, May 11, 2023. https://www.technologyreview.com/2023/05/11/1072865/how-sodium-could-change-the-game-for-batteries/.
8 Emellie O'Brien, "Going Green & Saving Green: A Cost-Benefit Analysis of Sustainable Filmmaking," April 2014, PGA Green, https://greenproductionguide.com/wp-content/uploads/2020/06/Going_Green_Saving_Green.pdf
9 "Are Rechargeable Batteries Bad for the Environment? Trends and Facts." 2024. GreenMatch.Co.Uk. April 16, 2024. https://www.greenmatch.co.uk/blog/rechargeable-batteries.
10 Rennie, Alex. 2024. "The Best Rechargeable Batteries in 2024, Tried and Tested." CNN *Underscored*, January 11, 2024. https://www.cnn.com/cnn-underscored/reviews/best-rechargeable-batteries.
11 Witman, Sarah. 2024. "The Best Rechargeable AA and AAA Batteries." Wirecutter: Reviews for the Real World. August 7, 2024. https://www.nytimes.com/wirecutter/reviews/best-rechargeable-batteries/.
12 Morin, Brandi. 2023. "In Nevada, Indigenous Land Protectors Face off With a Canadian Mining Company." IndigiNews. September 14, 2023. https://indiginews.com/news/in-nevada-indigenous-land-protectors-face-off-with-a-canadian-mining-company.
13 "Batteries | Ethical Consumer." 2024. Ethical Consumer. August 4, 2024. https://www.ethicalconsumer.org/energy/shopping-guide/batteries.
14 Battery Council International. *Recycling Programs.* https://batterycouncil.org/recycling/recycling-programs/
15 Electronic Recycling Act of 2003, Public Law 108-67. https://www.congress.gov/108/plaws/publ67/PLAW-108publ67.pdf
16 Call2Recycle. *Recycling Locations.* https://www.call2recycle.org/locator/
17 United States Environmental Protection Agency (EPA). *Battery Recycling.* https://www.epa.gov/recycle/battery-recycling

17 Editorial or Postproduction

What can we do to be green after everything is already shot? At first glance, it might not seem like there's anything else to do in terms of sustainability in postproduction, but it starts with your setup, and the technology you choose, and goes to the way you edit, stream media, archive, screen cuts, and even the film festivals you enter. There are so many green opportunities for someone in postproduction to get their hands on outside of the expected task of "fixing it in post."

Whether or not you have a dedicated space, and regardless of how many individuals are working in a post on a project, you do have an official "editorial department." Some of your editorial department's green behaviors can come from the suggestions offered for the Production Office in an earlier chapter (printing, water use, eco-browsers, etc.). But some behaviors are unique to post – you may have others to add to the list too.

We should note that in this day and age, the pipeline is almost entirely digital, which saves a lot of material waste. There are certainly no workprints, mag film, and splicing tape from the film days, and there are no tapes, DVDs, plastic cases, sleeves, or labels used anymore, which saves lots of packaging and transportation energy. There is a lot less stuff used in editorial than ever before, but some of the digital tools and services that we use in post are things that are not always visible in the room, or they have an energy cost that is greater than you might think.

Set Up Your Space

As shooting begins, an editor might be on set helping to distribute dailies or organize media, or more likely, you may just be waiting for media to come in. Either way, take care to set up your space in a comfortable and efficient manner regarding your lighting and power use. You've got your ergonomic chair (or gamer chair), your monitor, and your keyboard set up for good posture and to counter back pain and carpal tunnels, maybe you even have

DOI: 10.4324/9781003425441-17

light gray walls and something on the wall for acoustics. What will you do for air conditioning (AC)? What kind of light source will you have? You'll probably want a soft, warm bounce off the ceiling – energy-efficient, flicker-free dimmable LED (some Feit or Phillips brand lights dim well for example), as well as two modes in your lighting: a dim ceiling bounce for editing, and a brighter mode for when you are plugging in cables or swapping out drives under your table. Incandescent, tungsten lights look great and dim nicely but they'll use too much energy and generate too much heat. Better yet, keep overhead lights off and open the shades a bit to let some daylight in. Get some of those top-down, bottom-up blackout blinds so you can have some overhead light coming in from the top instead of using electric lights.

One other thing about the editing department is that it is sometimes located in an office building with the practice of leaving lights on in hallways and shared spaces all the time. It's a huge waste of energy. If the studio, office building, or facility is doing it for safety reasons, or some other reason, they might not have thought about the power use. Nowadays, more buildings are starting to have lights with motion sensors and timers on them to turn them on and off. That way, the lights are only burning power when someone is around to trip the sensor.

New Stuff

If you are using new computers, furniture, and electronics, you might experience off-gassing or out-gassing from your set-up. That "new car smell" may be VOCs (volatile organic compounds) being released from adhesives, resins, paints, and electronics dust from manufacturing.[1] Some people like to keep windows open and have maximum ventilation while new furniture or gear is being set up and tested. You can also reduce off-gassing by purchasing furniture and components that are made from natural materials.

Live plants can help to physically and psychologically clean the room of some toxins and contribute to a healthy environment (see "live plants" in the "art department" section). It's true. It's scientifically proven that plants are good for you,[2] help with mental health, stress reduction, healing, heat exposure, air pollution, and moods.[3,4,5] Have a couple of low-light plants in the room like a snake plant or red-edged dracaena. Plants are nice.

Of course, you'll need power strips (power bars, extension leads, or surge protectors) for your editing station, too. You may want a UPS (uninterruptible power supply) to give you some time to save your work if there is a power outage as well.

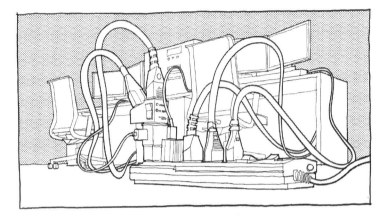

Figure 17.1 "Be careful of electricity vampires that use power even when computers are shut off. Turn off the power strips or breakers too."

Power

More than ever, we are reliant on a continuous supply of quality power. And the more power that is available, the more we use, it seems. You'll use power strips to plug in all your devices of course, but don't forget to turn them off when you are not using them. So many of our devices have AC/DC power adapters, illuminated charging blocks, and other mysterious units attached to the cord that are power vampires. They suck power and use electricity even when your computer or other devices are off. Ever notice how warm some of these things get even when they are not powering anything? They are still using electricity and converting it into heat and sometimes light if they have a little LED on them. So, if you have them plugged into a power strip, you can just shut the whole thing down and stop the electricity vampires in their tracks. Make it a habit to shut off the power strips at the end of your work day.

During peak electricity hours, the electric grid gets the most use, there is the greatest danger of electrical failures, and power rates are the most expensive. These hours are usually in the morning when people are starting their days, between 7 am and 11 am, and again in the evening between 4 pm and 9 pm. If you have the luxury to avoid using or starting up power-heavy systems during those hours, it could be beneficial. Your laptop or desktop doesn't use as much power as a circular saw or an old, inefficient air-conditioning unit, but electricity use does add up when you start adding a second and third monitor, servers, additional hard drives, and other things. You can buy a simple Kill-A-Watt meter (or one from Emporia, Sense, or Eyedro) and use it to measure just about any electricity use in your editing room.[6]

Many devices now have energy-saving settings that can be useful. Use them, but use with caution. Some energy-saving settings will affect the performance of your systems, including things like processing speed, monitor brightness, color, and other functions. There is a time to use them and a time to leave them off. Color correction, director screenings, and major effects rendering are probably times to let your machines do their work unhindered.

Luckily, these settings are usually easy to activate and deactivate. Starting with your computers, you can go into your settings and look for energy-saving or battery-saving modes. There will be different options in there that you can try out. Your displays may also have energy-saving modes – if they don't, you can always turn down the brightness a little. You don't need it at maximum all the time.

One area that we don't always think about while editing is the energy that we are using in other rooms. Down the hall in the server room, you might have a backup of your work running, or something being archived, rendered, or exported. If you have cloud storage, a Google Drive, a backup service, or use some kind of file transfer site you should think about the energy that is used in your streaming, cloud archiving, servers, and render farms. In a collection of articles by Marks, Clark, Oleksijczuk, Livingston, and Hilderbrand,[7] the authors highlight the adverse effects of streaming media. Marks calculates the energy generated from 1 hour of streaming media creates the CO_2 emissions equivalent to burning just under a gallon of gasoline and offers ways to mitigate this use. Clark looks at the huge environmental impact of archival footage and storage, Oleksijczuk examines the health and environmental effects of all the electromagnetic fields generated from this technology, and Hilderbrand looks at the repercussions and best practices of streaming in teaching. Streaming uses a lot of energy. "That consumption, driven by data servers, networks, and consumer devices, currently emits 2.7–3.3% of global greenhouse gases (Belkhir and Elmeligi 2018[8]; Lorincz, Capone, and Wu 2019[9]) and is cautiously projected to comprise 7% of global greenhouse emissions in 2030 and 15% in 2040 (Belkhir and Elmeligi 2018). Streaming media contributes more than any other sector to this increase (Cisco 2020[10])."[11] It makes sense – all those servers and drives and hubs need electricity – like the much-discussed energy use of Bitcoin mining. Some studies have the CO_2 footprint even higher. We forget that even sending one simple email uses electricity – and has approx. 0.3 g CO_2 emissions to be precise.[12] And cc-ing or sending an attachment adds a little more. So, think about that the next time you "reply all."

Limit Your Cloud-Based Data Storage and Transfers

Streaming and cloud-based processes use more energy than you would think. The DocSociety's Green Documentary Protocol uses a more dire prediction: "by 2025, cloud storage will be responsible for a fifth of the world's CO_2 emissions."[13,14] If accurate, that's a shocking percentage.

Can you use solar in your workflow? From the major studios to sustainable innovators like Tage Studios in Portugal, Penzig Studios in Germany, or Electric Owl Studios in Decatur GA, there are a number of production companies experimenting with solar trailers, solar units, and zero-emission sustainable facilities. Just remember the Javons Paradox – the more efficient power is available, the more we tend to use. Check with your power utility to see if you can specify a preference for using sustainable power. Many power companies will gladly switch you to green power – for a little extra money.

One thing that computer rooms need is air conditioning (AC). Just like the hot lights that we use in the studio, the irony is that we use electricity to create unneeded heat, which we then need to use more electricity (from fans and AC units) to get rid of. If we were designing a space from the ground up, we could probably figure out a great way to put the computers in the cool basement and let the heat rise to warm the rest of the building or configure heat pumps to efficiently move the heat where it needs to be – take a look at some of the newest sustainable studios out there.[15] Your editing station is probably more modest than that – so we can just do our best. Maybe you could work in the cooler times of the day and take a break when it's hottest, and power down the AC and computers for peak hours.

Mixing sound, sound design, visual effects, and music will use additional processing power and workstations. How can these areas be managed in a green manner? Some of the same tips may come into play for these areas as well. It may be that in some cases doing effects practically on set instead of digitally will be greener. Can the same be said of recording sound effects and music in production? It could be that *how* green a process is might affect our workflow in the future as countries in the EU (like Germany most notably) have green mandates and state-sponsored green initiatives.

Psychological Setup and Self-Care

Editors can keep brutal hours. Like writers, when you're "in the zone," time flies and you can find yourself wide awake in the middle of the night at your computer and you have an exam in four hours. Set boundaries for yourself. Get good sleep, take walks outside, talk to people. The first and greatest natural resource is yourself. Be sure to treat your mental health like an important ecosystem too. Going for a short walk outside and looking at trees and plants can be far more restorative and productive than having a "working lunch" at your edit station. According to a collection of studies, there are a tremendous number of benefits from just having trees nearby in a city.[16] Human interactions with nature and trees can make you happier, lower cholesterol, improve healing, and even make people more generous to each other.[17] It's science – trees and plants help.[18] Can we cut to a tree every now and then in our film? There is no study about that effect yet, but maybe you can take up that project.

E-Waste

Stuff breaks or finds its built-in obsolescence. How do you keep your broken printers, cables, monitors, and computers out of the landfill? (see also Chapters 7, 8 and 18). Your sustainability coordinator or postproduction supervisor can help you with this. Some donation centers like Goodwill Industries or Electronic Recycling Association are pretty good about recycling old computers, VHS tapes, or broken cables. Some other items can be sent via mail to places like greendisk.com. The United Kingdom has a waste electrical and electronic equipment (WEEE) take-back system at many merchants and other venues that diverts items from a landfill or incinerator and recycles them instead.

Green Seals and Logos

Your amazing Sustainability Coordinator, or Eco-Rep has put a green filmmaking plan into effect, and taken the team through the tough and tussled battlefire of green filmmaking. They have undoubtedly asked for your ideas and are keeping track of the production's green strategy using a calculator or checklist like PEACHy, or one from albert, DocSociety, or the like (see Chapter 4). And as the film marches on through the night of darkened edit rooms and approaches the editors' dawn benchmarks of rough cuts and picture lock, you'll need to take stock of your accomplishments. Now that you are finished with production and are in post, this is the time to make sure you've completed the "at wrap" and "postproduction" sections of your checklist and ticked all the boxes that you can for post.

If all went to plan, you've probably earned a green seal of some kind. Congratulations! Maybe it's a sustainability seal from your school, maybe it's from the Environmental Media Association or another group. Whoever it is, don't forget to have the data certified by the appropriate person, and approved so you can get your certificate and download the official green seal to put in your credits. Make sure you're keeping notes on your green accomplishments and adding data to the record for posterity.

Exhibition

While not strictly a subset of postproduction, screenings are an important part of the postproduction process, for quality checking (quality control or QC), screening notes, and all kinds of technical testing. Student and low-budget productions may not have too many options in regard to low-emissions, high-efficiency projection, but there are a few angles to consider. There is new technology like Christie and Barco laser projectors "providing energy savings of as much as 70% vs. traditional Xenon-based illumination, operational efficiency, and the elimination of waste from consumables" according to a Toho Studios exhibition-related site.[19]

Here is a more heart-healthy solution: use a bicycle-powered projector! There are a number of music festivals, special events, and equipment rental places that feature this technology. These groups have done some amazing screenings and events:

- Bike Power – UK bike cinema bike-power.co.uk/services/bike-powered-cinema/
- CicloCinema – Pedal-powered nomadic cinema in Italy ciclocinema.org/en/the-pedal-powered-nomadic-cinema/

- Little Projector Company – cinema in a cargo bike – Melbourne littleprojectorcompany.com/l-p-c/projector-bike
- Make your own Cinebike – hackaday.io/project/5665/instructions
- Electric Pedals – small bicycle cinema – London – electricpedals.com/hire-us-cinema

It's literally a circular system! The pedal crank set and wheels are actual circles, of course. But it's also a self-contained system, the only energy used is that generated from the dynamo connected to the bicycle. There are some systems that will run on the voltage that you produce, and some with straight cut-off switches if you don't keep something moving.

> **Million Dollar Idea: Make your own people-powered projection systems!** Attach it to a bicycle or treadmill. Keep it in the editing room for when you need to motivate yourself. Or maybe it's punishment for someone at the screening who didn't pull their weight recycling or composting this week. Or it could be a reward – who will earn the great honor of turning the golden pedals for dailies today? They can wear the Yellow Jersey and everything. Have some fun with it. Some tinkerer in your group will surely have a way to attach something like this to the viewing monitor in your cutting room, or the coffee maker, or connect it all to a mini treadmill under your desk or something. That's gold! A million Euros at least!
>
> *Low Tech Magazine* has an article about making your own bike and a video showing a projector.
>
> https://solar.lowtechmagazine.com/2022/03/how-to-build-a-practical-household-bike-generator/

Green Film Festivals

Do you have a festival strategy for your film yet? There are so many interesting green film festivals that you may be eligible for now. Some of them even have bicycle-powered screenings too! If there are environmental actions or messages in your film, or climate storytelling, or green production practices, you may want to screen at a green film festival. Here are some to think about:

- Small File Media Festival – "raising awareness about the environmental impact of streaming media and bandwidth imperialism by creating original small-file movies."
- Jackson Wild – "celebrating excellence in storytelling that illuminates our connection to the natural world and collective responsibility to the wild."
- Environmental Film Festival in the Nation's Capital – DCEFF – Has been around for over 30 years and strives to "advance understanding and stewardship of the environment through the power of film."

- Ecocine in Brazil – An international environmental film and human rights festival since 1992.
- CinemAmbiente – Italy – Founded in 1998 "with the aim of presenting outstanding environmental films that promote cinema and green awareness."
- Ekofilm in Prague – "an international film festival about the environment, natural and cultural heritage."
- Portland EcoFilm Festival – "the premier environmental film festival in the US Pacific Northwest, showcasing some of the world's best new films about nature and ecology, environmental justice, frontline communities, conservation, and outdoor pursuits."
- One Earth Film Festival – Chicago "the Midwest's premier environmental film festival, creating opportunities for understanding climate change, sustainability, and the power of people."
- Green Film Festival of San Francisco – goal is "to celebrate the blue marble we all live on and also confront the challenges we face in maintaining a livable planet."
- CMS VATAVARAN in New Delhi is a "pioneering international festival of films on the environment and wildlife, initiated in 2002."

Postproduction knows how to deliver – literally. But so many tasks fall on editors these days that were not part of the job description in the past. From credits, to visual effects, to dailies, mixing sound, music, screenings, and beyond – it's almost unfair to ask one more thing of editorial. But it's precisely because of all the postproduction department's magic that its footprint needs to be measured too. Besides, it's where the smartest teammates on the film work, right cutters? Who else is going to save the day this close to delivery? It's the editors.

Exercise

1 Research some of the green film festivals listed above. How are they different from each other? Is there one that is suitable for the project that you and your team are working on? Are there others out there that might be a better match? Give it a go – fill out the application and submit it!

Notes

1 "Volatile Organic Compounds' Impact on Indoor Air Quality | US EPA." 2024. US EPA. August 13, 2024. https://www.epa.gov/indoor-air-quality-iaq/volatile-organic-compounds-impact-indoor-air-quality.
2 Wolverton, B. C., Anne Johnson, and Keith Bounds. 1989. "Interior Landscape Plants for Indoor Air Pollution Abatement." NASA Technical Reports Server (NTRS). September 15, 1989. https://ntrs.nasa.gov/citations/19930073077.
3 Kathleen L. Wolf, Sharon T. Lam, Jennifer K. McKeen, Gregory R. A. Richardson, Matilda van den Bosch, and Adrina C. Bardekjian. 2020. Urban trees and human health: A scoping review. *International Journal of Environmental Research and Public Health*, Vol. 17, No. 12, p. 4371. https://doi.org/10.3390/ijerph17124371

4 *The Little Known Physican and Mental Health Benefits of Urban Trees.* https://yaleclimateconnections.org/2023/02/the-little-known-physical-and-mental-health-benefits-of-urban-trees/
5 K. T. Han, L. W. Ruan, and L. S. Liao. 2022. Effects of indoor plants on human functions: A systematic review with meta-analyses. *International Journal of Environmental Research and Public Health*, Vol. 19, No. 12, p. 7454. https://doi.org/10.3390/ijerph19127454. PMID: 35742700; PMCID: PMC9224521.
6 PCMag. 2023. "Power-Hungry PC? Here's How Much Electricity Your Computer Consumes." PCMAG. September 20, 2023. https://www.pcmag.com/how-to/power-hungry-pc-how-much-electricity-computer-consumes.
7 Laura U. Marks, Joseph Clark, Jason Livingston, Denise Oleksijczuk, and Lucas Hilderbrand. 2020. Streaming media's environmental impact. *Media + Environment*. https://doi.org/10.1525/001c.17242
8 Belkhir, Lotfi, and Ahmed Elmeligi. 2018. Assessing ICT Global Emissions Footprint: Trends to 2040 & Recommendations. *Journal of Cleaner Production*, Vol. 177 (March), pp. 448–63. https://doi.org/10.1016/j.jclepro.2017.12.239
9 Lorincz, Josip, Antonio Capone, and Jinsong Wu. 2019. Greener, Energy-Efficient and Sustainable Networks: State-Of-The-Art and New Trends. *Sensors*, Vol. 19, No. 22, p. 4864. https://doi.org/10.3390/s19224864
10 Cisco. 2020. Cisco Annual Internet Report (2018–2023) White Paper. https://www.cisco.com/c/en/us/solutions/collateral/executive-perspectives/annual-internet-report/white-paper-c11-741490.html
11 Laura U. Marks, Joseph Clark, Jason Livingston, Denise Oleksijczuk, and Lucas Hilderbrand. 2020. Streaming media's environmental impact. *Media + Environment*. https://doi.org/10.1525/001c.17242
12 Mike Berners-Lee. 2011. *How Bad Are Bananas?: The Carbon Footprint of Everything*. Profile Books.
13 DocSociety green protocol. https://docsociety.org/greendocprotocol/; Justin Adamson, 2017, May 15. Carbon and the cloud: Hard facts about data storage. *Stanford Magazine*; Nicola Jones. 2018, 12 September. How to stop data centers from gobbling up the world's electricity: The energy-efficiency drive at the information factories that serve us Facebook, Google and Bitcoin. *Nature*. https://www.nature.com/articles/d41586-018-06610-y; https://www.theguardian.com/environment/2017/dec/11/tsunami-of-data-could-consume-fifth-global-electricity-by-2025
14 Reporter, Guardian Staff. 2021. "'Tsunami of Data' Could Consume One Fifth of Global Electricity by 2025." *The Guardian*, August 25, 2021. https://www.theguardian.com/environment/2017/dec/11/tsunami-of-data-could-consume-fifth-global-electricity-by-2025; Climate Change News 'Tsunami of data' could consume one fifth of global electricity by 2025, published on 11/12/2017.
15 Scott Roxborough. 2023, May 18. Two new studios represent the future of green filmmaking. *The Hollywood Reporter*. https://www.hollywoodreporter.com/business/business-news/portugal-tage-studios-europe-first-all-green-shooting-facility-1235353500/
16 K. L. Wolf, S. T. Lam, J. K. McKeen, G. R. A. Richardson, M. van den Bosch, and A. C. Bardekjian. 2020. Urban trees and human health: A scoping review. *International Journal of Environmental Research and Public Health*, Vol. 17, p. 4371. https://doi.org/10.3390/ijerph17124371
17 "Why Trees Can Make You Happier." n.d. Greater Good. https://greatergood.berkeley.edu/article/item/why_trees_can_make_you_happier.
18 D. Nuccitelli and D. Nuccitelli. 2023, March 10. The Little-Known Physical and Mental Health Benefits of Urban Trees. Yale Climate Connections. https://yaleclimateconnections.org/2023/02/the-little-known-physical-and-mental-health-benefits-of-urban-trees/.
19 "TOHO Cinemas Advances Sustainable Cinema With Expansion of Laser Projection." n.d. Barco. https://www.barco.com/en/about/press-releases/toho-cinemas-advances-sustainable-cinema-with-expansion-of-laser-projection.

18 Wrap

"That's a wrap!" is what is triumphantly called as the last shot is concluded on set. It's a great thing to hear, and a fun thing to say if you are the one calling it. It's the culmination of all your hard work and very satisfying to applaud and celebrate with your collaborators. There are actually several times you might celebrate a wrap – after an actor's last scene, for example, or as you finish up in a particular location. "That's a wrap on Michelle!" might happen the day before "That's a wrap on sound!" or later, "That's a wrap on post-production!" The wrap on the wrap party might be the ultimate wrap. Whenever it happens, wrap means that it's time to clean up.

With some good planning and a little luck, you might not have much to clean up (see the chapters on Pre-Production and the Production Department for more on planning for less waste). But most productions end up with more to wrap up than they thought they would have. Yes, there is equipment to put away safely and carefully. The gear gets packed away nicely for a return to the rental house, your equipment room, or cage. If you leave a cable behind, or a special mounting screw or lens cap, you'll likely get fined or reprimanded. If you left behind all your audio on a drive or card, you're likely to face the wrath of the entire cast and crew. If you leave behind food wrappers or coffee cups, you might not notice – and the stuff will either stay there, or it'll get eaten by an animal, or someone else will be forced to clean up after you. Instead, act like you would on a camping trip in the wilderness and "leave no trace." That means cleaning up as you go along, cleaning up at the end, and checking to make sure you aren't forgetting anything before "tail lights" (aka when people drive home … or take mass transit). Sometimes cleanup takes an hour, but more likely than not, it will take longer to return, break down, recycle, give away, donate, or otherwise take care of all the odds and ends before you can watch the premiere.

Don't Throw It All in the Dumpster or Rubbish Bin

Some shows at some production places don't plan time to properly wrap and end up with humongous trash piles at the end of the shoot. Rule number one is to build a realistic wrap time into your production schedule. Let's say that

DOI: 10.4324/9781003425441-18

you are shooting some reenactments for a big documentary about Pharoah Ramesses III and his tree-planting campaign in Ancient Egypt. At wrap, there are sets to get rid of, props, food, costumes, supplies, and trash, not to mention infrastructure like desks, office chairs, Wi-Fi equipment, touch-up paint, a make-up table, cables, safety equipment, signage, and all of the other things that make a production happen smoothly. If you are at the end of a day and have to get out of the building in 1 hour, it will be tempting to tilt the whole place into the trash bin and run for it. A smart producer or filmmaker will schedule a whole day (or more) for wrap. If you are renting a studio facility, you might get a cheaper rate for a wrap day since there will likely be fewer people, less energy used, and less overall fuss. This is a big day for a sustainability coordinator, the producer(s), and/or a production assistant or two.

Figure 18.1 Donate as much as you can at wrap.

Donate as Much as Possible

Some leftover food can go with the crew as they pack up and leave, but remaining packaged snacks, drinks, and compostable plates can be donated to the next production or given to a food bank or homeless shelter (in which case you or the production company may be able to write off the donation as a charitable tax deduction). More importantly, giving things to others helps them as well as the Earth. Those flats (set walls) from Ramesses III's palace can be donated to another film, a local theater group, or maybe an elementary school. Better yet, you already had an end in mind for the set pieces when you built them, and you constructed them in a way to break down easily for the daycare center that will come pick them up in their van. If nothing else, maybe you've found a use for the lumber or other materials. In a city like Los Angeles, you have companies like EcoSet or Recycled Sets. In Savannah, Georgia (formerly in NYC), Film Biz Recycling might take your used flats, or even take them back if you sourced from them in the first place. A sustainability coordinator on a larger show may have a whole network of people to donate things to and charities that might take your items. Thrift stores and secondhand stores are good places to send things. Charities like Goodwill in some areas of the United States even accept worn-out clothes and cloth for ragstock, old electronics, and the like for refurbishing or e-recycling. Other thrift stores may just keep the treasures and trash the rest.

The Expendables Recycler (open by appointment only) is a Los Angeles area business that has for years accepted used and barely used expendables, like rolls of gels, diffusion, tape, and all kinds of cast-offs from the crew. "We've had one simple goal" says the retiring owner "to reduce waste in the industry by buying and selling leftover expendables." It's a great idea.

Recycle

Recycle everything you can. It seems obvious, and by now it feels like you've been recycling like mad, but at wrap is when you realize how much stuff you still have. It's surprising. It's more than bottles and cans and cardboard too, of course. Those props and set pieces need to go somewhere. Some things like remaining office supplies, reusable cloth bags, or coffee mugs you can give away to crew members, but recycling all the stuff and sending it for reuse is the name of the game.

Mixed Construction Waste and Old Sets

Old sets, construction materials, etc., can be recycled and reused. The major studios and production companies try to donate, reuse, and recycle their sets, props, and materials. For the wrap of the TV show *Westworld*, a Sustainability Coordinator from Warner Brothers contacted the Green Film School Alliance and other groups to see who might need anything in the warehouse filled with used set dec, flats, and office furniture that they had finished with. A number of schools and theater groups came away with desks, tables, safety equipment, cleared set pieces, wardrobes, and all kinds of materials to give them a second life. If you want to work in sustainability on a film production, that may be a big part of your job – getting items cleared for donation, finding storage, ensuring that they aren't destroyed before give-away, keeping track of who got what, etc.

Mixed construction waste is a huge problem and is tough to dispose of properly. Some of the trickiest stuff to get rid of is paint, adhesives, solvents, and other toxic waste that will need to be dropped off at a hazardous waste disposal site if you can't find anyone to take them. Students can use city toxic-waste sites or services to get rid of some things at no cost, but businesses are not supposed to use free services. Check your local options. Check your local public works department, or demolition and recycling businesses. They may be able to take your old lumber with no nails, glass bottles, scrap metal, and other stuff too. Building materials salvage centers like Big Reuse in NY, or a franchise like The Junkluggers in Los Angeles will schedule an appointment to come to you, find a place to donate the items, and give you the receipt – for a fee. Some places will even take your stuff for zero disposal fee. If you look hard enough you can find clearinghouses that take surplus items in large lots. Look at green vendor lists (like the one on the Green Production Guide website) for vendors in your area.

Toxics and E-Waste

According to the US Environmental Protection Agency, "for every million cell phones we recycle, 35 thousand pounds of copper, 772 pounds of silver, 75 pounds of gold and 33 pounds of palladium can be recovered."[1] That's a lot of stuff you don't need sitting around in a landfill leeching into the groundwater.

If you haven't done it already, set aside a cardboard box and write "Toxics and E-Waste" on it. Put all the old batteries, paint, busted phone cables, expired medicine, old glue bottles, and the like can all go in there. It might take you a Google Search or two, but there is likely a toxic-waste drop-off point, hazardous waste disposal, or e-waste center in your area. Some places have permanent collection sites called SAFE (Solvents/Automotive/Flammables/Electronics) where you can drop off items. In the European Union, there are commissions that take care of the regulation of waste electrical and electronic equipment (WEEE). Take-back centers and merchants in the United Kingdom will take your e-waste, and so will places like Recyclum in France.[2,3] Batteries can be recycled at places like Currys, Pep Boys, Walmart, Auto Zone, Home Depot, Staples, and Lowe's – just call before you go in. Many supermarkets and town councils have battery recycling bins now.[4] Canadian Tire and Canadian Energy are recycling sources too.

If you're starting a production company of your own someday, consider that you might need to actually pay for toxic-waste disposal sometimes, and factor it into your budget.

Collect Data

Keep track of all that you reuse and recycle. Your behind-the-scenes documentation of your green behavior will come in handy later. You might use it for a documentary on your sustainability efforts – or your department or school might want it for promotional use. The data can also be used on your PEACHy scoresheet, which can be evaluated against other films' data to reach conclusions about best practices. Getting the word out about the hard work that you did in the service of sustainability in film is part of your "bragging rights," but more importantly, your practices, and eco-story are inspiring for others who will make the next films. Once the film is finished, you may get an interview request or an article written on your sustainability efforts, which might inspire people to see your project and maybe hire you for the next one. When you do good, it comes back to you. More than that, in order for us to show that this work is making an impact now and, in the future, we'll need to show some meaningful evidence and conclusions and that means keeping good data.

Exercises/Homework

1 What is your favorite wrap and clean-up music? "Dirty Deeds Done Dirt Cheap?," "Taking Care of Business?" "9 to 5?" "Beds are Burning"? Make a playlist that you can use for wrap. There might be some great inside jokes from production to take advantage of for your song list too. Why did you include each song?
2 Make bingo cards for a wrap with things like "recycle an aluminum can," "compost it!," "coil a cable properly," "donate to charity," "properly recycle a battery," "divert from landfill," "medical waste," or "radioactive hazard." The winner gets to take a coveted prop home for reuse or gets to pick the music for the day. Sometimes you have to gamify it and bring the fun with you.

Notes

1 "Electronics Donation and Recycling | US EPA." 2024. US EPA. July 16, 2024. https://www.epa.gov/recycle/electronics-donation-and-recycling.
2 "Waste From Electrical and Electronic Equipment (WEEE)." n.d. Environment. https://environment.ec.europa.eu/topics/waste-and-recycling/waste-electrical-and-electronic-equipment-weee_en.
3 "Can LED Light Be Recycled? | Any-lamp." n.d. https://www.any-lamp.com/blog/can-led-light-recycled.
4 Jayme Sauer. 2023, 18 July. Recycling. *Canadian Energy*. www.cdnrg.com/services/battery-recycling

19 Green Filmmaking Case Studies and Jobs

Switching to green filmmaking doesn't have to be that hard. The practice of incorporating sustainable practices can be as easy as looking at a checklist or reading an article about green production. Just being aware of the issue and having the intention to begin using sustainable production techniques puts you on the path to doing it. Half of doing a checklist like PEACH or the Green Doc Protocols or the Code of Best Practices for Sustainable Filmmaking[1] is in the learning of new ways of working. Once you start to think about it, you start to see it everywhere. You'll start to do it because it's on your mind. Eventually, all productions will use more sustainable practices just like all cars now have seatbelts. Starting the practice is not as big a deal as it might seem.

It's Easy Being Green

A 2019 New York University Tisch study examined one senior-level student production's switch to sustainable practices in an advanced production class. The study reported on a number of successful, effective practices and also found that even though the majority of those polled found that they had to make changes to their normal routine, over 90% of them found that sorting and disposing of waste was "easy" or "extremely easy," and 100% of those polled had a positive feeling about being on a green set and were likely to continue this behavior in the future.[2]

Similarly, a 2023 survey from a California State University, Long Beach project found that the overwhelming majority of respondents felt that sustainability was "important to them," that it was "easy" to practice, and that it was "very likely" that they would carry sustainable practices on to the next project they worked on.[3]

DOI: 10.4324/9781003425441-19

Student Sustainable Filmmaking Case Studies

From my article "Sustainability in Production and the Green Film School Alliance" in the FilmForum 2022 publication, *The (Un)bearable Lightness of Media, Critical Approaches to "Sustainability" in Film and Audiovisual Production, Circulation and Preservation*.[4]

In one class of third-year undergraduates, students Jillian Dorsey and Kalia Wilkins put together a comparison study of three short film productions in our intermediate production class and created a sustainability report. They identified five practices that they wanted to track throughout each 3-minute production: "power down when not in use, reusable water bottles, less paper on set, reusable utensils and plates, and rechargeable batteries."[5] *High Heat Showtime*, a film about waiting in line for the opening night of a long-anticipated sci-fi movie, was judged green for turning off lights and gear between takes, offering reusable cutlery at meals, and communicating a green plan in preproduction. *Hanging Out*, a film about friendship without social media, did particularly well with separating trash and limiting paper use (including printing half and double-sided sheets). The final film, *Sound of the Air*, was the control of the study with no attempt to reduce its footprint. One of the greatest challenges at the third-year level of student filmmaking is just learning the roles and routines of production. Because of the demands of filmmaking and the limit of only one day of shooting student films for practical reasons, best practices and best intentions were challenged. Despite some missteps with printing errors and accidentally throwing out reusable metal flatware, the group committed to some effective habits in powering down equipment and the use of rechargeable AA batteries for audio gear. The green practices they implemented helped to offset the unavoidable waste generated by COVID-19 testing and prevention protocols.

Another case study is a sustainability project put together for the 2018 California State University, Long Beach senior film *Don*,[6] by students Jessie Butera and Claudia Villalta-Mejia. That semester I gave students a sustainability assignment that could replace any other assignment in the Senior Narrative Production class: make one of their films a sustainable production and document the data as a presentation. Claudia (a film and environmental science double-major), Jessie, and I brainstormed practices with a small group of students and decided to do a short behind-the-scenes film about the making of one of the senior film productions as a green film. Their behind-the-scenes video project, called *Sustainability in Filmmaking: Entertainment with a Conscience*,[7] won an honorable mention at the university's sustainability fair, and Claudia, the producer of the short, got a job in the school's sustainability office and then at Sony Pictures as a sustainability trainee.

In the course of production, they collected over 15 pounds of compostable food waste. The crew used only 18 plastic single-use water bottles over the three-day shoot by using refillable water bottles, saving roughly 120–180 plastic water bottles.[8]

As a part of this effort, they made the beginnings of a student checklist – before we even knew about the PEACH tool or any other checklist. It was simple, but it worked. It broke down actions by department: writing, camera, make-up and wardrobe, grip and electric, etc.

Each department had a few boxes to check off. For example:

Transportation:
- *Set up a carpool*
- *Use public transportation*
- *Use hybrid and electric vehicles*

Art Department:
- *Re-use and recycle sets*
- *Use non-toxic paint*
- *Buy props, wardrobe, and other items at thrift stores, or borrow them*[9]

Later, we discovered that our short checklist was similar in spirit to the Green Production Guide's PEACH (Production Environmental Action Checklist) tool, some Canadian and German initiatives, and those made by like-minded people at places like the American University and the American Film Institute.

Another case study of a student assignment to track green filmmaking practices was presented at a university-wide sustainability event (Figure 19.1).

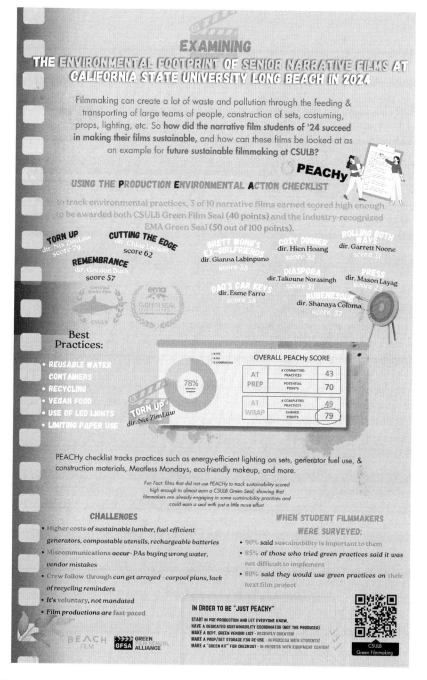

Figure 19.1 A CSULB class assignment to present green filmmaking practices at a campus-wide green showcase sponsored by the university's Sustainability Office. Three of ten films used the PEACHy to track green efforts, and the other seven used it after completion even though they weren't able to employ green practices. The top scoring films earned a green seal from the school, an EMA green seal for students, and a prize at the showcase. Data and analysis from the FEA342 class, with design and execution by Gasia Baghdassarian, Jamie-Ann Aranda, Habiba Hassaan, and Soo Ahn.

Green Filmmaking Professionals Around the World

BIBESH ROY
Executive Director, International Academy of Film and Media, Bangladesh

Q: How is Bangladesh seeing the effects of climate change?

We are suffering greatly. First and foremost, we are losing our six seasons. Bangladesh is known as the "Six Seasons Country": Summer (Grisma ritu), Rainy (Barsa ritu), Autumn (Sarat ritu), Late Autumn (Hemanta ritu), Winter (Shitt ritu), and Spring (Basant ritu).

Climate change disproportionately affects the poor and vulnerable. Tropical cyclones cost Bangladesh about $1 billion per year on average. A third of agricultural GDP may be lost by 2050, and 13 million people may become climate migrants.

Q: What made you start the International Academy of Film and Media and the ECO Film Lab project?

Bangladesh lacked a proper film school to provide our youth with world-class film education. We began our journey in 2006 by bringing in international film professionals to teach.

In 2022, to protect our environment and raise awareness about the effects of climate change, we launched the ECO Film Lab: An International Film Residency program. This engages our young talents in expanding their knowledge of sustainable film production to save our planet. Today's young talents will be tomorrow's industry professionals.

Q: Why is green filmmaking important to you?

Bangladesh requires sustainable production to reduce costs while also reducing carbon emissions. This is very important for the next generation, but we need a call to action now at the mass level.

Q: What successful green practices have you implemented at the IAFM?

IAFM began practicing green filmmaking with six short student films in 2022. In accordance with GFSA guidelines, the Eco Film Lab projects started with a paperless production (we used script software); told environmental-themed stories; tried to avoid plastic; used real, green locations rather than artificial sets; shot in daylight in just one location and in one day; didn't use makeup; relied on only local public transportation; provided organic food without food waste; and incorporated other initiatives. In fact, we shot three short films with a very small amount of money based on the green filmmaking initiative.

Q: What advice do you have for young filmmakers (green solutions or other advice)?

To reduce costs and carbon emissions, I encourage all young filmmakers and professionals to adhere to green filmmaking practices. Every indie filmmaker faces financial challenges early in their careers, so a sustainable film production approach is the best way to get started. At the same time, as future film professionals, you have made a commitment to the planet to make it more environmentally friendly.

Q: What do you hope to do next in the area of sustainability and film?

My next project is to develop two filmmaking courses focused on environmentally friendly filmmaking, the first for university students and the second for professionals. These courses will teach the best-practice tools for sustainable film production and involve more young people in the journey of green filmmaking. We also want to continue our ECO Film Lab with more collaborations and participants from abroad.

LENA WELCH

Owner of green production group Next Earth and consultant to numerous Netflix and HBO shows, Los Angeles

Q: What does the sustainability in film job landscape look like?

There are more and more jobs out there as studios start to require it thanks to sustainability mandates. People who are passionate about sustainability will flourish in these jobs. But if you're only doing it as a stepping stone to something else, then it might be more demanding and dirtier than you are ready for. If you have passion, a sense of urgency, and a love of order, it's a very viable career path with skills that are transferable to other industries. As far as the film industry itself, there's a lot of need. Right now it's the sustainability department doing this work, but eventually, it will hopefully be part of each department; for example, props and grip and electric will each have a head sustainability person of their own.

Q: Why should filmmakers use checklists like PLUM, PEACH, or PEAR?

PEACH, PEAR, and PLUM are good because they allow us to standardize things. But standardization is user-determined, so the numbers can be fudged; for example, using PEACH, you can get the same points for using one electric vehicle for part of one day as for using 20 vehicles for 20 days. It's an imperfect tool – but it is still a tool. It's a way to recognize blind spots as well as get a pat on the back and encouragement. It's also a way to archive the process for others to look at later and make comparisons.

We have this discussion all the time. For example, is the production composting? If the production department has a bin, then hypothetically, yes. But if you don't have the bins on location near the places where the food is, then you're not composting. Or maybe you have the bin and just throw trash in it. Either way, if you have the bin, you still get the point on the PEACH checklist. So, it's imperfect. PEAR uses real data, so that's concrete. PLUM is good, but only as good as your lumber source.

And it doesn't help that some players can ask for the moon and get it. There are creatives who get anything they want, good or bad – but usually it's bad for the environment. Big actors, for example, can ask for seven trailers, accommodations for their entourage, and have everyone travel together for one appointment if they want to. It can become about privilege and egos. We need to get by with less, as Jonathan Wang [producer of *Everything Everywhere All at Once* and other films] said at the Hollywood Climate Summit.

Q: What do you do in your job?

I consult for productions, specifically about fuel use. Using PEAR, I look at the amount of fuel used in generators and vehicles. That involves taking lots of telematics [digital systems that instantly update vehicle data such as speed and location, for example], logs, and forms and compiling those into estimates to figure out what is using the most fuel. Vehicles like passenger vans are the most fuel-use intensive, probably, because there's almost no time they are not being used in a 12-hour day. However, 20% of that fuel is used in idling. That's one place where change can happen.

Q: Do you have any advice to students and young people?

I came up in the ranks in a different climate, where you needed to bust your ass and not take time off and secretly suffer. I hope that is not the case anymore, but you do have to get onto set. If it's a good culture on set, then talk to everyone in every department and be present. Have them see you 20 times a day. Check-in with them, go to the head of a department, and ask what you can do to get to the next level, or hone your skills, or get better.

Ask if you can shadow the sustainability person. Be open to opportunities even if they involve some hardship. Some sacrifices will need to happen. Don't get siloed into one thing.

BIRGIT HEIDSIEK
Founder/CEO of *Green Film Shooting* magazine about sustainable production practices and projects in the film and media industry, Hamburg, Germany

Q: What made you interested in green production in the first place?

I have been working in the film and media industry for many years, which has been very different from my personal lifestyle as a vegetarian. It bothered me how much energy, resources, materials, and food are wasted, so I decided it was time to bring two worlds together: the film and media world and the eco-conscious people. In 2013, this suggestion sounded bizarre for most people in the industry, but I was convinced that actors could become role models for a greener lifestyle. Meanwhile, more and more people understand the necessity to fight climate change, but there is still a huge gap between what people realize what kind of impact their actions often have.

Q: Do you have a favorite scene in a film or TV production that has an environmental message?

An impressive scene is in Todd Haynes's *Dark Waters*, when the attorney played by Mark Ruffalo comes home and throws out all the pans in the kitchen that are coated with Teflon after he realizes the impact of the "forever chemicals" PFAS (per- and polyfluoroalkyl substances), which are present in paper, cosmetics, textiles, carpets, and even foam from fire extinguishers and strongly suspected of being harmful to the human liver as well as being carcinogenic.

Q: What advice do you have for film students who are interested in green production?

Green film production starts with the script. If a film takes place at many exotic locations, it means cast, crew, and equipment have to get there. Local stories can have a global impact. Students can also keep their budget down by shooting with available light, and by actors wearing their own clothes. Filmmakers can also ensure that filming takes place at real locations with the props which are there, and that the movie is shot within a distance of 30 kilometers (about 20 miles), with local actors and crew members. And, very important, the cook or catering service needs to be good and serve delicious vegetarian food.

Inside the Role of a Sustainability Coordinator

Tyler Confoy
Associate Producer and Sustainability freelancer who worked on *The Undoing* (2020)

Nina Farmer
Freelance Sustainability Coordinator who worked on HBO's *Gossip Girl* (2021–2023)

Olive Ryan
Freelance Sustainability Coordinator and Makeup Artist who worked on *Mean Girls* (2024)

Q: What brought you to sustainability in film?

Tyler Confoy: I was working as a Production Assistant on live events when a friend heard that HBO was looking for Eco PAs. I had a general interest in sustainability, so I interviewed and got the job. In this first job, I worked under a Sustainability Consultant from Green Spark Group. I ended up learning so, so much about waste and sustainability programming (how to teach crews) as an Eco PA. Whatever I lacked in knowledge in the beginning, I made up for by speaking to waste haulers and eco vendors, reading, and learning from our Green Spark Group consultant.

Olive Ryan: For *Mean Girls*, one of my NYU professors (Harry Winer, who directs student sustainability efforts) recommended me for the job. I had never worked a sustainability job before, but I understood all of the policies and efforts because my mother is *extremely* passionate about sustainability and raised me in a household that is extremely eco-conscious, so I had a sort of personal background in it!

Q: What does the day-to-day of a Sustainability Coordinator look like?
Tyler Confoy: A Sustainability Coordinator is someone who institutes a waste reduction program on set for a film crew, while also arranging institutional changes with department heads. Waste reduction on set has three components, usually overseen by a PA: instituting a landfill-recycle-compost system, implementing a no-single-use plastic rule, and organizing daily food donations. Working with department heads on department-specific plans to reduce waste involves examples like, with Production Design, transforming sets instead of throwing them away; with Transportation, using renewable diesel; and with Writers, getting sustainable plot points put into scripts. There is also a lot of donation coordination involved for all departments (costumes, set design, construction, office).

Olive Ryan: The job entails helping each department follow a certain set of guidelines known as the PEACH, PEAR, and PLUM documents. This includes sourcing supplies sustainably (e.g., thrifting costume pieces, using preexisting props rather than making and buying new, using supplies that are FSC certified, buying wood from sustainable forests, donating leftover food, etc.) as well as using sustainable energy sources and setting up recycling.

Q: What do you like best about this job?
Tyler Confoy: It's interesting to see people's minds change over the course of a six-month production. Some crew members who never knew what compost was (or cared) will become uncomfortable throwing leftover food into a landfill bin by the end of production. They'll look around for the compost bin. It goes to show that you can really change people's habits if you make doing the right thing easy for them.

Nina Farmer: My favorite part of the job is donations. The film industry can be quite wasteful because they will only use a large quantity of materials during production. So … where does that material go? It is my job to advocate avoiding these things going to the landfill. Sometimes, I get to see the reactions of recipients getting the material and it is always so positive!

Olive Ryan: What I liked best was that it gave me an opportunity to become familiar with each department and almost the entire crew and their processes since the job stretches over every aspect of production.

> **Q: What is your advice for a college student who is interested in sustainability and wants to work in film?**
>
> **Tyler Confoy:** My advice would be to become an Eco PA and be eager to learn everything you can about waste reduction so you can go above and beyond in the role. Being a strong Eco PA lays the foundation for being a good coordinator. Let people see that you really care about sustainability, and they will be more likely to listen to you and get on board with the mission.
>
> **Nina Farmer:** To be transparent, you need to have a whole lot of passion and patience to do sustainability in film. Depending on the production, the work can be an uphill battle since this is a relatively new concept to an industry that is over 100 years old. However, people will notice your passion and respect it – if you put in the work.
>
> **Olive Ryan:** My advice would be that although it may not seem like a glamorous job at first glance, it's actually a great way to familiarize yourself with the film industry and how all aspects of production function. There are also tough parts about the job – departments do tend to push back on what you're asking of them because it can seem like an extra step of work or inconvenience to them. To avoid that pushback, it's important to initiate the sustainability expectations very early on in preproduction so that you aren't jumping in and changing routines once everyone has started their prep on the film. But above all, it's a very important job and the fact is that this is absolutely going to become the norm for productions nowadays, so it's a growing job market with lots of room for opportunity and growth.

Exercise/Homework

1. Pick your own action item: do a social media campaign, make an activist project, show a film with Q&A, make a case study of your own, do a poster of your study or campaign, look for sustainability jobs in your area. Whatever you choose to do – share it with the world, let us all know about it.

Notes

1. "It Started in Jackson Hole: The Code of Best Practices for Sustainable Filmmaking." 2020. American University. October 3, 2020. https://www.american.edu/soc/news/it-started-in-jackson-hole-the-code-of-best-practices-for-sustainable-filmmaking.cfm.
2. V. Keowmang, B. Sachs, and H. Vaxer. 2019. *Taking Action: Sustainability in Tisch Film Productions. Advanced Television Production.* Kanbar Institute. https://tisch.nyu.edu/content/dam/tisch/film-tvs/Green%20Production/Green_Production_Presentation_web.pdf
3. K. Hayward. 2023. *Lunar Estates*. Green Filmmaking Survey.

4 K. Hayward. 2024, November. "Sustainability in production and the Green Film School Alliance." In *FilmForum 2022 XXIX Udine International Film and Media Studies Conference – (Un)Bearable Lightness of Media (cfp 2022), Critical Approaches to "Sustainability" in Film and Audiovisual Production.* Mimesis Circulation and Preservation, Udine, Italy.
5 Jillian Dorsey and Kalia Wilkins. 2022, May. *Sustainability in Filmmaking: A Comparative Study of Three FEA336 Junior films Using Green Checklists from the Green Film School Alliance, CSULB Student Assignment for FEA336.* The three student films were "*High Heat Showtime,*" dir. Josiah Armstrong. https://www.youtube.com/watch?v=k4NXYh4UhK0. "*Hanging Out,*" dir. Jennifer Hoehn, and "*Sound of the Air,*" dir. Miki Inoguchi.
6 Jessie Butera. 2018. *Don.* https://vimeo.com/350634352
7 Claudia Villalta-Mejia, Jessie Butera, Xochitl Torres, and Karlie Casas. 2018. *Sustainability in Film: Entertainment with a Conscience.* CSULB student behind-the-scenes video. https://youtu.be/URvoT9L0MbA
8 Claudia Villalta-Mejia. 2018. *Student Sustainability Report from Don.*
9 Kent Hayward and the FEA classes of 2018–2019. 2019. *CSULB Green Filmmaking Checklist.*

20 Looking to the Future

We end as we began, with the acknowledgment that the climate crisis is real and that there are plenty of ways that we filmmakers can participate in addressing the problem. The fact that you are reading this means that you are interested in participating in a paradigm shift to a different kind of storytelling that incorporates sustainable development goals, social justice, the three Rs (reduce, reuse, and recycle), and a smaller footprint. You've learned some practical strategies for action and have some tools to achieve change.

Kim Stanley Robison's cli-fi novel *The Ministry for the Future* embraces the idea that a new worldview must be adopted to reverse the effects of climate change and celebrate the earth, nature, and the interconnectedness of everyone on the planet. Scientist and American Musical and Dramatic Academy (AMDA) teacher Brian Ashenfelter writes in his sustainability class materials *How We Got to Now* that responding to climate change requires a new model for storytelling. Perhaps what is needed is a new model that no longer champions a colonialist Western machismo with a white male protagonist who is in opposition to nature, but instead embraces all of humanity and acknowledges its place within nature – a new kind of storytelling that no longer relies on an extractive, exploitative means of production, but is instead in sympathetic kinship with the natural world.

In this chapter, we zoom out to touch on some of the bigger issues at play when it comes to making film more sustainable, discuss how to cope with the anxiety that can accompany committing to the fight against climate change, and wrap up with hope for a greener film future.

Bigger Picture Policy Changes

Sustainability in film is a big subject, and there are factors beyond the scope of this book to consider. For example, this book doesn't get into a critique of capitalism or settler-colonial ideology and their roles in the movie business, or discuss policy-based green mandates versus voluntary green practices in film. That said, addressing bigger picture issues certainly plays an important part in making film more sustainable long term.

DOI: 10.4324/9781003425441-20

What are we missing in film's sustainability movement? In their chapter on environmental media management in *The Routledge Handbook of Ecomedia Studies*, Pietari Kääpä and Hunter Vaughan write:

> The challenges for transforming practice and policy are multi-fold. Key amongst them is what we refer to as the "responsibility deficit" in media management, that is, a lack of coordination between organizations, regulators, producers, and creatives, leading to gaps in accountability over the design and implementation of environmentally sound policies.... Challenges arise from competing measurement tools (especially as these incentives have now become commercialized), lack of unilateral standards (heavily problematic for co-productions or runaway shoots for example), different environmental regulatory regimes, and diverse creative and managerial practices.... [With] this lack of a transparent trail of governance...responsibility becomes someone else's problem.[1]

In the March 2023 Sustainability Issue of the *Hollywood Reporter*, editorial director Nekesa Mumbi Moody argues that the "adjustments that are being made ... put us on the path to change, but may not be fast enough. Certainly, the movement needs more buy-in overall."[2] Meanwhile, the UN's Intergovernmental Panel on Climate Change 2023 report warns that the "choices and actions implemented in this decade will have impacts now and for thousands of years."[3]

What is the future of sustainability in film? As production gets more and more digital, how can we ensure that we build green practices into future workflows and technologies? Human ingenuity is ongoing – it seems that there is no end to new technology, which brings with it new kinds of waste and new ways to mitigate waste and pollution. How can sustainability keep up with technology, and how can technology keep up with sustainability? Searching for future solutions can feel like a moving target.

As Kääpä and Vaughn put it in their 2022 book *Film and Television Production in the Age of Climate Crisis: Towards a Greener Screen*,

> the advent of the digital age and the vast electrical and Information and Communication Technologies (ICT) infrastructures required to support digital production, distribution, and archiving has resulted in the rapid expansion and diversification of the industry's resource use, infrastructure construction, energy dependency, and consequent waste and emissions production. Addressing these structures is essential to alleviating their environmental and social impact and ensuring that the industry's rhetoric on environmental responsibility is reflected in its practice, especially at a time when these processes – resource extraction, manufacturing, and grid deployment – continue to follow mostly environmentally destructive twentieth-century protocols.[4]

In fact, as Kääpä and Vaughn ask in the 2023 study "Sustainable Digitalization: Ensuring a Sustainable Digital Future for UK Film and Television," are digital solutions *actually* environmental solutions?[5] Going forward, we will need to implement what they call "sustainable digitalization": In addition to *policy changes*, they recommend the use of *life-cycle assessments* as a part of the regulation of digital media, reasoning that the electronic manufacturing industry is a part of global digital convergence and that the manufacturing side needs to come up with some answers too. A final recommendation is to bring in *social sustainability* to the mix. Part of that charter would include key principles like equal representation, social benefits, community impact assessment, an AI taskforce (like the 2023 work of the Screen Actors Guild for their strike), environmental justice assessments, and a look at labor and waste.

As it stands, film production mainly relies on self-reporting and self-regulation, with a varying amount of regulation from governments depending on what country you are in. Given the scale nature of the climate emergency, it seems that both top-down and bottom-up sustainability efforts are needed for the greater good.

Climate Anxiety

A paper published in *The Lancet* in 2021 suggests that "climate change, climate anxiety, and inadequate government response are all chronic stressors that could threaten the mental health and wellbeing of children and young people around the world.... Climate anxiety is a collective experience, and based on our results, children and young people would benefit from having a social discourse in which their thoughts and feelings are respected and validated, and their concerns are acted upon by people in positions of power."[6]

Climate change and related issues can be overwhelming at times. Climate anxiety is real.[7] In a recent study of 10,000 young people from 10 countries, 75% said that the future is frightening when it comes to climate change.[8] Getting involved with others who share your concerns in a group like Greenpeace, the Environmental Defense Fund, the Green Film School Alliance, YEA! Impact, or any of the others mentioned in this book can be empowering and healing. Start a green film fest at your school. Offer to talk to other filmmakers about what steps they can take toward a more sustainable shoot.

That said, while getting your hands busy and your brain engaged in the effort is rewarding, volunteer burnout and fatigue are also real. Sometimes, it can seem that volunteering for the greater good is a hard choice while others in the world seem to be rewarded for choosing the least amount of work for the maximum personal profit. Know that your choice to help is the more healthy and ethical choice. Joining activist and advocacy groups can help you process anxiety with others who share your concerns. Make sure to balance your volunteer activity with self-care and personal recharging. Talk about it with friends.

Attend a help group like The Good Grief Network, or find a specialist through the Climate Psychology Alliance or Climate Psychiatry Alliance. Go to the movies. Take a walk in nature. Being amongst plants and trees and creatures in the outdoors can be tremendously restorative.[9] Just looking at nature is good for our mental and physical health.[10,11] According to an article from the New York State Center for Environmental Conservation, "numerous studies show that both exercising in forests and simply sitting looking at trees reduce blood pressure as well as the stress-related hormones cortisol and adrenaline. Looking at pictures of trees has a similar, but less dramatic, effect."[12]

Environmental psychology is an entire field related to human interactions with the environment. Check out environmental engineer and climate action designer Katie Patrick's *How to Save the World* book and podcast or her *Why Optimism and Creativity (Not Doom) Will Save the Planet* TEDx Talk on YouTube for motivation.

"I'm done with doom," says Patrick in her TEDx Talk. "We need a beautiful optimistic vision of the amazing future we are making…. At a deep soul level we are craving a new story for a future that we can believe in." She continues,

> Optimists are happier because in the brain, optimism releases dopamine – the chemical responsible for happiness and motivation. Happiness matters in our quest to save the world because a positive mood allows us to solve complex problems and come up with great ideas. Researchers also say that images that are frightening and scary largely fail to motivate us to take action – and we need to take action. Creativity is all about taking action to do things that have not been done before, and that is what makes changing the world an inherently creative act.[13]

Hope for the Future

"Right now, we have a stage that is occupied by people living in the past," says actor, producer, and climate activist Robert Redford. "They're so frightened about change. I think particularly as younger people come into the business of filmmaking, they're coming in with a different point of view that is more progressive."[14]

Olive Ryan, who was hired as the Sustainability Coordinator on *Mean Girls* (2024) just a year out of college, agrees.

> If you begin work in film sustainability, you will soon see that productions can be *extremely* wasteful and have a massive carbon footprint even with a single short production. I think people have the urge to say "I don't want to follow these policies because it's not making an impact anyway," but that's simply not true – *any* sustainability impact makes a difference, even if it's just donating leftover food at the end of the day. Something is always better than nothing, and that's the first step in doing better as an industry.

There are plenty of reasons for optimism. A 2022 BAFTA albert report tells us that 40% of programs that participated now feature "climate, sustainability, or the environment in the dialogue or commentary" or "environmental narratives or sustainable lifestyles."[15] Furthermore, in 2022, albert trained over 2,300 production professionals on sustainable production.[16]

The studios and streamers are committing to sustainable practices, the tracking of emissions data, and bringing green technology into sound stages, as some recent data shows from the Sustainable Entertainment Alliance and the Green Spark Group.[17] Good Energy and Natural Resources Defense Council studies have shown an increase in climate mentions and story elements too.[18] Good Energy's Climate Reality Check showed that climate change was present in twice as many films released during the second half of the decade that they examined (2013–2022) – so that's progress compared to the first half of the decade! There were still only about 10% of films released that portrayed climate change as a reality (*The Glass Onion*, or *Don't Look Up*, for example), but progress is progress. Furthermore, climate mentions were present in episodic TV shows like *Ted Lasso*, *Unstable*, *Extrapolations*, *Reservation Dogs*, and *Abbott Elementary*.[19] Time will tell if this is a trend or just wishful thinking.

In the meantime, students and teachers have action items to pursue. Download and use a checklist like PEACHy, DocSociety's protocol, or albert's toolkit for your production. Make the Sustainability Coordinator a job on your set or in your school. See how high you can score on the checklists. Make it a competition with the other films in your cohort. Who can make the greenest film? Have a fun prize for the winner! Send your films off to green film festivals and attend them.

Now that you have knowledge and experience with greening film production, you are employable in the growing field of sustainability in film. Independent films, studios, and production companies are looking for students with experience in using checklists like PEACH. Policymakers, environmental groups, and nonprofits are looking for people like you to help them get to the next level of sustainability.

Join social justice and environmental groups in your area. Get involved. The old adage "think globally, act locally" is true. Vote. Your involvement matters. Your voice matters.

Stay positive. The world is a complex place, and positivity is infectious. Make each day count and keep your head up. It makes a difference. You make a difference.

So, here's looking at you kid, may the force be with you, and just keep swimming.

Notes

1 Pietari Kääpä and Hunter Vaughan. 2024. *Environmental Media Management: Overcoming the Responsibility Deficit*. Routledge Handbook of Ecomedia Studies.
2 Nekesa Mumbi Moody. 2023, March 22. Letter from the Editor – For Hollywood to truly heed the crisis call for our planet, every level must be involved. *The Hollywood Reporter*'s 2023 Sustainability Issue.

3 UN. 2023, March. UN's intergovernmental panel on climate change. *AR6 Synthesis Report: Climate Change 2023*. https://www.ipcc.ch/report/sixth-assessment-report-cycle/
4 Pietari Kääpä and Hunter Vaughan. 2022. *Film and Television Production in the Age of Climate Crisis: Towards a Greener Screen*. Springer Nature, p. 4.
5 Hunter Vaughan and Pietari Kääpä. 2023, October. *Sustainable Digitalization: Ensuring a Sustainable Digital Future for UK Film and Television*. Minderoo Centre for Technology and Democracy. https://doi.org/10.17863/CAM.101504
6 Caroline Hickman, Elizabeth Marks, Panu Pihkala, Susan Clayton, R. Eric Lewandowski, and Elouise E. Mayall. 2021, December. Climate anxiety in children and young people and their beliefs about government responses to climate change: A global survey. *The Lancet*, Vol. 5, No. 12, pp. E863–E873. DOI: https://doi.org/10.1016/S2542-5196(21)00278-3. https://www.thelancet.com/journals/lanplh/article/PIIS2542-5196(21)00278-3/fulltext
7 Schwaab L, Gebhardt N, Friederich HC, Nikendei C. Climate Change Related Depression, Anxiety and Stress Symptoms Perceived by Medical Students. Int J Environ Res Public Health. 2022 Jul 27;19(15):9142. doi: 10.3390/ijerph19159142. PMID: 35897512; PMCID: PMC9332784; https://www.ncbi.nlm.nih.gov/pmc/articles/PMC9332784/
8 Elizabeth Marks, Caroline Hickman, Panu Pihkala, Susan Clayton, Eric R. Lewandowski, Elouise E. Mayall, Britt Wray, Catriona Mellor, and Lise van Susteren. 2021. Young people's voices on climate anxiety, government betrayal and moral injury: A global phenomenon. *The Lancet Planetary Health*, Vol. 5, No. 12, pp. e863–e873. Available at SSRN: https://ssrn.com/abstract=3918955 or http://dx.doi.org/10.2139/ssrn.3918955
9 Mph, Stephanie Collier Md. 2022. "If Climate Change Keeps You up at Night, Here's How to Cope." Harvard Health. June 13, 2022. https://www.health.harvard.edu/blog/is-climate-change-keeping-you-up-at-night-you-may-have-climate-anxiety-202206132761.
10 Kathleen L. Wolf, Sharon T. Lam, Jennifer K. McKeen, Gregory R. A. Richardson, Matilda van den Bosch, and Adrina C. Bardekjian. 2020. Urban trees and human health: A scoping review. *International Journal of Environmental Research and Public Health*, Vol. 17, No. 12, p. 4371. https://doi.org/10.3390/ijerph17124371
11 S. M. Labib, Matthew Browning, Alessandro Rigolon, Marco Helbich, and Peter James. 2021. Nature's contributions in coping with a pandemic in the 21st century: A narrative review of evidence during COVID-19. *Science of the Total Environment*, Vol. 833, p. 155095. https://doi.org/10.32942/osf.io/j2pa8
12 New York State Center for Environmental Conservation. *Immerse Yourself in a Forest for Better Health*. New York State Center for Environmental Conservation. https://dec.ny.gov/nature/forests-trees/immerse-yourself-for-better-health
13 Katie Patrick. 2020. *Why Optimism and Creativity (Not Doom) Will Save the Planet*. TEDx San Luis Obispo. https://www.youtube.com/watch?v=GOWYwEtzeH4
14 Cynthia Littleton. 2019, September 10. Is Hollywood doing enough to fight the climate crisis? *Variety*.
15 Albert Report, 2022. https://wearealbert.org/wp-content/uploads/2023/10/06_ALBERT-ANNUAL-REPORT-v8.pdf
16 *Albert Annual Report*, 2022, p. 8.
17 "GPG in Action – Green Production Guide." n.d. Green Production Guide. https://greenproductionguide.com/in-action/.
18 "The Climate Reality Check." n.d. https://www.theclimaterealitycheck.com/.
19 Rowley, Melissa Jun. 2024. "How Hollywood Is Crafting a New Climate Change Narrative." *Rolling Stone*, February 22, 2024. https://www.rollingstone.com/culture-council/articles/how-hollywood-is-crafting-new-climate-change-narrative-1234972469/.

Appendix A
Top 10 Sustainability in Filmmaking Million-Dollar Ideas

It's a two-step process: (1) start/invent this, and (2) make a million:

1. Boutique/warehouse selling used expendables and sets clearinghouse in your area (like Film Biz Recycling (formerly in New York City, now in Atlanta), the Expendables Recycler or EcoSet in the Los Angeles area, or The Resource Exchange in Philadelphia, Pennsylvania
2. Biodegradable polystyrene for construction and fabrication
3. A mixed construction materials recycling company for all that construction and demolition waste
4. More efficient power supply units and transformers for computers and big equipment
5. Rechargeable batteries that aren't made from something that needs to be mined
6. Energy storage using gravity or water instead of chemical batteries
7. Collaboration with tech manufacturers to make electronics, computers, and cameras less disposable and more upgradeable, modular, and recyclable
8. Cool new public projects that create energy from people walking with kinetic energy dynamos, piezoelectric tiles, kinetic pavement, energy-generating stairs, or even energy-generating shoes
9. Concrete that uses carbon sequestered from the atmosphere - or absorbs carbon as it cures (instead of releasing it)
10. A substitute for plastic that's just as light and strong but is easily recycled and doesn't break down into microwaste

Appendix B

Sustainability in Film Teachers Guide

A "quick start" guide for including sustainability in your film curriculum

Problem: Climate change and environmental degradation due to human activity, including wasteful practices in the production, consumption, development, streaming, and archiving of film and television.

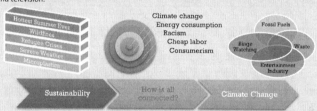

Solution: Get students engaged in Sustainability with forward-thinking teachers.

Sample topics and exercises:

Production – Making films can be wasteful, and some films have content that is counter-productive for the well-being of people and the planet. How can production students make a difference? Here are some ideas for your students:

- *Documentary, Reality, and Activism* – Look at the docsociety Green Doc Protocol for inspiration. How does climate change intersect with the documentaries your students are making now? Have a group make a PSA or short doc about an environmental issue that you see in your community as an assignment. Example: *The Canal, Sustainability in Film*
- *Climate Storytelling* – Most of us talk about climate in our daily lives, yet less than 1% of film and TV scripts use the phrase "climate change" according to a Good Energy study. Look at the Good Energy Playbook guide for writers. Rewrite a scene from a favorite film using three of the subtle or broad methods for incorporating climate in story.
- *Green Filmmaking practices by department* – Use the Production Environmental Action Checklist for young filmmakers (PEACHy) to get new ideas for "greening" your workflow. Reusable water bottles are just the start -- low-energy lighting, thrifting, and meat-less lunches are next-level. Try five new sustainable behaviors on your film. Keep score with PEACHy.
- *Green Filmmaking modules* – Use the Smashcut/NYU/GFSA "Make a Film, Save the Planet" online videos and course material in class or as an assignment.

Film History – The history of film and culture is complex and ongoing. A discussion of the history of movies must include a mention of the connection between humans, technology, and the natural world.

- Essay: Some Hollywood films have been shockingly abusive to the environment. Read a chapter from Hunter Vaughan's *Hollywood's Dirtiest Secret* and write an essay about a classic film's use of what we would consider a questionable environmental practice or message today.
- Discussion: Many early films showcased an appreciation of nature and animals in motion. How does the class feel about nature and the environment as represented by Muybridge's animals in motion? What about James Cameron's?

Appendix B

Film Theory and Criticism – Students studying the formal attributes of film or writing critical essays on scholarly approaches won't be disappointed by the fascinating variety of writing on Sustainability in Film.
Look at the body of work generated by "The (Un)bearable Lightness of Media" FilmForum 2022 XXIX Udine International Film and Media Studies Conference which looks at Critical Approaches to "Sustainability" in Film and Audiovisual Production, Circulation and Preservation. A description of the scholarly prompt is here. What would your presentation be about?

Ecocriticism and Ecocinema – These related disciplines investigate the relationship between humans and the natural world in literature and film.
Project: Make a slideshow presentation describing your take on the way that a film describes the Natural World. Consider Bong Joon-ho's *Okja*, Miyazaki's *Princess Mononoke*, Cameron's *Avatar* films, *The Day after Tomorrow*, *Don't Look Up*, or *Snowpiercer*.

Media Ecology and Environmental Media – What happens when we look at screen media by way of environmental studies, globalization, neoliberal capitalism, identity, social justice, science communication and related social issues?
Read/discuss/present: Have three groups of students read articles from the Journal of Environmental Media and then lead a class discussion on the topics.

Intersectionality – How does climate change, the environment, and sustainability in film intersect with racism, poverty, indigenous rights, colonialism, democracy, and representation?
Explore and discuss: How are the issues discussed at The Hollywood Climate Summit similar to the issues outlined the UN Goals for Sustainable Development?

Resources to explore:

The Green Film School Alliance (GFSA)
The Green Production Guide (GPG)
Environmental & Climate Change Literacy Projects (ECCLPs)
Center for Environmental Filmmaking
albert

Young Entertainment Activists! (YEA!)
The Hollywood Climate Summit
"Make a Film – Save the Planet" online course
NDN Collective – Indigenous movement
Indigenous Climate Action

Books:
The Intersectional Environmentalist, Leah Thomas
The Green Filmmaker's Guide: Sustainability for Students of Movie Making, Kent Hayward, (forthcoming) Routledge Press
The Book of Hope: A Survival Guide for Trying Times, Jane Goodall and Douglas Abrams, 2021

Articles:
"Sustainability in Production and the Green Film School Alliance" Kent Hayward, FilmForum 2022 XXIX Udine International Film and Media Studies Conference, 2022
"Why Optimism and Creativity (Not Doom) Will Save the Planet", Katie Patrick, 2020

Prepared by CSULB Prof. Kent Hayward for fellow teachers, the Green Film School Alliance (GFSA), and readers of my upcoming book on Green Filmmaking from Routledge Press.

This and other digital downloads are available on the Routledge website for this book: www.routledge.com/9781032545622

Index

Abbot Elementary (TV series) 53–54, 110
ABCs of Sustainability poster 34, 115
acousmatic listening 137
Acres, Birt 3
Adobe Acrobat 65, 74
advocacy group 70, 106
aerosol hairsprays 122
AFI Green Initiative 32
air conditioning (AC) 146
albert (environmental organisation) 11, 21, 24, 33, 42, 46, 98, 171–172
alternative fuel vehicles 125–127
American Beauty (1999) 9
American Film Institute (AFI) 100
American Musical and Dramatic Academy (AMDA) 12
Apocalypse Now (1979) 1
art department 85, 89, 158
Ashenfelter, Brian 12
Atkin, Emily 18
Attenborough, David 8–9, 39, 48
audio production 140
Avatar (2009) 7, 53, 138

Bangladesh, climate change 160
Barclay, Bridgette 5
Battery Council International 140
battery, rechargeable 68, 71, 75, 77, 99–101, 138–140, 154
The Beach (2000) 11
Beasts of the Southern Wild (2012) 46
Begalman, Allison 17–18
Bell, Art 7
Belli, Mary Lou 84
bicycles 128
"The Big Picture: Representing Our Climate-Altered World On-Screen" 54–56

Bike Power 147
biodiesel 28, 99, 126–127
Biophilia (1984) 89
Black Mirror (2011–) 119
Blue Oyster Cult (Rock band) 5
bounce light 93–94
Boyle, Danny 11
Bozak, Nadia 4
Brakhage, Stan 10
Brereton, Pat 3
British Academy of Film and Television Arts (BAFTA) project 11, 21, 24, 42, 172
Brunson, Quinta 18, 53, 110
BYO (Bring Your Own…) 108

Cagney, James 131
Call2Recycle 140
camera department 27, 66, 92–102
Cameron, James 53
Campbell, Joseph 2
carbon-arc lights 97
carbon emissions 7, 21, 47–48, 69, 99–100, 125, 133–134, 145, 161
carbon footprint 7, 9, 33, 39, 42–43, 76, 98, 108, 140, 171
carpool 76–77
casting process 53, 107–108
catering 110, 115
Chasing Coral (2017) 9
Chasing Ice (2012) 39
checklist 27–28, 30–31, 33–37, 41–42, 162
The Checklist Manifesto (Gawande) 27
Chion, Michel 137
Christie and Barco laser projectors 147
CicloCinema 147
Cinebike 148
cinema, history of 3

CinemAmbiente 149
cinematographers 49, 61, 85, 93–94
CITES (Convention on International Trade in Endangered Species of Wild Fauna and Flora) Management Authority 21
clean energy 100–101
The Clean Energy Toolkit 34
Clean Energy Working Group 129
Clean Water Act of 1972 45
climate anxiety 170–171
The Climate Book (Thunberg) 123
climate change 3, 7, 10, 12, 31–33, 45–48, 53–56, 64, 75, 106, 112, 160, 168, 170, 172
climate issues 54–56
climate justice 15, 17–18, 40, 49–50
Climate Reality Check 172
cloud storage 145–146
CMS VATAVARAN in New Delhi 149
Cobo, Nalleli 18
Code for Best Practices in Sustainable Filmmaking 41–42
coffee and tea 114
coffee pod 78–79
Cohen, Hillary 115
Cohen, Jem 9–10
Common Ground (2023) 106
community 15, 17, 23–24, 39, 42, 50–51, 62, 106, 126
Confoy, Tyler 164–166
convenience 66, 68, 79, 107, 139
cost efficiency 139
Cousteau, Jacques Yves 43
COVID-19 pandemic 19, 107, 116, 157
Cox Automotive study 125
craft service 66, 110, 112, 116
Crenshaw, Kimberlé 14
CSULB student study 159
culture 15, 51
Curtis, Jamie Lee 106

Dark Waters (2019) 163
Darlington, Sophie 95
data collection 154–155
Dawson, Rosario 106
The Day After Tomorrow (2004) 7, 35
daylight shooting 49, 93, 143
Days of Heaven (1978) 7
"Decolonizing Climate Storytelling: From Hip-Hip 50 to Land Back" 49
"Demarginalizing the Intersection of Race and Sex" (Crenshaw) 14
department heads 30, 61, 65–66, 71, 98, 165

Dern, Laura 48
diesel generators 98–100, 129
Diesel, Rudolf 125
diesel vehicles 126–127
digital copy 74
digital *vs.* film 96
digital workflow 74–75
Directors Guild of America (DGA) Sustainability Pro Tips 34
Directors Tell the Story (Belli and Rooney) 84
documentary filmmaking 8–9, 39–44, 47–48, 79
DocuSign 74–75
Don (2018) 157
donation, food 115–116, 152–153
Don't Look Up (2021) 51
Dreams (1990) 8
Drescher, Fran 106
dry cleaning 120
DuVernay, Ava 43

e-bikes 128
EcoBaze 100
Ecocine in Brazil 149
ECO Film Lab 160–161
eco-foam 88
eco-friendly: detergent 120; devices and computers 75–76; products 67
ecohorror 5
ecomedia 3, 10
EcoProd 34
Eco-Rep 37, 147
Ecosia 75
Ecosphere (2020) 8
Ekofilm in Prague 149
electricity use 40, 78, 102, 144
electric kitchen composting 113–114
Electric Pedals 148
electric vehicles (EVs) 73, 125–127, 162
Electrocuting an Elephant (1903) 4
Electronic Product Environmental Assessment Tool (EPEAT) 75
Electronic Recycling Act of 2003 140
electronic waste (e-waste) 69–70, 82, 132, 139–140, 146–147, 154
Elson, Erica 28, 31–33
Elwes, Catherine 95–96
Emmerich, Roland 7, 35
energy efficiency 75, 96–98
energy savings 75, 139, 144–145
Engel, Larry 41
English, Jeanell 51
environmental film 48; festival 148–149

Environmental Impact of Filmmaking (EIF) project 133
environmentalism 14–15, 118
Environmental Management of the Media: Policy, Industry, Practice (Kääpä) 10
Environmental Media Association (EMA) 30, 38n6
environmental moments 48–49
Environmental Protection Agency (EPA) 138, 154
environmental psychology 71, 171
Escobar, Tania 95
Ethical Consumer 139
ethics/ethical 4, 20, 39
European Film Commission Network 34
Every Day Action (EDA) 115
Everything Everywhere All at Once (2022) 17, 73
exhibition 147–148
expendables and materials use 102
Expendables Recycler 101, 153
exterior and natural light 93–94

Fairtrade 114
Farmer, Nina 164–166
fashion 118–119
Fashion Reimagined (2022) 118
Film and Television Production in the Age of Climate Crisis (Kääpä and Vaughn) 169
film history 3
film production 2, 11–12, 14, 28, 35–37, 127, 138, 140, 153, 157–158, 160–161, 164, 170, 172
Fisk, Jack 86
Fitzcarraldo (1982) 1
Flaherty, Robert 4
fluorescent lights 97
food 110–116; catering 110, 115; coffee and tea 114; composting process 113–114; craft services 66, 110, 112, 116; donations 115–116, 152–153; meat industry 112; safety 116; vegetarian 53, 112; waste 113–114
Forest Stewardship Council (FSC) 73, 87
Foster, Craig 85
From Surma 127

The Garden in the Machine (MacDonald) 9
gasoline vehicles 128–129
Gates, Bill 101
Gawande, Atul 27

Gay, Roxane 54–56
Global Inheritance 86
Gods Behaving Badly (2013) 138
Godzilla (1954) 5
Godzilla 3 6
Godzilla 3D IMAX treatment 5
Go-Green Checklist 34
Going Green and Saving Green 20, 138
Gone with the Wind (1939) 1, 35
Goodall, Jane 43
Good Energy playbook 15, 46, 52
Goodwill 153
Gore, Al 21
The Graduate (1967) 89
green cleaning products 82
green content 94–96
Green Council Initiative 106
Green Doc Protocol 34
Green Documentary Protocol 42
The Green Documentary Protocol 42
greener packaging 122
Green Film Festival of San Francisco 149
green film festivals 148–149
green filmmaking professionals 160–164
green film production 2, 14, 164
The Green Film School Alliance (GFSA) 23, 28, 30–33, 80–81, 115, 153
Green Film Shooting 100, 115
greenhouse gas emission 7, 23–24, 35, 92, 113–114, 145
greenlight checklist 27–28
Green Production Guide 67, 76–77, 80, 115–116, 123, 154
Green Rider campaign 106
green room 122–123
Green, Sam 137
Green Screen: Environmentalism and Hollywood Cinema (Ingram) 10, 95
green seal 71, 147
Green Spark Group 79
green vendors 67–68, 77
greenwashing 10, 22–23, 34–35, 76, 114
grip and electric department 66, 92–102

Hanging Out (2000) 157
#DocsGoGreen 42
Haynes, Todd 163
Healthy Living app 121
Heidsiek, Birgit 133, 163
High Heat (2022) 157
Hip Hop Caucus 50, 52
HMIs 97
Hoffman, Dustin 89

Index

Hollywood 7–8, 10–12, 35, 45, 53, 77, 84–85
Hollywood Rides a Bike (Rea) 128
Hollywood's Dirtiest Secret (Vaughn) 11, 35
Honest Beauty 121
How to Avoid a Climate Disaster (Gates) 101
How to Save the World (Patrick) 23, 171
humanity 5, 9, 12, 45, 168
hybrid 125–127, 129

IAFM 160–161
An Inconvenient Truth (2006) 21
Indigenous people 15, 51–53, 68, 108
Ingram, David 10, 95
International Documentary Association (IDA) 42
intersectional environmentalism 14–15
The Intersectional Environmentalist (Thomas) 14
intersectionality 14, 17, 55
Ivens, Joris 9

Jackson Wild 148
Jevons paradox 73, 145
job training 21–22
Junkluggers in Los Angeles 153–154

Kääpä, Pietari 10, 169–170
Kidao, Sinéad 119
Killers of the Flower Moon (2023) 18, 86
Kingdom of Plants (2022) 8
King of the Monsters (2019) 6
Klein, Naomi 10
Koyaanisqatsi (1982) 9
Kurosawa, Akira 8, 94
Kwan, Daniel 17

Landscape and the Moving Image (Elwes) 95–96
The Last of Us (2023) 7, 106
Lawson, Angela 18
Leonard, Franklin 54–56
life-cycle assessment (LCA) 133–134, 170
A Life on Our Planet (2020) 39, 48
light emitting diodes (LED) 32, 97–99, 101, 134, 143–144
lithium batteries 15, 68, 101, 139
Little Projector Company 148
Little Women (2019) 119
live plants 89, 94, 123, 143
local shopping 77

logos 147
Lonewolf, YoNasDa 18
The Lorax (2012) 35
Lost Book Found (1996) 9–10
Luu, Samantha 115

MacDonald, Scott 9
Mad Max: Fury Road (2015) 11
makeup and hair 118, 120–123
Malick, Terrence 7, 94, 137
The Mandalorian (2019) 133–134
March of the Penguins (2005) 9
mass transit 62, 127–128
McKee, Robert 47
Mean Girls (2004) 164, 171–172
mica powder 122
microfiber lens cloths 102
The Ministry for the Future (Robinson) 12, 168
mixed construction waste 153–154
Miyagawa, Kazuo 94
Miyazaki, Hayao 7
mobilespace, Germany 100, 127
money, save for 19–20, 22, 49, 66, 93
Moody, Nekesa Mumbi 169
Mothlight (1963) 10
Mukharjee, Siddhartha 36
Mutual of Omaha's Wild Kingdom (1963 to 1988) (TV series) 8
My Neighbor Totoro (1988) 7
My Octopus Teacher (2020) 9, 85, 95

Nanook of the North (1922) 4
National Resources Defense Council (NRDC) 45–46
"Native American Representation Across 1,600 Popular Films: The Lily Gladstone Effect" 53
nature sounds 136–138
negative fill 94
Nomadland (2020) 7
nontoxic beauty products 121
Nye, Bill 24

O'Brien, Emellie 17, 138
OceanHero 75
One Earth Film Festival 149
organic: cleaning 120; coffee and tea 114; foods 111
Origin (2024) 43
original equipment manufacturers (OEMs) 126
Our Planet (2019–2023) 9
outdoor lighting 93

paper documents 75
paperless 49, 64–65, 73–74, 106–107
Patrick, Katie 23, 171
PDF (Portable Document Format) 49, 65, 74–75, 107
PEACH+ 33
Personal Protective Equipment (PPE) 132
Pielot, Mareike 71
Pilcher, Lydia 129
Pirates of the Caribbean: Dead Men Tell No Tales (2017) 11
Planet Earth (2006) 9
plasma lights 97
plastic 111; bags 81; coffee pod 78–79; packaging 70; pollution 111; water bottles 21, 75, 78–79, 107, 110–111, 158
Plastic Pollution Coalition 111
"The Playbook for Screenwriting in the Age of Climate Change" 46
The Polar Bear Hunt in the Arctic Seas (1910) 4
pollution 23–24, 28, 47, 68–69, 134, 138
polystyrene materials 102, 112–113
Ponyo (2008) 7
portable electric 100, 102
Portland EcoFilm Festival 149
post-production 142–149
power use 98–100, 105, 138–140, 143–145
Powney, Amy 118
premade signs 81, 115
preproduction 60–71
Princess Mononoke (1997) 7–8
principles and practices checklist 33
production department 73–83, 149
production design (PD) 84–90
Production Environmental Accounting Report (PEAR) 33, 162
Production Environmental Action CHecklist (PEACH) 28, 33, 162
Production Environmental Action Checklist for Young filmmakers (PEACHy) 28–33, 37, 62, 132–133
Production Lumber Materials (PLUM) 33, 162
Programme for the Endorsement of Forest Certification (PEFC) 87
Psihoyos, Louie 39, 47
psychoacoustics 136
pump sprays 122

Racing Extinction (2015) 9, 39, 47
Rain (1929) 9
Ramsey, Bella 106
RARE Conservation 7
Rashomon (1950) 94
Reasons for Hope (2023) 40
Rea, Steven 128
rechargeable battery 68, 71, 75, 77, 99–101, 138–140, 154, 157
recycle and reuse 6, 42, 64, 69–70, 73–74, 76, 82, 88, 90, 101–102, 107, 115, 140, 153–154
recycling bins 48, 80–81, 115, 154
recycling e-waste 139–140
reduced waste 138
renting 89; studio facility 152; vehicle 127–128
Reservation Dogs (2021–2023) 53
Robinson, Kim Stanley 12, 168
Rodriguez, Faviana 50–52
Rogers, Brian 5
Rooney, Bethany 84
Rough Sea at Dover (1895) 3–4
The Routledge Handbook of Ecomedia Studies (Kääpä and Vaughan) 169
Roy, Bibesh 127, 160
Ruffalo, Mark 163
Ryan, Olive 164–166, 171

SAFE (Solvents/Automotive/Flammables/Electronics) 154
safety 76, 92, 98, 128, 132
Samsara (2011) 9
Saniset Fleet 127
Sasquatch Sunset (2024) 7
Scheinert, Daniel 17
Scorsese, Martin 18, 86
Screen New Deal (2020) 11
Scriptation software 32, 49, 65, 74, 107
Seaspiracy (2021) 39, 48
secondhand stores 119, 153
The Secret World of Arrietty (2010) 7
Seventh Generation Principle 2
shooting film 67, 92–96, 133–134, 142
signage 115
The Silent World (1956) 40
Singing in the Rain (1952) 35
single-use: dishes 112; plastics 32, 66, 106, 111; plates 113; pods 114
Skin Deep Cosmetics Database 121
Small File Media Festival 148
smart power management 140
Smith, Stacy L. 53
The Smog Monster (1971) 5

social media 14, 64, 79, 126
social sustainability 170
sodium battery 100–101, 138
solar panels 40–41, 73, 77–78, 86, 99
SolarPunks 100
Song of the Cell (Mukharjee) 36
sound design 136–138
Sound of the Air (2022) 157
Soylent Green (1973) 26
special effects 131–132; makeup 121
Steward, Karen 84
storytelling 1–2, 15, 46, 50–51, 53–55, 93, 148, 168
Strange World (2022) 138
streaming media 68–70, 107, 145
Strieber, Whitley 7
styrene products 88
Succession (2018–2023) 46
sustainability 2–6, 10; culture of 15; definition 2; digitalization 170; million-dollar ideas 174; teachers guide 175–176
Sustainability Coordinator 3, 61–65, 71, 86, 98, 115, 146–147, 152–153, 164–166, 171–172
Sustainability in Filmmaking: Entertainment with a Conscience 158
Sustainable Entertainment Alliance 2021 42, 125
Sustainable Entertainment Society in Canada 100
sustainable film production 19–20, 31–32, 36–37, 41–43, 156–161
Sustainable Production Alliance (SPA) 98

talent 105–108
Thacker Pass Lithium Mine 139
Them! (1954) 5
The Thin Red Line (1998) 7, 94, 137
13th (2016) 43
32 Sounds (2023) 137
This Changes Everything (Klein) 10
Thomas, Leah 14
Thorn, Randy 136
Thunberg, Greta 123
Tidwell, Christy 5
Titanic (1997) 11
T-marks 102
Toho Studios 147
toxic waste 82, 87, 90, 96–97, 132, 153–154
transportation 76, 125–130, 140, 158

trash 76, 80–82, 85, 95, 112–113, 115, 151–153
The Tree of Life (2011) 7, 94
tungsten lights 97–98, 143
Tutu, Desmond 12

UCLA 31, 79
The Undersea World of Jacques Cousteau (1968 to 1976) (TV series) 8
Unstoppable (Nye) 24
The UN Sustainable Development Goals 14–16, 40, 87
the US Department of Energy 99, 126
utensils, reusable 8, 108, 112, 116

Varga, Thomas 138
Vaughan, Hunter 11, 35, 169–170
vegetarian and vegan food 53, 112
VFX production 131–132
virtual production (VP) 129, 133
visual effects 129, 131–132
volatile organic compounds (VOC) stand 88, 132, 143

Waititi, Taiko 53
Wang, Jonathan 73, 84, 162
wardrobe 108, 118–120, 122–123
waste electrical and electronic equipment (WEEE) 146–147, 154
water bottles, reusable 20–21, 57, 66–67, 78–79, 85, 107–108, 110–111, 115, 158
Welch, Lena 15–17, 100–101, 161
Well People 121
Westworld (TV show) 153
wet signature (ink signature) 65, 75
Wilson, Edward O. 89
The Wizard of Oz (1939) 118, 131
workflow 49, 61–62, 64, 67–68, 78, 134
wrap 90, 151–155

Yearwood, Lennox 50, 52
Young Entertainment Activists (YEA!) 17–18, 170
Yunus, Siti Syuhaida Mohamed 133

Zabriskie Point (1970) 35
Zhao, Chloé 7
Zoo Quest (1954–1963) (TV series) 8

Printed in the United States
by Baker & Taylor Publisher Services